NEW ZEALAND POLITICS IN ACTION
The 1960 General Election

New Zealand Politics in Action

The 1960 General Election

R. M. CHAPMAN
Senior Lecturer in History
University of Auckland

W. K. JACKSON
Senior Lecturer in Political Science
University of Otago

A. V. MITCHELL
Lecturer in History and Political Science
University of Otago

LONDON
OXFORD UNIVERSITY PRESS
WELLINGTON MELBOURNE
1962

Oxford University Press, Amen House, London. E.C.4

GLASGOW NEW YORK TORONTO MELBOURNE WELLINGTON
BOMBAY CALCUTTA MADRAS KARACHI LAHORE DACCA
CAPE TOWN SALISBURY NAIROBI IBADAN ACCRA
KUALA LUMPUR HONG KONG

Printed in Great Britain at the Villafield Press, Bishopbriggs, Glasgow

PREFACE

Psephology, the study of elections, is a comparatively new arrival in New Zealand. It should take firm roots in the dominion. A small population, an open society, a generous supply of official documentation and a basically simple governmental and economic system have provided the ideal environment for the study of the social sciences. Added to these the political scientist has the advantages of election results published in polling-booth units which cover only a small area, and a straightforward and well-documented electoral system. The only possible obstacle to study, the reluctance of some politicians and officials to allow questioning on 'party matters', is one which should be attenuated as a tradition of impartial academic enquiry is established.

This book is therefore offered as an attempt to utilize these outstanding natural advantages so as to provide a description of New Zealand politics and parties as seen through a decisive event on the political scene, a general election, the triennial political climax. It is, so far as is possible when three authors collaborate from centres so far apart as Auckland and Dunedin, a joint effort. Each chapter has been written by one of the three authors but revised after collective discussion and criticism. It is also, indeed inevitably, a work which owes much to the co-operation of others and for which many acknowledgements have to be made. The whole study was made possible by research grants from the Carnegie Committee for Research in the Social Sciences and the Council of the University of Otago. Fifty-eight students and staff of the University of Otago deserve our thanks for their successful efforts at interviewing in Dunedin Central, and the inhabitants of that electorate for their kind co-operation. We are naturally very grateful to the politicians and party officials who gave up so much time to interviews ('the toughest grilling I've ever had' as one described it) both during and immediately after the election, at times when they were also extremely busy with other matters. The help of people all over the dominion is also acknowledged with gratitude, whether they be the candidates who filled in our questionnaires and sent in leaflets and information about their local campaigns or those students of the Universities of Auckland

and Otago who helped by sending in voluminous piles of pamphlets, Press cuttings and eye-witness accounts. The publishers of the eight main centre morning and evening newspapers and of the *Nelson Evening Mail* very kindly agreed to provide free copies of their newspapers during and after the campaign. Several students generously devoted considerable amounts of time and energy to helping with various aspects of this work and the efforts of Peter Aimer in Auckland, Brian Bellringer in Taranaki, Barry Brailsford and Jack Dowie in Christchurch, and Alister McKillop, Alister McMurran and Dick Matches in Dunedin were invaluable. The manuscript of the book was read in whole or in part by Professor Willis Airey, Mr. W. J. Gardner, Senior Lecturer in History at the University of Canterbury, Mr. Ian Main, National Party Publicity Director, Mr. Martin Nestor, National Party Research Director, Mr. Fraser Coleman, Labour Party Assistant Secretary, and Mr. A. J. McDonald, Labour Party National Secretary. Their suggestions and corrections have been extremely useful, although naturally responsibility for remaining shortcomings rests with the authors alone. We thank Mrs. Chapman, Mrs. Olwynne Green and Miss Glenys Hammond for their care in typing the manuscript and their patience in coping with the numerous revisions and corrections which have been necessary since the first drafts were written. Finally the generous help, advice, and encouragement of Professor E. A. Horsman and Professor W. P. Morrell, helped to make publication of this book possible.

R. M. Chapman
W. K. Jackson
A. V. Mitchell

March 1962

CONTENTS

PREFACE

NEW ZEALAND TERMS

Though this book is to some extent bilingual in that it is written by two Englishmen and a New Zealander, it is possible that some of the terms used in it may not be immediately clear to readers outside New Zealand. Possible difficulties are:

Car Conversion: Would be known as 'car stealing' in the United Kingdom, but in New Zealand the penalties for conversion are lower than those for theft.

Caucus: The parliamentary party assembled in private to take management and policy decisions.

Electorate: Constituency.

Group Housing: Houses built for sale in groups by private builders, the building being supervised by the State Advances Corporation which takes over unsold houses at approved prices.

Householder: Leaflets distributed through the post 'to the householder'.

Informal Vote: Invalid vote. Voting in New Zealand is by crossing off all names on the ballot paper except the one supported.

McKenzies Chain store on the pattern of Woolworths.

Main Centres: The four largest cities; Auckland, Wellington, Christchurch and Dunedin.

Mana: Prestige, influence, authority.

N.Z.B.S.: New Zealand Broadcasting Service.

Paddock: Field.

Pakeha: Maori description of the white man. Now in general use to distinguish European from Maori.

Remit: Resolutions sent in to the annual party conferences by the branches.

Section: Building plot.

State Housing: Housing built and owned by the Government though also available to occupiers for purchase. A local version of the British 'council house'.

PART ONE

THE BACKGROUND

I

THE ELECTORAL FRAMEWORK

A GENERAL election is one of the biggest single administrative enterprises undertaken by the modern state. In size, scale, timing and the need for accuracy and impartiality, it is a unique and costly operation. In New Zealand the cost to the country exceeds £250,000 in the year of the election together with some £30,000 for the two intervening years, and the administration of the election depends on close as well as sympathetic co-operation between different Government departments. More important, elections necessitate diligent constitutional provision to balance the three conflicting aims of giving the same value to each vote, creating realistic electorates, and providing for a stable Government.

In view of the scope of these problems, it is hardly surprising that the electoral system has been the subject of controversy and altercation throughout the country's history and that in a little over a hundred years of self-government, more than seventy bills directly pertaining to representation have been introduced into the New Zealand General Assembly, an average approaching one a year. The heyday of experiment was in the 1880s and 90s when, in the ten years 1884–94, no fewer than nineteen Bills dealing with electoral arrangements were introduced into Parliament, although only three survived to become law. For most of the latter part of the nineteenth century, only finance and liquor excited more discussion and controversy in the House of Representatives.

Today the electoral system, the first-past-the-post system of single-member constituencies, is much the same as that used in Britain, from whom New Zealand inherited her original electoral arrangements. Yet British example has never been slavishly followed. From the outset when the British property franchise was enshrined in New Zealand by the 1852 Constitution Act, British models were adapted to local purposes. The original property-holding qualification was the occupation of a dwelling with an annual value of £10 in a town, or £5 in the country, together with freehold and household provisions. Inevitably with a property franchise, some people had no vote at all but there can be little doubt that, from the 1850s onwards, despite the similar property provision, the vote was more widely based than in Britain. Property distinctions meant much less in a pioneering community, the voting age of 21 much more, since a high proportion were under that age limit.

The original situation sets the tone of later development. Although New Zealand copied some of its original ideas from the British system, generally speaking it has been in the vanguard of developments since. Many years in advance of Britain, before the end of the nineteenth century, New Zealand attained the principle of 'one adult, one vote'. Manhood suffrage based merely on a residence qualification was adopted in 1879 together with triennial Parliaments, whilst in 1889, plural voting was abolished and in 1893 New Zealand helped to pioneer the way in votes for women. Thus by the end of the century the basis of the present-day system had already been firmly established.

Yet though the electoral record is an enviable one by any standards, its implications are possibly misleading. It appears to represent a steady conscious striving towards perfection. In fact development was far more haphazard and less influenced by long-sighted motives than a mere recital of the record would suggest.

An illustration of this is the granting of adult male suffrage to the Maori population in 1867 before it had been legally obtained for Europeans. The expressed purpose of offering the Maoris such generous provisions in 1867 was to safeguard their interests. English precedent had been of little help in deciding if and how the Maoris should be represented and the 1852 Constitution Act had been studiously vague in this respect. The problem was doubly complicated because not only were the Maoris in a comparatively primitive state of development at the time, but, in addition, most of them held their land in common, thus posing difficult problems where a property-holding franchise was in vogue. The 1867 Maori Representation Act conceding separate representation through four seats to the Maoris, represented an attempt to overcome these difficulties which, it was hoped, would go far in pacifying disaffected tribes, and, in providing a stepping-stone to a form of political unity which was believed to be inevitable and very near at hand. This double act of faith, the belief that the Maoris were worthy of taking part in Parliament, and confidence in the ability of the two races to merge their political future, was expressed in a double action—parliamentary representation coupled with manhood suffrage. The New Zealand Government not only modified existing procedures to meet local needs, it also courageously pioneered new ground with manhood suffrage in difficult circumstances. Unhappily this pioneering has never been followed up. This experiment which under-represented the Maori, at first in number and then in influence, has continued largely unaltered for nearly a hundred years. Today, four seats out of eighty are still reserved for Maori candidates and voters, a European is not entitled to be registered as an elector of a Maori district and a Maori (other than a half-caste) is not entitled to be registered as an elector of a European district. A half-caste Maori may choose to be registered either for a Maori or European district, and special rules are laid down to govern a change from one to the other. If the framers of the Act saw it as an important step towards political unity, as expressed in a common roll, Maori representation today is still treated as a subject somewhat apart from European electoral arrangements.

Another aspect of this pragmatical development of the New Zealand electoral system may be seen in the 1893 Act by which votes were granted to women. Only the State of Wyoming outside the British Empire, and the Isle of Man within it, preceded New Zealand in this bold experiment which was not to be emulated by Britain for another twenty-five years. This, it is tempting to believe, provides ineluctable proof of the deeply ingrained sense of fair play and almost radical striving for political equality which New Zealand's electoral record might entitle us to expect. Undoubtedly such qualities were in evidence, but in the event it was more by good fortune than design that the issue was carried at all. The electoral reform which gave women the vote was the result of the work of a large and determined group of women led chiefly by the Women's Christian Temperance Union, which had for years been demanding the vote for women. Mr. Ballance, leader of the Liberal Government, had supported them and committed his party to adopting the measure, but after his death most of his colleagues were 'publicly tepid and privately warmly opposed to it'. However in 1893, when an electoral Bill was before the House, Sir John Hall moved an amendment to enfranchise women and Mr. Seddon let it pass in the expectation that it would be rejected in the Upper House, earning for that body the consequent opprobrium. To the surprise of everyone, not least of the Government of the day, the Bill passed. Women had the vote.

Thus conscious striving for perfection has played but a comparatively small part in building up an electoral system which has grown up piecemeal, moulded by many different influences. Study of electoral arrangements in the present century shows that much has been achieved by methods quite as haphazard as those employed during the last century. The old 'country quota' system, introduced in 1881 after the abolition of the Provinces, existed well into this century, thus artificially strengthening the position of conservative governments by giving a special weighting to country voters. Town electorates were given one-third more voters than country areas, thus producing a marked disparity in the value of the votes. Under the terms of the Representation Commission this quota was fixed at 28 per cent for many years, until it was abolished by the Labour Government in 1945. The same Labour Government, with its support waning, also changed the basis of representation from 'total population', which favoured the National Party since rural areas tend to have a larger population of non-voting age, to 'number of electors', which was more helpful to Labour's chances. The National Party, when it was returned to power, deemed it undesirable to restore the 'country quota', but it did revert to 'total population' as the basis for dividing the electorates. Change has thus been continuous and often the result of self-interest; it was not until 1956 that an attempt was made to raise the whole matter of electoral arrangements to a non-partisan level in the Electoral Act passed that year.

This Act is not designed to produce strict mathematical equality of electorates, though it is intended to produce, as far as is possible, a just result. Under the Act, which provided the framework for the 1960 General Election, the Representation Commission meets after each quinquennial census and uses this as the basis in drawing up the electoral boundaries which are thus liable to change every five years. The commission consists of the Surveyor-General, the Government Statistician, the Chief Electoral Officer and the Director-General of Posts and Telegraphs as official members, together with one representing the Government and one the Opposition, nominated by the House of Representatives and appointed by the Governor-General, as unofficial members. In addition a further person, appointed by the Governor-General on the nomination of the official and unofficial members of the commission, acts as chairman. Its most important task is to divide the Dominion up into seventy-six European seats on the basis of an average population figure, but having due regard for size, topography, transport, facilities, nature of the roads, distribution of population and community of interest, these being the considerations specified for the Commission by the Act. Here it is quite clear that although the principle of 'one vote, one value' is the basic consideration, the framers of the Act realized that even today it is difficult to apply this test strictly throughout the country without creating ridiculous anomalies. Hence a reasonable latitude, now fixed at 5 per cent $\pm$ tolerance over or below the average electorate figure, may be invoked. Triennial elections mean that two general elections can be held under some effective redistributions. Where this happens the second election, as in 1960, exhibits more inequalities than the first. The New Zealand system is also unique in the sense that the decisions of the Representation Commission are final in law.

The whole structure of election procedure, from the planning of the election to the casting and counting of votes, is also dedermined by the 1956 Electoral Act. This Act prescribes the three-year maximum for the term of Parliament, the provisions for administering elections, the qualifications of electors and the compulsory registration system with the main and supplementary rolls drawn up before the election together with the quinquennial reregistration after each redistribution. It covers all eventualities such as by-elections, the death of a candidate, the maintenance of order at elections and the provision of a corrupt practices list. In nearly every case its provisions and definitions are simple and straightforward. Thus the qualification for electors is simply British nationality and one year's residence in New Zealand: that for candidates is registration as an elector and the payment of a £10 deposit, repayable if more than a quarter of the total votes of the successful candidate are secured.

These comprehensive provisions were agreed upon by both major parliamentary parties after discussion and negotiation so that the Act was passed unanimously. Certain provisions are subject to limited safeguard within the Act itself. Thus Section 189, Sub. 2 states: 'no reserved provisions shall be repealed or amended unless the proposal for the amendment or repeal (a) Is passed by 75 per cent of all members of the House of Representatives: or (b) Has been carried by a majority of the valid votes cast at a poll of the electors of the European and Maori Electoral Districts.' The main reserved provisions relate to the life of Parliament and the composition of, and instructions to, the Representation Commission. The effect of this form of entrenchment is subject to question, for, legally, it hardly amounts to a safeguard. It draws its force at present from the binding character of a 'gentleman's agreement', but it could eventually come to be recognized as a constitutional convention.

The comprehensive provisions of this Act and its efficient administration by the Electoral Department ensure that all that can be done administratively to secure fair play, is done. As a result, positive misdemeanours tend to be of a stupid rather than a serious nature. During the 1960 election, in one of the very few corrupt practices reported, a young freezing worker was brought before the court on a charge of plural voting. The charge arose from a scrutiny of the roll which had revealed that the accused had voted at two separate booths. In defence the accused said that it was the first time that he had voted and that he did not know much about it. He had been drinking (the stock New Zealand excuse for a misdemeanour) on the morning of the election, and a man at the hotel told him that each man was allowed two votes—'I am pretty sure that I voted for the same candidate both times,' he said. In reply to a question, accused said that he knew now what the votes were for—'One is for beer, and the other one is for the Parliament thing.' This particular culprit was fined £25 and £1 10s. costs for his fault and put on the Corrupt Practices list, suffering loss of voting rights for three years.

Unhappily, although the European electoral system provides as close an approximation to fairness as is possible under the circumstances, this conclusion is less evident when the Maori electoral arrangements are considered. For example, the Maoris did not have the secret ballot until 1937, sixty-seven years after the Europeans. It was not until 1950 that an Amendment Act was passed by the New Zealand Parliament providing that European and Maori elections should be held on the same day. Previously Maori elections had been held on the day preceding European elections. Not until 1951 did a further amendment provide for the polling hours in Maori electorates to be extended to 7 p.m. to conform with European electorates, and the system of compulsory registration which had been in operation for Europeans since 1924 was not introduced for the Maoris until 1956. In some cases there have been sound reasons for such delays, but the element of un-intentional discrimination, implying that Maori electorates are less important than their European counterparts, cannot be denied. The practical importance of this is to be seen in the different methods employed to delineate electoral boundaries. European electorates are redivided by the non-partisan Repre-sentation Commission every five years, a system first inaugurated in 1887. Maori electorates are still redivided by the old mid-nineteenth-century method, much criticized when it was intro-duced—a proclamation by the Governor-General in Council. Thus whilst European electorates have been regularly redivided for nearly eighty years now, only one major change has been made in the Maori electorates. This occurred in 1952 when the boundaries were redefined to reduce numerical inequalities, but even this merely modified an abuse which had existed longer than the present century.

The lack of correlation between the two systems may be clearly seen by comparing the numbers of voters on the rolls in European and Maori electorates:

Electors on roll to nearest thousand in 1960

Thousands	9	10	11	12	13	14	15	16	17	18	19	20	21
Maori Electorates (No.)	1			1	1	1							
European Electorates (No.)					1	8	13	15	21	10	5	1	2

Clearly there is no direct comparison here in terms of one vote, one value. A vote in Southern Maori (9,319 on roll) is worth twice as much as a vote in Waitakere (21,244 on roll), or Manukau (21,458 on roll), yet judged in terms of total population the Maori electorates are, on average, larger not smaller than the European electorates. The result is that, by continuing with this system of special representation, Maori interests on many occasions have been left to the four representatives who form an ineffectually small part of a House of eighty members. With a present-day Maori natural increase rate of 35·27, compared to the European rate of 15·67, it is clear that this inequitable situation cannot be allowed to continue for much longer. Within a few years the decision will have to be taken either to merge the two systems, or to enlarge Maori representation.

Electoral arrangements of the type used in New Zealand inevitably favour a two-party system and power has long alternated between Labour and National with third parties making but a very slight impression.

	Labour Votes	%	National Votes	%	Social Credit Votes	%	Other Votes	%
1946	537,000	51·3	507,100	48·4	—	—	3,100	0·3
1949	512,600	47·6	553,800	51·4	—	—	10,300	1·0
1951	490,100	45·8	577,600	54·0	—	—	2,000	0·2
1954	484,100	44·1	485,600	44·3	122,600	11·2	4,600	0·4
1957	559,100	48·3	511,700	44·2	83,500	7·2	3,100	0·3
1960	508,200	43·4	557,000	47·6	100,900	8·6	4,400	0·4

The swings between elections have been comparatively slight and impressively regular, reflected to an exaggerated degree by regular changes in the seats in Parliament:

	Swing			Seats Labour	National
1943–6	1·2%	to National	1946	42	38
1946–9	3·3%	to National	1949	34	46
1949–51	2·2%	to National	1951	30	50
1951–4	4·0%	to Labour	1954	35	45
1954–7	2·1%	to Labour	1957	41	39
1957–60	4·1%	to National	1960	34	46

However, an inevitable disadvantage of the first-past-the-post system of single-member constituencies is that the distribution of seats does not always accurately represent the division of votes, especially if an important third party exists. In 1954 National, with just over 50 per cent of the two-party vote, won forty-five seats and Labour with the support of a fraction under 50 per cent of the two-party vote, secured only thirty-five. The National Party could have won the election on a marked minority of votes, for as the boundaries were drawn, even 48·5 per cent of the two-party vote would have been sufficient to return between forty-one and forty-three members for National. As a result of the further boundary changes in 1956 this bias was much reduced in the 1957 and 1960 elections, but it was still noticeable, for in 1957 in the seventy-six non-Maori electorates the Labour Party obtained 51·4 per cent of the two-party vote and only thirty-seven seats, whilst the National Party with 48·6 per cent, won thirty-nine seats.

In part this bias to National is due to a factor on which the 1956 Act was a compromise and over which the two parties still differ: the respective merits of 'total population' and 'number of electors' as a basis for the division of electorates. The 5 per cent latitude in redistribution also favours National since it is mostly used in an endeavour to prevent the creation of sprawling rural electorates. Finally there is the tendency for Labour to pile up large majorities in city electorates while National's support is more evenly spread and therefore more effective. The combined result of these factors is a handicap which may amount to as many as six seats against Labour.

A final noteworthy feature of the working of the system is the regularity of high polls. Unlike Australia, New Zealand does not have compulsory voting, yet the average poll at general elections is consistently high, usually about 90 per cent, and far higher than the average poll in Britain. This consistently high poll may be partly attributable to the referendum, held jointly with each election, at which the voter is asked to decide between 'National Continuance', 'State Purchase and Control', or 'National Prohibition' of the sale of alcoholic liquors. Other factors affecting the high polls may be the comparatively small size of the electorates, the generous provision of polling booths, the closing of the bars at midday on polling day, and the somewhat practical nature of New Zealand politics. There is also a special factor in the very extensive facilities for 'envelope votes', for some 10 per cent of the total vote is normally cast in this way. Under the provisions of the 1956 Electoral Act, a person may apply as a special voter if: 'He will throughout the hours of polling on polling day be travelling under conditions which preclude him from attending to vote at any polling place in the district', or 'He satisfies the Returning Officer, or Deputy Returning Officer, that on any other ground it will not be possible for him to vote at a polling place in the district without enduring hardship or undue inconvenience'. In addition to these generous provisions and the usual stories of polling officers collecting votes by rowing-boat or other methods, many votes are recorded overseas and on ships at sea. Thus no effort is spared to collect votes and provisions regarding the casting of votes are made as easy as possible, so that high polls are to be expected.

The efficient functioning of the system goes far to ensure that it has widespread acceptance. After a long history of changes New Zealand does seem to have arrived at a system which maximizes the opportunities for voting, is reasonably just, and also tends to favour the possibilities of a clear result. The state of Maori representation, which contrasts rather unhappily with this, is due not to conscious principles of discrimination, but rather to the same pragmatical development which has characterized the European system, coupled with undue neglect.

II

DRAMATIS PERSONAE: THE PARTIES

THE 'modern' period of New Zealand's brief political history, a period which begins in the late nineteenth century, has been characterized by a basic continuity. Conflict between Right and Left, between the defenders of the *status quo* and the advocates of change and reform has been the dominant political dialectic for most of the period since the Liberals took office in 1891. Both the major parties which contested the 1960 election were founded comparatively recently, Labour in 1916, National in 1936, but the actual dates are unimportant beside the fact that both are the present-day exponents of this traditional conflict.

Labour's line of inheritance is an indirect one. Formed in part because of the failure of the Liberal Party to maintain the radical momentum of the 1890s, Labour eventually replaced the Liberals as the party of challenge to the established order. On coming to power for the first time in 1935, Labour's electoral majority was distributed both over the Dominion as a whole and within the towns, in much the same way as the vote which had brought the Liberals to power in the 1890 election and supported them there until 1912. Labour's reformist policy was also similar in some respects to that of the Liberals in their prime so that the Labour leader, Michael Joseph Savage, embodied a good deal of truth in his claim that 'We intend to begin where R. J. Seddon and his colleagues left off'. The mantle was clearly inherited albeit indirectly. National's continuity is even clearer because the party is a physical descendant, the offspring of a union between the Reform and United Parties. Reform, growing out of the opposition to the Liberals, was the proponent of the conservative tradition while United, though actually descended from the Liberals, had become, by the time of the change of name, an alternative conservative party. In 1931 after several years of three-party confusion, Reform and United at last formed a Coalition Government to fight the depression and the Labour Party, the union being cemented into a new party, with a new title, and new organization, but many of the old parliamentary personnel, in 1936.

The degree of difference between the two traditions which Labour and National now represent, and the volume of the two-party debate between them, have both fluctuated with changing circumstances. They have been able to change the more readily because neither party is anchored by the firm ideological ties of some overseas parties. Both are in the main pragmatic, even opportunist in their policies. A political history which has lasted for just over a hundred years has provided no ideology for the party of the Right, and no institutions, other than a generalized *status quo*, for it to venerate. National, like its conservative predecessor, Reform, has tended to rally round the negative principle of anti-socialism and opposition to the activity and programmes of the party of the Left. To this negative basis have been added a somewhat generalized attachment to private enterprise, 'freedom', individualism, and opportunity. None of these principles has been erected into a dogma or doctrine for the party. Nor could they be, for the State has always played a major role in New Zealand politics and all sections of the community, even the most conservative, have been ready and willing to turn to it for protection, subsidy or intervention. A wide sphere of State activity is thus taken for granted and a party basing itself on doctrinaire opposition to the power of the State would receive very short shrift at the hands of the electorate.

Conservatism without any traditions save that of continued existence has been opposed by 'socialism without doctrines'. Labour received some of its initial stimulus in the ideologies of socialism and the class war, both found among the groups and unions anxious to break away from the Liberal Party and take an independent line. Once the break had been made and the party had achieved its own momentum these origins were of declining influence. The steady rise to major party status produced, as a necessary precondition of that rise, a gradual dilution of socialism. 'Socialization of the means of production, distribution and exchange' remained a part of the constitution right up to 1951 but in the same way as skeletons long remain in proverbial family cupboards. In fact, from 1925 socialism was mentioned but rarely. It was not disavowed explicitly: a party cannot disavow its own past completely, but it ceased to have any practical relevance to current policies. When Labour came to power in 1935 it was with a programme of reform within the capitalist system, based on what

amounted to Keynesian common sense with Douglas Credit overtones, rather than socialist prescriptions. Since that time the party
has remained ready to extend the power of the State but only so
far as is necessary to secure its real goals of welfare, equality of
sacrifice or benefit, and full employment.

Differing as they do in attitudes rather than fundamentals, and
lacking firm ideological roots, the two parties can the more readily
be buffeted apart or together by the winds of circumstance. Two
circumstances have had a particular influence. The depression,
discrediting prevailing policies and the party in power, allowed
Labour to introduce its panaceas: social security, equality of
sacrifice, insulation of the economy through State marketing
arrangements and price guarantees, and diversification through
the development of industry. With this, and encouraged further by
the war, went a close State regulation of the economy and overseas
trade through subsidies, price and other controls, and import
restrictions. Depression and war were followed by the second
major influence on the Dominion's modern politics: the prosperity
of the affluent fifties, a prosperity which, in New Zealand as
elsewhere, has produced a trend to the Right, as well as a tendency
for the two lines of tradition to converge after depression had
forced a divergence. The National Party came to power in 1949
but proved reluctant to court unpopularity by doing more than
tinker with the machinery of economic control and the welfare
State built up by its predecessor. Labour for its part proposed few
major alterations. A little more of the same pink pill was its
prescription for the fifties.

Wide or narrow, the differences between the two parties,
between the two lines of tradition, reflect in the main the differences between the sections of the community on which the
parties base themselves. Labour draws the bulk of its support
from the wage-earners, the unionists, and the less well-off sections
of the community to whom welfare and security have the most
immediate relevance. National bases itself on the farmers and the
better-off elements in towns and cities, people with a direct
interest in lowering taxation and encouraging enterprise. Though
both parties are essentially responsive to the needs of these
supporters both have also to appeal to intermediate sections of the
community and to make inroads into their opponent's strongholds in order to secure a majority. This need is a built-in

guarantee that differences will be minimized as both parties attempt to conciliate the maximum possible degree of support. In any case the social scale is a comparatively restricted one in New Zealand so that differences between parties based on sections of that scale will also be slighter than in less egalitarian countries. Add to this circumstance the fact that in the 1950s most sections of the scale have been reasonably contented, reasonably affluent, and a narrow range of differences between the political parties is seen as almost inevitable. And yet the tendency to converge is dependent on prosperity. Economic developments could readily force the parties apart again. Depression, affecting the base of the social pyramid more severely than the apex, could once again become a political catalyst. Population growth, creating a need for industrialization, could accelerate the divergence of interests between town and country and hence the divergence between an urban Labour Party and a National Party which has to straddle both sections.

Convergence in policy has been paralleled by the development of a growing similarity in organization, for both parties have tended to become centralized bodies. Power in each has come to rest with the parliamentary party and not with the subordinate machine of the mass organization outside Parliament. This is not to say that the party activists who man these machines do not get their necessary reward of influence in the party and on its policy, but rather to point out that uncontrolled parliamentary parties themselves decide just how much reward is to be given and that excessive generosity has not been a characteristic of their attitude. It would appear that Robert McKenzie's thesis on the basic similarity of the two major British parties in respect of internal power distribution is probably even more applicable to New Zealand. This similarity has, however, been developed by different influences in each party, and is maintained by different organizational devices.

The Labour Party constitution is a complex one for Labour is not only a party but also the political wing of the whole Labour Movement. Though relations between the heads of the political and industrial wings of that movement, Mr. Nash and Mr. Walsh, have hardly been marked by excessive amicability in the fifties, and though the trade unions have not been the active force of previous decades, party and unions still consult together through the Joint Council of Labour and other channels and the unions still provide over two-thirds of the party membership of approximately 180,000. Though these 'affiliated' members pay a lower subscription than the individual members, 1s. 6d. as compared with 5s., the unions provide the bulk of party finance through the very number of their members, and through their additional contributions. Yet while they are the backbone of the party, the role of the unions in the New Zealand Labour Party is less clearly defined, and is not as dominant as that of their counterparts in the British party.

The remaining members of the party, the individual members, some of whom are also members through affiliated unions, are grouped into about seven hundred branches distributed unevenly over the Dominion. Like the trade union affiliations, they tend to be concentrated in the towns. Labour is predominantly an urban party, and most of the urban electorates have four, five, or more branches, while many of the rural seats have but one or two. Branches vary in size and in activity and vigour, though generally speaking branch activity and enthusiasm have been low in the fifties, a factor which has assisted in the transfer of power to the centre.

Above the branches are the Labour Representation Committees on which both branches and affiliated trade unions are represented in proportion to their membership, a situation which usually gives trade union delegates a majority. The function of an L.R.C. is to act as the governing body for the party in its area, and normally this area is one electorate, though in the four main centres one L.R.C. controls several electorates: eight in the case of Auckland. When this happens the affairs of the party in each individual constituency are co-ordinated by the Inter-Branch Council, a body first established in 1955, and unique in the party in that the delegates to it are sent by the branches only and not by the unions. Though of secondary importance, it is the only body dominated by the individual members.

Branches, affiliations and L.R.C.s all have the right to send delegates to the annual conference of the party, though not all avail themselves of this right for average attendance has been about three hundred and fifty. The 1960 conference, the policy conference for the election, with an attendance of only 307, was the smallest to be held for some years past, and saw, like the 1959 conference, a decline in the number of branches and unions represented to 195 and 57 respectively.

Conference is in theory the 'Parliament' of the movement, and its 'supreme governing body' according to the constitution. In practice in spite of these high claims it is a fairly quiescent body and one which can normally be dominated by the party leadership. In part this is because the leadership has the regular support of many of the trade unions, particularly the more conservative ones, but other mechanical and constitutional means of influence are also available. One is the simple fact that conference cannot hope in its four-day sitting to deal adequately with the five hundred or so remits which are normally sent up to it. The remits have to be consolidated and reduced to about thirty groups by the National Executive Committee, which has a certain amount of latitude in its task. Pressure on time also means that at the conference the remits have to be dealt with by a series of committees, seven or eight in number. Not only are the members of these committees nominated by the executive, though changes are made by conference, but their conveners are always M.P.s or N.E.C. members, and each committee includes in practice three or more other members from these two groups. In a body which is normally only twenty strong the voice of experience can be expected to preponderate. This degree of control over the committees is crucial since approval by these bodies is the main hurdle which remits have to face. For radical remits or remits frowned on by the leadership it is a formidable hurdle. Such remits are either approved in neutered form, or recommended for rejection by the cautious committees. In either case the original remit has little chance of passing, for moves to disagree with the decision of a committee are not numerous, and very few are successful. At the 1960 conference there were only thirty-six amendments to the reports of the committees, and under a third of these, normally fairly harmless modifications, were successful. As a long-stop there is the president of the party who takes the chair, and whose influence could, if necessary, be used to steer the meeting. Since it is normally a fairly hectic, even slightly chaotic function, the conference does normally need a certain amount of guidance and control from the chair.

To emphasize only these means of influence would leave the impression that a legislative power is being frustrated. This impression would be erroneous. Means of influence are comparatively unimportant beside the all important psychological fact that conference is essentially a deferential and a submissive body. Labour has been in power for seventeen of the twenty-six years since 1935, and this has had a major effect both on the psychology of the party and on the internal distribution of power. It has concentrated power in the hands of a leadership which has for so long been the Government, and led to the development of a feeling that conference should neither dictate to nor embarrass this leadership-cum-Government. Based on an attitude, this state of affairs could change; and indeed in the past conference has, on a very few occasions, been able to secure the adoption of a policy which it has urged against the leadership. Yet at the moment the position of conference is best summed up in the words of a Labour Cabinet Minister who commented that it 'can normally be relied on to do whatever the platform suggests it should'. In the unlikely event of a clash, conference could if necessary be ignored. Unlike the conference of the British Labour Party it has little claim to control policy, and it has no constitutional claim to dictate to the Parliamentary Party. The limit of that body's responsibility to conference is to report annually on its treatment of the remits referred to it the previous year.

For the 361 days of the year when conference is not meeting, the title of 'governing body' passes to the National Executive Committee. To this body the conference elects the president, the vice-president, five representatives who must live in the Wellington area, and the woman representative. There are also a Maori representative, and thirteen area representatives elected by the branches and affiliations in the areas concerned through a postal ballot. These area representatives find themselves on the periphery of the executive since they normally attend the four statutory annual meetings and a very few others. The other eight or ten meetings held in the course of the year are mainly attended by the Wellington representatives and the officers. Thus an inner ring of leading party and trade union figures in the Wellington area is in a dominant position.

The most important function of the N.E.C. is to control and direct the party organization outside Parliament. In addition the president and the national secretary, a full-time official, have the right to attend caucus meetings of the Parliamentary Labour

Party, and to speak there, though not to vote. The N.E.C. is, however, essentially subordinate to the Parliamentary Party and tends to confine itself strictly to its organizational duties. Once again this is the result of a long period of office and a short period most of which was near to office.

Such a distribution of power in a party is probably inevitable in a modern democracy, and historically the nearer Labour approached to power the less influential did its outside organization become. Yet the distribution is also influenced by constitutional factors. Both the leader and the secretary of the Parliamentary Party have the right to sit, though not to vote, on the N.E.C., while in practice two or three of the other members have also been M.P.s, as has the president on occasions, so that there are voices to urge the views of caucus on the N.E.C. In addition parliamentary representatives dominate policy formulation. The policy committee which draws up the manifesto before every election consists of four N.E.C. representatives, who include the secretary and the president, and four representatives from the Parliamentary Party, the four being, in 1960, Mr. Nash, Mr. Nordmeyer, Mr. Skinner and Mr. Boord. A clash between these two sets of representatives would be unusual, but of the two it is the parliamentary representatives who have the dominant voice, through personal stature and because theirs would be the responsibility for carrying out the policy if elected. Caucus makes suggestions to the committee, which also considers the remits passed by conference in the previous three years. Even with these obligations the discretion accorded to the committee is almost absolute. It alone is the final arbiter of what goes into the manifesto, and the product of its deliberations is the only policy Labour has, since there are no permanent policy planks: 'the policy of the party shall be that submitted to the electors in the manifesto issued prior to each general election.' As such it is binding on all members even though they do not see it until the campaign opens and have minimal influence on its drafting.

Where power lies in caucus is a complicated question. Labour members naturally act as a disciplined body, but only after decisions have been made collectively in caucus. The influence of the leader on these decisions is impossible to assess, though with a leader of the stature and experience of Mr. Nash it must be considerable, even allowing for the theoretical attachment to the principle of collective leadership, and the formality of the re-election of the leader in the session before an election. In opposition the rank and file can play an active part in the collective deliberations of caucus. They also have a considerable initial influence when the party comes into power, for caucus decides who is to be in the Cabinet, the Prime Minister's task being merely to allocate portfolios to those selected. Once the Government is formed, however, the collective powers of caucus are inevitably reduced. Legislation and policy are still discussed in the regular caucus meetings but most of the policy formulation takes place outside, in cabinet and departments, while the need for governmental secrecy and discretion impose further checks on caucus influence. The attitude of Ministers and leaders to caucus varies; some are prepared to accept caucus views, others such as Mr. Nordmeyer have been reluctant to make concessions to the political expediency urged at times by caucus. Normally, however, the Government's collective voice predominates in caucus, partly because of the need for party solidarity, especially with a very narrow majority, and because the size of the Government, sixteen out of a caucus of forty-one or more, guarantees the basis of a majority. The caucus system certainly does not mean the domination of a Government by its backbenchers.

National has reached a basically similar distribution of power, but by a different route. Since the party has never had an actual physical alliance with bodies such as the trade unions there has never been any provision for extra-parliamentary influence. On the contrary, from the first the party adhered to the view that the parliamentary members should not be subject to control from outside. It is true that the machine was originally more powerful than it is now, for in 1936 when the party came into being there were strong elements in the organization opposed to a parliamentary section which had been discredited by the defeat of 1935, and the organization was later able to play a part in changes forcing the Hon. A. Hamilton out of the leadership. Yet this situation was due only to temporary circumstances. A new leader and the growing strength and prestige of the Parliamentary Party from 1940 onwards soon redressed the balance.

The basis of National Party strength is its enormous membership of 230,000 or just over 40 per cent of the party's total vote. Membership does mean some degree of identification with the party, though the subscription is only 2s. 6d. and such a low figure normally means a correspondingly low level of active participation. Attendance at branch meetings, even at the annual meeting to which several branches confine their activities, is usually a mere 5 per cent of membership in the towns, and about 15 per cent in the country areas, although the women's branches and the junior branches have a rather more active programme on the social side. The result of this low activity is that the executive of secretary, chairman and committee-men are the branch for all practical purposes.

Neither the huge membership nor the 1300 branches into which it is organized are evenly distributed over the Dominion. Rural areas, always solidly National, have the highest membership figures, the sprawling Wallace electorate in the south of the South Island having thirty branches and over 4000 members. Urban electorates, particularly in safe Labour areas, usually have smaller figures, Island Bay having only just over 1000 members. There are exceptions to this tendency for suburban Tamaki, had in 1960 a larger membership than any other electorate with just over 5000 members, and other prosperous suburbs also reached large figures. This distribution of support indicates that National is less monolithic than solidly urban Labour in the interests it represents. In its origins the party was a coalition of various anti-Labour elements, the main bond of union being negative. This characteristic is visible today in the way it has to straddle the support of both urban and rural groups, and reconcile the possibly divergent interests of each.

Above the branch is the electorate committee running the affairs of the party in each individual electorate. Once again power is concentrated in the hands of an executive consisting of the electorate chairman, and a small group who are usually branch chairmen, together with the electorate secretary, who is in a few cases full-time and normally receives an honorarium. Electorate committees in turn send delegates to the next stage of the pyramid, the divisional committee, New Zealand being divided up into five divisions which vary in size from the huge Wellington division covering twenty-five electorates to Otago-Southland which covers only ten. The division is an extremely important unit in the administration of a party which in some respects resembles a coalition of five semi-autonomous empires, each with its own organizers and its own methods, each jealous of its independence. Here again, as at the lower level, power rests not with the full committee which is often so large as to be called a conference, but with the inevitable oligarchy, the executive.

The pinnacle of the organizational hierarchy is the Dominion Council consisting of delegates from the divisions, which controls the affairs of the party outside Parliament. The full council meets only twice a year but an internally appointed executive of twenty meets more regularly, usually about once a month. The leading figures on it are the president and the five divisional chairmen. The five vice-presidents elected by the conference are rather less important. The council is served by the permanent staff at headquarters working under the general director, a full-time official.

National has evolved a party machine which encourages member participation more effectively than does Labour's. Officials at each stage are elected by the stage below, and there is nothing to counterweight the decisions of the individual members or induce in them a feeling of powerlessness in the way the trade unions tend to in the Labour Party. Inevitably, however, democracy is modified by the apathy of the mass of the members, and tempered by the tendency to oligarchy in the shape of the executives at each level with their power of co-option. It is also a democracy which does not reach all the way up the pyramid since it not only stops short of influence over the parliamentary section but is combined with a considerable deference to the leader.

The subordinate nature of the party organization is best demonstrated by the position of its annual conference. Attendance at this assembly is about the same as at Labour's, averaging about three hundred and fifty, though in 1960 just over four hundred attended, including the four delegates sent by each electorate committee, the Dominion councillors and the M.P.s, who also have the right to attend. Business on the other hand is not as great. In 1960 there were only 140 remits and, since the conference is only a two-day affair and there is no subcommittee system, only forty of these could be dealt with. Before they reach the conference the remits have already undergone a long filtering process and the divisions are asked to specify those which they consider to be of the greatest importance, the remainder, which conference is unable to deal with, being left over for Dominion Council. Conference has two main roles. It can be given an illusion of power by being used to decide questions on which there is a division among the parliamentary members, as it was used in 1960 to decide, by rejecting, a proposal for a second chamber. More important it is a sounding board, perhaps even a safety valve, for opinion within the party. The leadership can get to know what the rank and file are thinking and if necessary make concessions to their views, while the rank and file can let off steam. Naturally if the conference is to fulfil this role properly debate has to be free, and there is in fact less machinery for control than at the Labour Party conference. This in turn means that the leadership has to allow for the occasional embarrassment when resolutions are carried against its wishes and intentions, as in 1960 when a resolution was carried in favour of imposing a charge on medicine under the Social Security Act. Embarrassment is all that such an incident can cause, since conference decisions are binding neither on the Parliamentary Party nor on the policy committee. Obviously some are implemented. The 1959 and 1960 conferences both expressed support for the abolition of compulsory unionism, a plank which was included in the party manifesto, though at the last minute. The decision, however, rests with the leadership, which is perfectly free to accept, or reject, conference decisions.

Neither conference nor the Dominion Council, which is of more importance in the organization, can direct or control the Parliamentary Party. They have, indeed, no pretensions to do so because of the attachment to the constitutional propriety that M.P.s should not be subject to control from outside Parliament. In fact the prestige of the Parliamentary National Party has, since the thirties, been such that the party outside Parliament with its nominally separate sphere of jurisdiction has, in practice, been prepared to play a subordinate role. Parliamentary supremacy has also been strengthened by attachment to the leadership principle. In party organization inside and outside Parliament, and in party theology, the leader is allotted a more important role than is the leader of the Labour Party. He is a figure treated with considerable deference, and attachment to the leader is a major bond of unity in a party which, so far as its support is concerned, is not mono-lithically united.

Respect is reinforced by concrete powers. The leader is a member of the Dominion Council and its executive, thus securing a position of influence in the organization. Once elected by the

Parliamentary Party and approved by Dominion Council, he is not subject to re-election. In opposition he allocates members to the subcommittees of caucus which formulate policy on the different aspects of parliamentary activity. On coming into power he selects his own cabinet without reference to caucus. Probably his views are treated with a more automatic respect in caucus than are those of the Labour leader, and he can also claim more influence over party policy. This is formulated by a policy committee consisting of the president of the party, and two other representatives of the Dominion Council, the leader and two representatives of the Parliamentary Party appointed by him. The meetings are also attended by senior headquarters staff. The committee considers remits passed by conference, is advised by a Dominion policy advisory committee on which are leading figures in the organization and maintains full consultation with caucus, but in theory the leader is in a controlling position, partly because of his 'mana' and partly because the constitution states that 'the leader of the party shall from time to time, after consultation with the policy committee, announce outstanding features of the policy'.

Yet in spite both of great potential powers, and of the mystique of the leadership, the leader of the National Party is less powerful than theory might suggest. A leader ignores moods and attitudes in his party at his peril, and both Sir Sidney Holland and Mr. Holyoake have had to face considerable amounts of muffled criticism at moments of difficulty or defeat, while the treatment of Adam Hamilton provides an enduring warning that tenure is terminable. In any case the need to maintain unity and the firm establishment of the caucus system have acted as restraints on the leader. Despite the leader's theoretical powers over policy the wishes of caucus are in practice final since policy is discussed there as it is worked out and any plank rejected by caucus would almost certainly not be accepted by the policy committee. In policy formulation, both electoral and parliamentary, Mr. Holyoake has, like Sir Sidney Holland before him, declined to commit himself early in discussion, and given elaborate consideration to strongly held minority views. Occasionally this hesitation to impose majority or leadership views has led to an indecisive party attitude, even to the tail wagging the dog as it did on the question of joining the International Monetary Fund, about which no action was taken for many years partly because of minority objections.

The corresponding advantage has been the maintenance of a firm party unity. At the moment, therefore, in respect of the leader, theory and practice diverge. Yet so far as concerns the party supporters outside Parliament who approve the theory and know little of the practice, deference to the leader is a further factor strengthening the supremacy of the parliamentary Party.

The freehold claim on the political system established by the two major parties has made the lot of minor parties a hard one. Several have failed to establish themselves and withered after one election, as did the Democrats in 1935, the Real Democracy Movement and the Democratic Soldier Labour Party in 1943. The Social Credit Political League, formed in 1953, has, therefore, survived better than most, for 1960 was its third election contest. Survival does not, however, mean that the League has a firmly established machinery of organization, for it has only some 5000 members spread very unevenly over the Dominion. Only the fierce enthusiasm of the few maintains the rickety organizational framework which rises from the electoral branches, through the regional executives, to the annual conference and the Dominion council. Disruption appeared to threaten in 1958 when Mr. Wilfred Owen, a Christchurch manufacturer, and the leader of the League in 1954 and 1957, resigned after a series of disagreements on policy and the constitution, following this in 1960 by resignation from the League. The danger was averted by moving the headquarters from Christchurch to Wellington, appointing a new national secretary, providing new bonds of unity through a monthly periodical *The New Zealand Guardian*, and a series of points of principle, and forbidding the branches to discuss technique so that they could be kept clear of the quicksands of theoretical division. Social Credit was clearly settling down to a long-term political siege of Jericho. An even smaller party, the Communist, has been carrying on its own siege since 1921, but with a conspicuous lack of success. Branches are few, and the tiny membership is concentrated mostly in Auckland. Though a rise in membership was reported in 1960, the story of the party in recent years has mainly been one of dwindling membership, declining activity and continued appeals for financial support to fight elections and keep the party weekly, the *People's Voice*, going. The onslaught on capitalism has become a pathetic rearguard action.

New Zealanders, Maori and Pakeha, are one nation so that in theory the parties should have the same Maori organizations as they have for the European electorates. In practice, however, separate rolls and differing customs and attitudes produce organizational differences. Generally speaking Maori organization is much weaker, and depends to a great extent on informal personal contacts, and on the influence of tribal ties. Even Labour has not got an efficient Maori organization, though it has held the four Maori seats since 1943. Formal organization consists of a number of Maori branches and committees scattered over the country, and an elected Maori policy committee which was established in 1957 with power to elect a Maori representative to the N.E.C. The party also has the advantage of contacts with the chiefs and the leading figures of the Maori world, and of a connexion cemented in the 1930s with the Ratana Church. This Church, a movement to achieve Maori unity and reach parity with the Europeans with the aid of supernatural guidance, claimed, in 1956, the allegiance of 14 per cent of the Maoris though its influence may have been wider. The four Labour M.P.s in the Maori seats are all ministers of the Church and the maintenance of these 'four quarters' of a prophecy by Wiremu Ratana, is looked upon as a trust bequeathed to the Church. Difficulty was therefore caused in 1960 when Mr. Omana, M.P. for Eastern Maori, expressed the intention of retiring and signed the nomination papers for Mr. Steve Watene, a leading Maori trade unionist and a member of the N.E.C. of the Labour Party, but not a member of the Ratana Church. After a period of hesitation Mr. Omana decided to stand again, and the National candidate for Western Maori claimed that Mr. Watene's selection had been opposed by the Church and that to prevent it Mr. Omana had been prevailed on not to retire. If this claim was in fact correct, the problem of relations between Ratana Church and Labour Party is due for revival in three years.

The last National Maori M.P., Sir Apirana Ngata, was defeated in 1943. Having relied up to that time on the prestige and position of individual candidates, the National Party had to begin the work of building up a Maori organization almost from scratch. With strenuous efforts the number of branches has grown; there are now eight in Southern Maori, more elsewhere. Maori representation on divisional committees is provided for, there is a

Maori electorate committee on the European pattern, and in some cases a European type of candidate selection. At the top there is a Maori affairs advisory council set up in 1946, and a vice-president representing the Maori race is elected to the Dominion Council at party conference. Yet much still depends on informal contacts, even though increasingly these are among ex-servicemen and farmers rather than among the 'blue bloods' of Maoridom. The extent of the dependence on individuals is illustrated by the reluctance to make the advisory council an elected and not an appointed body. To turn to Social Credit is to repeat the same story, with the reservation that the dependence on individuals is even more marked because of the absence of formal organization.

A review of the framework, Maori and European, on which the New Zealand parties depend makes it clear that organizational differences are slight. In both major parties the organizations outside Parliament are primarily vote-getting machines, the 'handmaidens' of the parliamentary party. Naturally the parliamentary parties listen to the views of the organizations if strongly expressed, and naturally too these views are more influential when a party is in opposition than when it is clothed in the mantle of power, but never are they dominant. The decision on whether or not to accept the views offered by the organization rests with a parliamentary party which cannot be controlled. Such a situation is an inevitable product of the needs of democracy, for as Mr. Shand put it before the election, 'All political parties need some form of organization outside to help in the collection of funds and the management of their affairs so that they can fight elections, but it is fundamental to our democratic system that political control should stay with those in this house; a political party ceases to be a political party in the sense we accept in British democracy if it is dominated by some powerful group outside.'

This situation has been strengthened by two factors indigenous to New Zealand. The smallness of the parliamentary parties has made them more cohesive by supplementing party connexions with strong personal ties, and tended to reduce the possibility of disgruntled groups attempting to reinforce their views by appeal to the outside organization. Secondly the low temperature at which political debate has been conducted in the Dominion in recent years has damped political activity and enthusiasm, and made the party organizations somewhat less strenuous in their discussion and advocation of policy. Indeed in this situation the normal channels of communication upwards have tended to be reversed, for the flow of ideas, discussion and policy formulation has often been downwards from the parliamentary parties.

Within this basic similarity there are minor organizational differences but, like the policy differences between the parties, they are questions of degree and emphasis rather than fundamental opposition. National has been able to secure a rather higher degree of member participation, possibly a greater feeling of internal democracy, than has Labour with its trade union tie and its failure to maintain enthusiasm for further reform. On the other hand the Labour Party conference, though now fairly quiescent, is potentially more powerful than its National Party counterpart, partly because of the legacy of the past, partly because where National M.P.s and officials recognize the unimportance of their conference so far as policy formulation is concerned, the attitude in the Labour Party is rather more respectful and conference has more of a central role in the organizational year. Finally there is the difference produced by the enhanced position accorded to the leader in the National Party. In practice he may not use his powers to the full, and in 1960 Labour too may have had a powerful leader in Mr. Nash, yet there is a future potential for differences between a party expressly attached to collective leadership and the binding force of majority decision and one attached to the individual leadership principle. If, therefore, immediate differences are slight, those differences like the policy differences, could enlarge with a change in circumstances.

III

THE SCENE IS SET: 1957–1960

The 1957 Election; Results and Programmes

IN the general election of 30th November, 1957, the Labour Party won six seats from National which restored Labour to office after eight years on the Opposition benches. One sure National seat was left nominally undecided because the Labour candidate had been killed on the eve of polling. A by-election later confirmed the electorate's loyalty to National, leaving the new state of the parties in the House: forty-one Labour against thirty-nine National. Five of the six seats transferring their allegiance were in city suburbs of middling or mixed social composition: Roskill and Tamaki in Auckland, Lyttelton and St. Albans in Christchurch, and St. Kilda in Dunedin. The other Labour victory was Nelson, a constituency made up almost wholly of a provincial town.[1]

Labour held a majority over National of 4·10 per cent of the valid votes cast, or 57,000 in an electorate of one and a quarter million. Non-voting declined and altogether 93½ per cent of those eligible participated in the choice. Between the elections of 1954 and 1957 the third party, Social Credit, had lost approximately what Labour gained in 1957, 4 per cent of the votes. Meanwhile National passed from a 45:35 lead in seats to a 39:41 minority while hardly varying its share of the suffrages. The movement of votes to Labour was least in the country and the wealthiest city electorates. It was most powerful in the class of seat where the main changes of member occurred—the middling suburbs. The direction of the particular appeal exercised by the Labour programme, to judge from the results, was towards the family man, whether getting established in the new suburbs of city and town or living in the less well-to-do urban Labour strongholds.

It is obvious from Labour's 1957 platform that the party

---

[1] A more detailed treatment of these elections will be found incorporated in the analysis of the 1960 election in Chapter XII.

intended the result it got. A major plank was the increase of the family benefit from 10s. weekly to 15s. weekly for each child. In a renewal of a 1954 offer, loans for new houses were promised at 3 per cent interest, the neediest cases to be taken first. National's answer was to propose that, where the applicant already owned a section, loans should be granted covering 100 per cent of the cost of a new house, to a limit of £2500. By an intriguing development of the redistributive principle, families were offered by Labour the choice of capitalizing their child benefits for the future up to a limit of £1000, the money to be used to reduce existing mortgages or make a deposit. The child allowance was to be paid for a year in advance on the birth of the first child and again when children entered secondary school—to cope with outfitting new pupils. National offered a £25 gift to meet the latter contingency. Labour added a scheme for free textbooks.

For the pensioner, the universal superannuation benefit was to be raised by Labour to equal the age benefit so that, when 65 years old, the pensioner could opt for the former payment, which carries no means test. The age benefit itself was to increase somewhat and the allowance of capital before deduction of benefit was to rise. The National Government also promised to equalize the universal superannuation and age benefits, but there remained a measure of advantage for pensioners in Labour's proposals. There were other more general plans advanced by both parties. One big change was Labour's resolution to substitute a smaller, well drilled and equipped unit for compulsory military training. Another Labour proposal was of great local interest—a railway to join Nelson to the South Island main trunk system.

All taxpayers were interested in the concessions which would come with the introduction of the Pay As You Earn method of taxation. Both parties proposed to forgive the year which can be dropped out without a gap in the State's revenue when a country shifts from paying on past incomes to paying on present ones. There was still, however, one year's tax due in February 1958, one month before the P.A.Y.E. deductions would start. Labour's argument was that this overloaded the ordinary man, so Labour would rebate the first £100 of tax due in February. Naturally tens of thousands would have less tax due than £100, but these smaller sums at least they would not have to pay. National offered a 25 per cent rebate on all incomes up to a limit of £75 deductible from any one income. In addition this rebate was 'built into the P.A.Y.E.' tables enacted in 1957 for application in April, 1958. It was apparently to continue for three years, though there was some muddle over this and it was not emphasized. A provision was already embodied in National's tax legislation which deferred the payment by the self-employed of social security tax owed for the year 1957–8 and due during 1958. This was deferred until death or departure from the country. Labour proposed to collect in instalments. Overall, National emphasized its record as a party which had reduced the rates, if not the proportion of taxation.

Social Credit campaigned vigorously but again centred its effort on explaining the views of finance held by the party. People had turned to it on its first appearance in 1954. This time they turned away.

The net result of the forces at work was a Labour majority of two, or of one in a House of eighty when the Speaker was elected. Many were the predictions of an unworkable Parliament and an early election. These forecasts ignored decades of Tasmanian political history and the wonders of discipline accomplished in the Commons on a majority of seventeen. Certainly, so far as discipline in voting was concerned, Labour passed its long test with colours flying, while the National Opposition were co-operative in the matter of pairs. When the Labour caucus met, on 5 December, to elect the sixteen cabinet ministers, there were no complete surprises. The Prime Minister allotted major portfolios to four out of the five surviving ministers of the first Labour Government. But he upset calculations by giving senior posts to Mr. H. Watt (Works), Mr. P. N. Holloway (Industries and Commerce) and Mr. R. Boord (Customs), all of them relative newcomers to Parliament.

With the ample excitements of an overturn victory behind them and a plump programme of welfare benefits to confer, the second Labour Government turned to carve the duck only to find the bird removed. The rapidity with which the Cabinet had now to readjust its high hopes and think afresh must have dismayed all but the stoutest hearts. The new Government assumed office on 12 December, 1957. Three weeks later, one of those weeks containing Christmas and New Year, the Prime Minister went on the national radio network to proclaim the existence of an economic crisis over New Zealand's reserves of foreign exchange and to announce a policy for meeting it. Necessarily, some measure of austerity was back.

The Labour party, not just the beneficent party which had erected the welfare state but also the party of economic disciplines which had controlled, rationed and stabilized the country through the thin days of the war, was thus forced once more and immediately to present both aspects of its history to a public which had long since clamoured for the one and rejected the other. It was, in fact, quite uncanny how in three years the second Labour Government was driven to recapitulate the fourteen-year progress of the first Labour administration. First the conferment of benefits in the form of the £100 income tax rebate and 3 per cent loans for housing, accompanied by import control; then the middle period of austerity; lastly a gradual easing of curbs and the upsurge of a growing and somewhat redesigned economy. And as the events were recapitulated, so were the emotions they evoked: enthusiasm with benefits, foreboding at import selection, followed by discontent at taxation and doing without. The discontent lingered until it became impatience with remaining controls, resentful disbelief that *dirigisme* had ever been necessary, disbelief in the Government's capacity, and disbelief even of the evidences of returned prosperity.

The Parties Lay the Blame for the Foreign Exchange Crisis

Who was responsible? It was to this question that Mr. Nash addressed himself in the second sentence of his broadcast of 1 January 1958. 'The most urgent of these [concerns] has been a problem not relating to the Labour Government's policy but one which confronted us as a situation which must be met immediately . . .' Thus, even before he had described what was to make the new year so unhappy, Labour's leader was pointing straight back to the Nationalist past as the cause for policies Labour must reluctantly assume. It was inherently a defensive, apologetic gesture and it signalled a debate which was not stilled for three years.

The situation the Prime Minister described was certainly grim. New Zealand at the low point of the export-import year had funds to meet only six weeks' payments . . . You will agree that this is an astonishing situation in which to find ourselves after a period of eight years of unprecedented quantities and prices for exports, and yet these are the hard facts . . . Just recall those figures—£4 million down in September, £14 million down by October, £20 million down by November, £30 million in December—from £4 million to £30 million in a space of three months. That is the most rapid slide in the history of New Zealand trade and an indictment of the previous Government which in that short space allowed New Zealand's overseas reserves to fall from £83 million on 2 October to £45.5 million on 25 December . . . In addition to this sum we have a further £20 million invested for defence, which, although set aside for a special purpose, will not all be required during the coming year.

With righteous indignation the sometime Labour Minister of Finance, Mr. Nash, contrasted the reserves now with the reserves, relatively of double the size, left behind for National in 1949. He stigmatized the Nationalists' 'vacillation of policy, with firstly the importing free for all which developed into "crazy trading" (1950–52), then exchange allocation (1952–54), then free imports again (1955), then the credit squeeze.' Labour had criticized for years, the country was told, but to no great effect and the climax had been the last three months of excessive importing. The frightening figures were only now visible. However, insisted Mr. Nash, the responsibility for preventative action had been ignored much earlier. 'In the last two years there has been no effective action to build our overseas funds, to stop the flow of imports, and to build against or to offset the serious situation caused by the falling price of butter'.

Such was the Labour case; not simply for the necessity of immediate import controls, but also for the rigours of the Budget later in the year. When election time rolled round again Labour was still explaining that the reason the electors had been required to take the rough with the smooth, consumer taxes with benefits, rebates and loans, was the avoidable exchange crisis the National Government had handed on to them. The experiences of 1957–8 also underlay Labour's emphasis in the 1960 election campaign on the urgency of further industrialization. National's eight years of bounteous overseas prices had been so mismanaged, its opponents charged, that New Zealand had been left exposed to every tremor in the marketplace. Labour would shape what National had fumbled and encourage an expanded secondary industry to pull the country out of its dangerous dependence upon others.

A certain amount of this case was conceded at the time, if not by the Nationalists, then by those traditional critics of Labour, the metropolitan Press. And as with other aspects of this three-year period, it is remarkable how what was to follow was summed up at the start. The main leader in the *New Zealand Herald* for 11 December 1957, not quite a fortnight after the election, was headed 'Shadow of Import Control'. Noting that Labour was not pledged against such measures, the editor decided that:

The continued melting of overseas exchange reserves will give the new Government sufficient excuse for drastic action . . . Even if the election had gone the other way, the National Party would have been forced to adopt emergency measures in defence of overseas funds. The movements which have reduced the reserves to the lowest postwar figure began while the National Government was in office . . . Mr. Holyoake and Mr. Watts would probably have endeavoured to avoid the rigidities of import licensing, but stringent exchange rationing might well have been employed.

Thus while it was agreed there was a crisis demanding action and its genesis in National's term was pointed out, the newspaper distrusted from the outset the methods Labour would apply. Greater still was its dislike of what could be done under cover, as it were, of the method of import control. Starting from a recollection of what it termed Labour's normal 'doctrinaire policy of protection', the *Herald* anticipated the promotion of any and all home industry at the price of utilitarian styles, monotony and scarcity. In turn it expected political pressures against austerity to build up until controls were blown away.

Either way, however, immediate austerity there would be. If National had been in to repeat past measures, importers would have had their allocations of exchange reduced but would have continued to choose what was brought into the country. If Labour ran true to past form, the Government and its officers would plan centrally what classes of goods were to enter and allot licences accordingly, but still the overall quantities would have to shrink. For the figures were adamant. Instead of the £77 millions of the previous year there were £46 millions left at the end of December, 1957, with no predictable end to the rundown in sight. Reviewing the possible courses of action the Prime Minister found five. He rejected sole reliance on borrowing because London would not yield £50 or £60 million, interest rates were high and borrowing would leave the cause of the crisis untouched. To reduce purchasing power by cuts and unemployment would be too slow and, anyway, wrong. To alter the exchange rate sufficiently could add 30 per cent to the cost of living and start rocketing inflation. Exchange control was rejected as a blunt instrument, incapable of picking out needed goods. Mr. Nash was left, as expected, with a policy of import control.

The scheme, implemented from 1 January 1958, divided imports into licensing categories and the availability of exchange from trading banks was dependent on the possession of a licence. Raw materials for New Zealand's primary and secondary industries and certain foodstuffs and essentials like medical supplies were to enter virtually in 1956 quantities. Since four-fifths of a buoyant export income was normally spent thus, buying the usual essentials from a lowered income could only leave thin pickings for the rest. Nothing was to be allowed licensed entry which was already made or available in New Zealand. In between the shut and the open categories, a limited issue of licences was made for goods on the bases of general need and a recent history of importation. The chosen sacrifices were redolent of the previous prosperity: assembled cars and motor-cycles down a half, cars for New Zealand assembly down a quarter, no foreign-manufactured cigarettes or beer, spirits less by 60 per cent, a severe cut on overseas clothes and no imported footwear. As for foreign washers, irons, refrigerators or sporting goods, none were to enter. Only petrol was excepted. For the rest, New Zealand would henceforth process or produce its own luxuries and consumer durables, use more fully its clothing and leathergoods factories where employment had been slipping for two years, and once again assemble almost all of a smaller number of cars. Local manufacturers were delighted to be assured of materials and guaranteed a pressing home demand, and praised Labour for 'ensuring full employment and maintaining our standard of living'. The president of the Bureau of Importers, on the other hand, predicted more inflation, rising demand and widespread shortages.

Teething problems were inevitable. By far the most difficult to solve equitably was the problem of late ordering in anticipation of the clamping on of controls, subsequent scarcities and rising prices for stocks held in New Zealand. On 10 February Mr. Nash declared 'the Government has been forced to review all applications for "excess" import licences—that is, licences for goods over and above an importer's normal pattern of trade.' Goods shipped before 1 January 1958 were not affected, but the Government now reversed its original intention of licensing also those imports for which 'firm orders' had been placed and accepted overseas before the 1 January deadline. Since the sanctity of contracts and the importers' good faith were involved the step was a serious one, yet so was the continued exchange decline. The Prime Minister instanced cases of importers with a previous trade of a few thousand pounds ordering in November and December goods worth hundreds of thousands for 1958 delivery. And, indeed, on 3 December, the *Herald* had reported a bank official suggesting 'importers had anticipated the change in Government and for some six weeks had been "flat out" bringing in the full amount of current licences.'

The fact that there had been ordering against a possible change of Government was important also because the Nationalists made it a major point in their rebuttal of Labour's charges of financial fecklessness. The ex-Minister of Finance, the Hon. J. T. Watts, was early in the field against Labour's criticisms and controls. He at once declared that 'the position of New Zealand's overseas funds was nowhere near as serious as the Prime Minister, Mr. Nash, claimed.' He underlined what Mr. Nash had noted, namely, the existence of a further £20 million in the Defence Fund, put there for re-equipping the forces, and suggested that a last resort was provided by £10 million more of assets in earthquake insurance fund investments and Post Office Savings Bank reserves. This line of reasoning was developed by himself and his party in the course of the next two parliamentary sessions and the 1960 campaign. It became the countercharge that Labour had panicked, there was no real crisis, the overseas funds were more substantial than they seemed, and that Labour, keen for any excuse to slip a straightjacket on the economy, had done so while diverting and distracting the public by crying wolf about a crisis.

Mr. Watts was also the first to sound the theme that the prospect followed by the reality of a Labour administration had caused the real damage. Labour party speakers had threatened import control, he asserted, and in covering themselves against this eventuality importers had brought the reality closer. Moreover, after the election there had been rumours of an alteration in the exchange rate, so capital fled overseas. This theme was picked up and somewhat retuned by the ex-Prime Minister on 22 February: 'Until it became apparent to the business community that Labour had more than an even chance of winning the General Election . . . overseas funds were in a satisfactory position.' This was an unusual point for the National leader to make because at the date then mentioned, 4 September, the time when external assets were still above those of 1955 and 1956, Labour had two months yet to go before announcing the mass of its election-winning programme. The National leader agreed that the decline of £11½ million to the end of October was unanticipated and 'cause for some concern' but 'invariably' there was a seasonal drain then. 'Statistics indicate', he claimed, 'that it was during and after the General Election campaign that the rot set in. By the end of November [the election day was 30 November] our funds had declined to £58½ million.' Mr. Holyoake concluded by blaming Labour for taking three weeks to institute remedial action despite the ex-Prime Minister having let Mr. Nash know at once the position and the problem 'for which the [Labour] Government itself is largely responsible.'

The Nationalists' reply to the accusation of wasting eight years of big receipts and leaving low funds had to await the second, main session of Parliament in June. The Leader of the Opposition then drew a picture of a land 'in splendid heart'. The internal finances were sound, with the prospect of a 'prudently built up' £7 million surplus. A large public and private investment programme had utilized those past windfalls to raise production on farms and, even more, in factories. If New Zealand manufacturers could supply shortages under Labour's import control it was because of capital works under Nationalist guidance. External finances had certainly 'fallen to a dangerous level' but that, he repeated, was mainly after the election and undoubtedly after the last figure of £66·2 million—the figure for 6 November—which he had received during the campaign and commented on as cause for some concern but not panic. As for prevention, 'we were always taking remedial actions.' Mr. Holyoake illustrated this with the squeeze of credit and the remaining import controls, principally on cars. In the past, he contended, the National Government had acted efficiently and made a surplus in 1950, 1951 and 1953. There had even been an election year rundown in 1954 because 'traders and others were trying to insure themselves against the actions of a Labour Government . . . We dealt with it without giving these shocks to the economy and taking this drastic action with industry. We could have done it again.'

National's plea of 'not guilty' was little credited by the Press at the time and, in all probability, the general public's reaction at first was the same. The party's spokesmen, however, intertwined their arguments with references to the uncollected £21 million in income tax rebates and reiterated the charge that Labour had 'bribed itself into office.' By thus constantly linking the external rundown with the internal rebate, the future inflationary effect of Labour's internal programme was mixed up in the public mind with the past causes of an existing crisis over external assets. If the rundown of funds became 'the most contentious and least understood of the questions that confuse and confound people,' as Mr. Holyoake called it, then he had some part in creating that effective and skilful defence. After the Budget was announced in June, 1958, the public switched its attention to this new offence and began to accept the simple explanation that costly promises were being painfully redeemed. So when Labour continued to insist that the fall in overseas assets was the real cause of all that now befell, the disputed 1957 crisis grew to seem tiresome, remote and an arithmetical enigma about which accused and accuser could both be wrong or right.

The Pattern of the Improvident Fifties

Indeed, it was quite difficult to explain from a platform. In the first place there was no clear pattern in the public consciousness of what had been happening to overseas funds during the 1950s. Candidates could hardly illuminate the events of 1957–8 against the background of a past itself not understood. In actuality, the 1957–8 rundown was the third and worst of its kind, though this at no time became plain. When a fourth such plunge followed, in 1960–1, the electorate was scarcely any the wiser for the three years of oratory devoted to the topic. In 1958 Mr. Holyoake had mentioned the parallel rundown of 1954 and in December, 1957, the *New Zealand Herald* had remarked percipiently that a 'political cycle' was modifying the trade cycle. But these brief hints were not elaborated into common knowledge.

The facts necessary to trace the events of 1957–8, to measure the violence of the crisis against its immediate past, and to appraise the measures taken between 1958 and 1960 are gathered together in Table I. Columns D and F display the movements of New Zealand's assets over a series of trading years. The basic pattern follows from the fact that between the end of June and the end of January each year more is being bought than sold overseas, so the reserves are progressively drawn down. Between the end of January and the end of June the country's primary products bring mounting foreign returns so the funds build up. If the upswing cannot recover what is lost on the downswing this fact appears as a net loss in column H and New Zealand's overseas finances become more shaky, since the next rundown and recovery must begin that much nearer to exhaustion of the funds.

Naturally net gains are more probable if overseas prices move in the country's favour. If prices for exports rise or the cost of foreign imports falls, this is revealed in a rise in the terms of trade index in column J. The very high figures for 1950 and 1951, for instance, reflect the Korean War boom prices for wool. Changes in terms of trade ought to be the main short-term determinant of the annual result in overseas funds. With a healthy economy, rising production should keep ahead of population growth and, as trade expands and requires more finance and produces more reserves, the increment of production ought to show as a series of small plus signs down column K. If the terms of trade move severely against New Zealand in column J, as they did in 1952, then no gain or a small loss should appear, to be followed by substantial additions when terms of trade improve.

If columns J and K are compared, however, the predictable relationship hardly appears at all. With bonanza terms of trade figures of 119 in 1950 and 1951, New Zealand for successive years made a gain of £24 million and a loss of £13 million. In 1958, when terms of trade were at 85, the gain was £17 million, yet funds went down £29 million while terms were ten points higher in 1960. The bold years in the gain-loss column K are years affected by elections. It is obvious that those are, with the one exception of 1955, the years when loss occurs. Instead of a wave-like modification, corresponding to changing prices for our

TABLE I. Trends in Overseas Assets of Banks, on New Zealand Account; in £ million

A Govt	B Year June to June	C Funds at start	D DOWNSWING Cumulative from end June							E Funds in Jan.	F UPSWING Cumulative from end Jan.					G Funds in June	H Net gain or loss for June year	I Calendar year	Govt	J Terms of trade	K Net gain or loss Jan.–Jan.
			Jul.	Aug.	Sep.	Oct.	Nov.	Dec.	Jan.		Feb.	Mar.	Apr.	May	Jun.						
L	1949–50	80	−2	−9	−14	−18	−20	−20	−17	63	+4	+11	+19	+26	+24	87	+7	1949	L	92	0
N	1950–1	87	−3	−9	−16	−18	−24	−14	+4	91	+8	+9	+11	+23	+32	123	+36	1950	N	119	+28
N	1951–2	123	+1	−5	−12	−25	−37	−41	−45	78	+1	+1	−3	−1	−3	75	−48	1951	N	119	−13
N	1952–3	75	−5	−6	−10	−8	−8	−3	+5	80	+15	+22	+29	+37	+38	118	+43	1952	N	88	+2
N	1953–4	118	−10	−11	−16	−19	−17	−14	−11	107	+15	+22	+30	+32	+32	139	+21	1953	N	104	+27
N	1954–5	139	−8	−15	−28	−41	−48	−52	−52	87	+7	+7	+11	+14	+17	104	−35	1954	N	107	−20
N	1955–6	104	−6	−11	−16	−28	−39	−39	−37	67	+12	+18	+24	+33	+33	100	−4	1955	N	111	−20
N	1956–7	100	−3	−6	−13	−21	−24	−23	−23	77	+8	+12	+23	+33	+36	113	+13	1956	N	105	+10
N	1957–8	113	−10	−15	−26	−41	−54	−67	−70	43	+4	+7	+6	+9	+10	53	−60	1957	N	100	−34
L	1958–9	53	+3	+3	−1	+1	+5	+2	+7	60	+9	+15	+25	+33	+41	101	+48	1958	L	85	+17
L	1959–60	101	+3	+8	0	−3	−4	−13	−16	85	+8	+13	+22	+32	+34	119	+18	1959	L	100	+25
L	1960–1	119	−4	−13	−19	−29	−44	−53	−63	56	−3	−2	−2	+1	+6	62	−57	1960	L	95	−29
N	1961–2	62	−9	−10	−9	−13	−10	−14	−13	49	+5	+8	+14	+20	+24	73	+11				
N	62–3	73	−1	−2	−4	−7	−8	−11	−9	64	+10	+20	+30	+31	+32	96	+23				
N	63–4	96	−8	−10	−15	−27	−31	−36	−33	63											

Brace figures (H column): +52, −86, +9.
Brace figures (K column): +44, −64, +13.

Sources: Asset figures from *Monthly Abstract of Statistics*, the official, annual *New Zealand Economic Survey* for 1960 1950–61. Terms of trade index numbers show purchasing and 1961. power (in units of imports) of 100 units of exports, taking N.B. The proceeds of overseas borrowing are included among 1957 as the base year, i.e. 1957 = 100. These figures are from gains in assets.

exports and imports, what shows up is the operation of a politically induced cycle.

This cycle is even more obvious if the results for June-to-June years are examined. Then the effects of the characteristic swift outrush of funds in the months before elections and of the typically weak pickup afterwards are joined together instead of being offset by non-election gains. Column H reveals fully the extent to which election years have become years of crisis for New Zealand's financial reserves overseas. Between-election years are years of recovery, with the now minor exception of 1955–6. In these years Ministers of Finance apply exchange allocation (1952), credit squeeze (1955), or import control (1958). As the table demonstrates, the two more direct controls result in sharp recoveries; the indirectly acting credit squeeze works weakly. Then, with trial by election once more in sight, the pressure relaxes, allocations increase and the import orders flow out, carrying away with them the hard-won funds of the preceding two years.

It is apparent from the table that changes in the terms of trade—economic changes—can widen or contract the political cycle. What ought to have been a feeble post-election upswing at the end of 1951–2 was converted to a slight drop by the violent fall in export prices. The 1957–8 crisis was undoubtedly worsened by the contemporaneous fifteen-point sag in the terms of trade and so also with the case of 1960–1. But the 1954–5 election spree was conducted amid improving conditions and still cost £39 million in all.

Particularly ominous is the fact that, since the June 1954 highpoint of £139 million for overseas funds, the overall trend has been strongly downward. After mid 1955 terms of trade also began to decline. The recovery under credit squeeze policies was so poor that New Zealand approached the 1957 election in a vulnerable condition. Worse still, the cost to funds of each election was rising. Allowing for adverse and then beneficial terms of trade, in 1951–2 and 1954–5 respectively, the loss in each election year was about £40 million. By the end of the decade the average cost of an election in external funds was somewhere between £50 and £55 million. Continuation of these trends would wipe out New Zealand's funds in 1963.

The overseas fund figures testify that New Zealand's politicians had correctly concluded that the voters demanded more than their economic effort had earned. The figures demonstrate how the politicians catered to this demand, though only in election years. Financial risks mounted as the decade advanced but, ironically, rewards to politicians declined. The 1954–5 debauch was the last which satisfied the electorate sufficiently to allow of the Government surviving, and then the governing party dropped a punishing 10 per cent of the vote and crept back for reasons extrinsic to this process of bribe and fall.

Though this general situation was not properly understood by the public in 1957, the Cabinet, which had experienced the rundown twice already, might be expected to have watched for the pattern to reappear and to have acted at once if it could muster the courage. The pattern certainly gave evidence of appearing from the very first return—that for July, 1957—which would have been known to Cabinet, on Mr. Holyoake's estimate of a three-week lag or a two-week delay in a crisis, by mid-August. Funds were down £10 million. This compared, as column D of the table shows, with −£8 million in the last emergency and −£6 million and −£3 million in the intervening years. Perhaps Cabinet took the result for another 1953, −£10 million at this point, but by mid September there could have been little doubt. In the middle of October, three weeks before Labour's platform was announced, the downswing had proceeded farther than all but the plunge of 1954.

If Cabinet had its eyes on other indicators, these, too, showed danger early. Export prices, which had been rising in early 1957, turned sharply downwards in the third quarter. Cheese fell throughout the first two quarters; butter and wool sank from June onwards; meat went down from September. But more critical than these danger signals was the trend in the quantity of imports landed in the country.

Table II places the monthly import figures in 1957 and 1958 against a moving average of the results for the two previous years. There were two good months in 1957 (see line C for March and October) when imports fell distinctly below the preceding level, and in one month, June, there was a slight fall. For three-quarters of the year, however, each month saw a worsening of the position. By mid June, 1957, the Cabinet knew imports were £3·6 million higher over the period since January. At the time of the 1957 Budget the Minister of Finance said he was expecting increased

TABLE II.

Trend in Importing 1957–8; in £ million

	Jan.	Feb.	Mar.	April	May	June	July	Aug.	Sept.	Oct.	Nov.	Dec.
A Mthly Ave of '55 + '56	22·6	21·2	23·0	21·1	23·9	23·0	21·9	25·1	24·3	25·4	26·2	22·4
B 1957 Mthly	23·6	22·1	20·1	25·3	24·3	22·3	24·5	29·4	28·2	22·6	27·6	26·7
C Difference + or − of A:B	+1·0	+0·9	−2·9	+4·2	+0·4	−0·7	+2·6	+4·3	+3·9	−2·8	+1·4	+4·3
D Cumulative Increase	+1·0	+1·9	−1·0	+3·2	+3·6	+2·9	+5·5	+9·8	+13·7	+10·9	+12·3	+16·6
E Latest Mth Orders were placed	Oct. '56	Nov.	Dec.	Jan. '57	Feb.	Mar.	April	May	June	July	Aug.	Sept.

(ELECTION — annotated across the Mar.–April columns)

	Jan.	Feb.	Mar.	April	May	June	July	Aug.	Sept.	Oct.
A Mthly Ave of '56 + '57	23·1	21·0	20·7	22·7	23·3	22·7	24·1	27·2	26·4	23·7
B 1958 Mthly	24·0	23·8	24·4	24·1	26·7	22·8	20·7	24·0	22·8	21·4
C Difference + or − of A:B	+0·9	+2·8	+3·7	+1·4	+3·4	−0·1	−3·4	−3·2	−3·6	−2·3
D Cumulative Increase	+17·5	+20·3	+24·0	+25·4	+28·8	+28·7	+25·3	+22·1	+18·5	+16·2
E Latest Mth Orders were placed	Oct '57.	Nov.	Dec.	Jan. '58	Feb.	Mar.	April	May	June	July

(CONTROLS — annotated across the April–May columns)

imports and the most he hoped for was 'to break even'. By the middle of September imports were known to have soared £9·8 million over the eight months, and a month later, the increase above the average for 1955–6 was £13·7 million. By then prices for exports were well on their way down and overseas funds had dropped £41 million since June. The triennial storm was blowing mightily.

Imports take time to order, to manufacture or assemble in Britain, and then to load and ship. An efficient and expeditious importer allows three months at a minimum between cabling his order and taking delivery. The piled imports which confronted Cabinet before they began to campaign had been ordered at the very latest by June, 1957, a fact which, all by itself, casts a cold light on the explanation that the business community saw which way the November campaign was going and thus caused the import rush. The table suggests that the increase in imports before news of the election result could affect orders amounted at least to the additional £20·3 million delivered by the end of February 1958, and probably to some millions more. Controls on new orders were imposed on 1 January 1958, and could, at the earliest, have taken hold on the April deliveries. Yet only in the month of June 1958 did deliveries fall below the previous level.

The editor of the *Auckland Star*, confronted with Mr. Holyoake's exculpatory statement of 22 February, 1958 was quietly savage: 'Whether there was cause for "alarm" may be a matter of opinion, but by the end of September, if not before, there was cause for action of some kind.' Recalling the Reserve Bank's warning in October that third quarter imports were 24 per cent greater than for the previous year—a fruitless warning—the editor incredulously noted that, 'If Mr. Holyoake's position is understood correctly, it is that the Government of the day cannot be held responsible if there is a dangerous draining-away of overseas funds caused in an election year by expectation of political change.'

It is a nice judgement whether the National Cabinet should have acted in September to batten down the hatches, or whether they should have acted half a year earlier to ensure that there would be no fresh breeze of credit bellying out importers' sails in the spring. Either way, what was primary was not the importers' anticipation of political alterations, but the Government's estimate of what it would have to do to prevent a political change and its parallel decision to ride out the consequences until election day. Three years later a Labour Government made an estimate of almost the same magnitude as to what was needed to survive and similarly held to it. Each Government thereby bequeathed a major problem to its successor, a problem sufficient to make the three years all too short a period in which to find an attractive answer.

For Labour's action in controlling imports, though decisive in shaping its answer to the problem of low funds and high living, was but a beginning. New Zealand's assets remained too near exhaustion for the Cabinet to take the risk that import control by itself would raise funds to a safe level from which to commence the next seasonal downswing. Mr. Nash visited Australia and secured an advance of £7·5 million from the Commonwealth Bank of Australia to the Reserve Bank of New Zealand. In April 1958, before import control took a real grip in June, a loan of £20 million was raised in London at the expensive rate of 6 per cent. Later, a standby credit of £10 million was arranged for two years with the Midland Bank, London. Finally on 1 October it was announced that J. P. Morgan & Co. of New York, with other bankers, had granted £12·3 million worth of dollars, secured by gold, and a revolving one-year credit of £4·1 million.

Nothing could have been more opposed to Labour's instinct for self-sufficiency, more unlike its history of reducing debt held overseas, more contrary to its frequently voiced dislike of high interest and distrust of foreign banking. Altogether £45 million was officially borrowed between March 1958 and March 1959, which provides a measure of the compulsion exerted on Cabinet and party by the exchange emergency. The very next year, as soon as the Government could manage it, there were official capital movements outwards which reduced New Zealand's indebtedness to the rest of the world by £28 million. To Labour stalwarts, within Cabinet and without, the posture of overseas borrower was inherently undignified and unsafe, and besides, Social Crediters were abroad in the land.

The electorate's desire to live beyond its overseas means was still there, however, and the cash and credit to use up stocks quickly was still in the public's hand. Even if New Zealand's production was maximized in 1958–9 it could hardly rival past plenty derived from the combination of an already fully employed home economy plus rich incoming cargoes added to by high prices for exports. If inflation had occurred then, what was to happen now?

Left Hand, Right Hand: Rebate, Housing and Budget

Inevitably, Labour's second action, enacting the income tax rebate of £21 million in February, added to the inflationary problem within the country, as the Nationalists correctly insisted. Labour men pointed out that National's intention to leave certain taxes on the self-employed uncollected till death or departure would likewise have left £18·5 million at large. This reply, nevertheless, did nothing to ease the immediate difficulties of Mr. Nordmeyer, though he did manage to take in £15·2 million of it in instalments over the next two years. Moreover, the rapid implementation of Labour's promise of 3 per cent loans for housing—begun by instruction to the State Advances Corporation on 12 February—was bound to complicate matters. House building, which had hesitated when credit was tight for small businesses and domestic borrowers, now picked up speed. Although it used local labour and timber there was a considerable overseas component, from galvanized iron to electric cable, in this form of capital investment. Stocks would need replacement from overseas and, internally, there was the indubitable embarrassment of a new flow of cheap credit to lower-income families. Otherwise some would have been forced to double up on accommodation, thus leaving builders' stocks intact and allowing builders' labour to find less remunerative and therefore less mildly inflationary occupations than working at their own trades in a housing boom.

Had Labour broken its promises of low-cost housing and an easy rebated conversion to P.A.Y.E., it would still have been faced with a sizeable problem of too much money chasing too few goods. Mr. Nordmeyer tackled one aspect when he requested the trading banks to reduce bank overdraft accommodation. Overdrafts had been permitted to climb £15·1 million since March 1957. Now that March 1958 tax payments had been negotiated, overdrafts were to come down from £184 million to £156 million, though in such a way, Mr. Nordmeyer requested, as not to force traders to realize stocks suddenly nor to deprive manufacturers of the working capital for expanded production. Increasing the ratio of reserves which the trading banks must hold with the central Reserve Bank was the customary mechanism for slowing down the issue of credit, but by this time the lining of the brake was worn with use. During 1957 reserve ratios had been tightened three times, reaching 28 per cent of demand liabilities and 15 per cent of time liabilities, yet Reserve Bank lending to trading banks, to the State and to marketing organizations meant that the brake simply would not hold. Instead of a squeeze there was a £49 million expansion of credit in the year ended March 1958. Nor was Mr. Nordmeyer more fortunate in his first experiences of increasing ratios and making appeals. As Budget time approached advances remained high at £178 million. Something drastic and effective was plainly necessary to meet the probability of internal inflation and the prospect of continued adverse terms of trade.

The consequence was the 1958 Budget and, in turn, the 1960 election result followed largely from that document, as later chapters will indicate. Writing the Budget must have been a cheerless task. Wherever Mr. Nordmeyer looked the statistics were daunting. Funds were down £60 million on the previous June, the flood tide of imports had not yet begun to ebb, bank credit had scarcely dropped, while the indices for export prices and for terms of trade had reached the low points of the decade, 79 and 74 respectively. The one slim hope was provided in May by Great Britain's request to butter-dumping countries to cease overloading the world's single free market for dairy products. Whether this would suffice to clear New Zealand stocks in England and raise returns far was matter for guesswork. Only a supreme optimist could assume that future butter prices would go so high as to pull New Zealand's funds right out of the depths. In any case, such future external improvements would not lessen present tendencies to internal inflation.

On 26 June 1958 Mr. Nordmeyer, having just half an hour before informed the Labour caucus and the bulk of his Cabinet colleagues, rose in the House to announce that the duties on beer, cigarettes and petrol and the sales tax on cars were all, within a fraction, doubled. Cash in hand was to disappear in return for goods in stock. The basic income tax rates of 1954 were restored as from 1 October and personal exemptions for single people and working couples were so reduced that, although income tax increased generally, it fell with particular heaviness on those without family commitments. A single taxpayer earning £1000 was now to pay £130 in tax in a full year instead of £78. A married man with two children on the same salary saw his tax rise from £37 to £49. Thus the fundamental family bias of the welfare state appeared in the Budget in two ways. The larger, freely disposable income of the single was the more sharply reduced by tax. At the same time duties rendered expensive those pleasures which a family man might be expected to have pared down already.

How far this last assumption remained correct in a prosperous age is a moot point, for New Zealand lacks adequate social research on such matters. One can hazard a guess that cigarette duties struck fairly evenly while costlier beer and spirits did annoy the less wealthy and the unmarried in the main. As to duty on petrol, this undoubtedly taxed the major luxury and pride of the young earner, but it cannot have left unmoved the longer established families who had attained to middling income and the maintenance of a car as the principal joy of the household.

One reaction was common to all groups: these doubled duties were highly visible and simple to comprehend. Income tax under P.A.Y.E. was being converted for the vast majority of people from a painful annual loss to an accustomed transaction effected in the front office by others. Psychologically the old 'indirect' taxes were now acquiring the colourful immediacy of the former 'direct' income tax. The tax issue thus continued to be self-dramatizing and of popular concern.

The Budget gave as well as took. It served notice that forthcoming legislation would, in the Government's first and critical year, raise the age and similar benefits to £8 per week for a couple and £4 10s. for single persons, increase allowable income for age beneficiaries to £3 per week and, of widest significance, raise the weekly family benefit from 10s. to 15s. per dependent child. This, said Mr. Nordmeyer, represented more than a similarly sized wage increase since it went untaxed. He did not remark that there was no increase for the single and childless. They might look forward some day to enjoying the fruits of a programme of rises in universal superannuation from the existing £110 per annum through two annual increments to £208 in April, 1960. Otherwise their satisfactions were confined to the assurance of full employment without lowered wages in a time of dragging export prices and unemployment overseas.

So far as most electors went, that was the end of the most

5   N.Z.P.A.

stirring Budget since the war. The major pledges in Labour's election programme, with the exception of capitalization of the family benefit, already stood redeemed. Yet they did not come with any triumphant flourish. Necessity, apology and explanation were the notes sounded in the Budget speech, and that document was remembered, not on receipt of family benefits, but as Mr. Holyoake joked, in each puff of smoke and at the bottom of each glass. Whether it was a necessary Budget will always be disputed. It was well received by economists who voiced an opinion, and the Treasury and Reserve Bank certainly inclined strongly towards such policies. The newspapers loudly registered the shock increases but were not disposed to quarrel with them so much as with the increased cost of welfare provisions. No one proposed as an alternative that Mr. Nordmeyer should have deferred raising taxes while he gambled on the returns from some future export revival. It was also obvious that if surplus purchasing power was to be rapidly siphoned off it would have to come from where it was, in the pockets of lower-income spenders as well as in thick wallets. Here a major Labour tradition was offended, even while another Labour tradition—redistributive taxation on behalf of the aged and the children—was being implemented.

Other economic decisions were taken at the same time. State investment in hydro-electricity, land settlement, railways and roads was kept high, or increased, for the double purpose of supporting growth in production and of stretching local resources to the uttermost. Dividends were now taxed as income and an Excess Retention Tax was planned to prevent evasion. Gift duties were to be raised, and death duties increased on estates of over £12,000. Although this last affected but a tenth of the number of estates, it attracted a great deal of adverse publicity, farmers' organizations proving themselves particularly sensitive to the change and prone to see the increases as a general disinheritance.

The Underlying Problem of Markets

For the farming sector had already suffered a considerable setback. Since the high point of 1955, dairy produce prices had dropped 45 per cent, which compared with the 47 per cent drop in the depression years from 1929 to 1934. Under the legislation of 1956, a Dairy Products Prices Authority determined the cost of production and fixed the prices to be paid to producers in New Zealand at the start of each season. It was agreed that the price should not be cut in any one year by more than 5 per cent of the previous price. Notwithstanding the fact that such a cut was made in the 1957 determination, the payout at 36·25 pence a pound for 1957–8 absorbed all the remaining dairy reserves, which had stood at £27 million at the start of the 1956–7 season. Not only did the reserves vanish but the Reserve Bank had to advance £7·3 million against as yet unsold produce in order to finance the payout. Indeed, at the time when the determination of the guaranteed price for the next season was first under consideration, it was predicted that this indebtedness might climb to £12 million. The Reserve Bank advances for the 1957–8 payout were converted into a proper loan and, as a deflationary move, the Minister of Finance in this Budget loaned £5 million from the Consolidated Fund to the industry so that a 'reasonable price' could be paid for the next season of 1958–9.

What reason might be in such difficult days was disputed between Government, marketing organizations and farmers for some months. In the end a cut of 10·4 per cent was made in the guaranteed price for butter, which necessitated a hard-fought Act to suspend the statutory prohibition against large reductions. Even then, the commentators of the quarterly, *The Round Table*, concluded that this 'did not represent a truly realistic acceptance of market conditions.' Farming members of the Opposition, however, did not accuse the Government of diluting their remedies by leaving the guaranteed price too high, but of being too severe with this one section of the community whose production for export was vital. Aerial top dressing of pastures did fall away in 1958, which indicates that some price in loss of productivity was paid for compressed overdrafts and decreased receipts, but neither the Minister for Agriculture, Mr. Skinner, nor Mr. Nordmeyer felt he could avoid it.

Behind the conviction that hard times required hard measures lay a growing disillusion about the regulation of New Zealand's primary market, Great Britain. The governments of Western and Eastern Europe in a normal season proved able and willing to flood the British market with dairy products at an artificially low price. European agricultural protectionism demanded that home consumers pay highly for their butter, part of the proceeds being used to make up the price fetched by the surplus which was dumped in London. The wholesale price of a hundredweight of butter in Eire was 430s., in Finland 600s., and in Sweden 515s. when the same butter fetched 240s. in the United Kingdom. The price of New Zealand and Danish butters was thus at the mercy of protected rivals unless the United Kingdom would step in to help the two countries which produced at a naturally low cost.

The British Government itself shared in the policy of subsidy. It was, for instance, the forced growth of British cheese production which threatened this particular section of New Zealand's exports. Pressure from dumping on the London market could not be met by diverting New Zealand's dairy products towards the U.S.A., Canada or the European countries with high living standards, since they were the chief exponents of protection. Meanwhile the Common Market of 1957 represented the gradual exclusion, not the expansion, of New Zealand's dairy and meat exports to that increasingly wealthy part of the world. As yet there was no question of Britain joining the European Economic Community, for Britain was still engaged in trying to set up a wider Free Trade Community for industrial products only. Certainly, though, there was writing of some kind on these trade walls. The meaning gradually became all too plain between 1956 and 1961.

While the British Prime Minister was visiting New Zealand in January, Mr. Nash discussed dumping with Mr. Macmillan. Then, in February 1958 New Zealand formally requested the invocation of the United Kingdom Customs (Dumping and Subsidies) Act, 1957. This Act provided for the imposition of British counter-vailing duties on dumped butter equal to the foreign subsidies behind dumped butter's low price. Speedy action by the United Kingdom was not forthcoming, so New Zealand's Minister of Agriculture journeyed to England. On 22 May 1958 the British Government went some of the way to meet the Dominion's case, a case supported by Denmark and the British National Farmers' Union. The United Kingdom asked Finland, Sweden and Eire either to keep their exports within agreed limits or to cease subsidizing them. Imports of Polish butter were also limited on Britain's initiative. The target of the suggested decreases was a reduction over the next year by 40,000 tons or 10 per cent of the total supplies to Britain for 1957. It was hoped that this would cause the price of butter to rise by sixpence a pound. The New Zealand Government was frank in its disappointment that no dumping duties had been imposed and expressed its decided doubt that the British requests would suffice to return prices to an economic level.

Accordingly, the Labour Government attached all the more importance to the revision of the Ottawa Agreement, also negotiated while the Skinner mission was in England. The agreement, which had institutionalized mutual preferences exchanged inside the Commonwealth, was a quarter of a century old in 1957. It dated from a time of deep economic depression, from an era of enforced hope in the Commonwealth and from the last abrupt change in British policy towards external trade. Twenty-five years of world-wide inflation had gravely lessened the value of the preferences accorded to New Zealand by Britain because those preferences had been expressed in fixed money terms. New Zealand's preferences to Britain, on the contrary, had remained the same, being expressed as percentages *ad valorem*. So the opportunity to correct and equalize preferences might have been used to scale up New Zealand's advantages to the British level if 'the spirit of Ottawa' yet prevailed. Alternatively, preferences to Britain in the New Zealand market could be brought down to the level of New Zealand's margins in the United Kingdom.

It was the latter choice which emerged in the Heads of Agreement signed in November 1958. New Zealand preferences to United Kingdom products, which had either been 20 per cent or close to it, came down to 5 per cent on essentials for industry, $7\frac{1}{2}$ per cent on 'welfare and producer goods' and 10 per cent on all others. With Commonwealth protection going out of favour in the metropolis itself, Britain's fifth largest customer, New Zealand, was taking steps to protect itself, to industrialize and to gain more bargaining power for the reorientation of its trade. Preliminary notice of how the London negotiations must be faring had in fact been served two months earlier when a trade agreement between Japan and New Zealand was announced on 9 September 1958. Unconditional most-favoured-nation treatment was reciprocally extended in respect of custom duties, import licensing and foreign exchange while other clauses secured to New Zealand a growing portion of the Japanese meat, hides and casein markets and protected New Zealand's share in Japan's wool imports. In return

New Zealand allocated import licences to those Japanese manufactures which offered no threat of 'serious damage' to New
Zealand's domestic industry.

The Trade Agreement with Japan was not unprecedented. It
followed the lines of Australia's agreement with Japan of July
1957. It was also preceded by the Japanese Prime Minister's
visit to New Zealand, a visit arranged by the National Government. So also the Labour (Skinner) Mission to the United
Kingdom came one year after the Nationalist (Holyoake) mission,
while New Zealand's reduction of preferences to Britain was
agreed to just twenty-one months after Australia brought her
preferences to Britain down to $7\frac{1}{2}$ per cent for production machinery
and industrial raw materials and 10 per cent on all other goods.
What was significant was that New Zealand's essays at readjust-
ment were beginning—in the context of an impaired British
market—to add up to a basic change. The painter which tied the
New Zealand cockleshell to the British merchantman had been
allowed to go slack and there were those who thought they
detected in the darkness a knife at work on the rope. Rather than
find themselves adrift and quite helpless, New Zealand producer
organizations, Crown servants and politicians were rigging a
rudder and casting about for a mast and sail, on the Australian
pattern if necessary.

Labour Acquires a Doctrine: Manufacture in Depth

Import control, the Budget, the drop in the guaranteed price, the
renegotiation of the Ottawa Agreement and the Japanese Trade
Agreement were thus interrelated one with another and with the
recurring crises over foreign exchange and with the radical
worsening of export prices. They were all connected, too, by their
implications for New Zealand manufacturing. If the basic grass-
lands industries had now to sell in new countries and be ready to
suit new customers with increased flexibility as between products,
then New Zealand's manufacturing and service industries had to
bear fresh loads by delivering substitutes for imports and making
a larger contribution to the gross national product. Neither was
an easy bill to fill. The reorientation of primary production and
marketing would mean the end of many fixed and treasured
concepts. So too would the hastening of industrialization. Yet

inexorably the logic of New Zealand's situation in the late 1950s was pushing the Labour administration towards a policy which it cannot be said to have possessed when it came to office.

Like most conversions of large institutions this one was slow, had many points of origin and carried forward from the past an almost unchanged mass of people and ideas. It would be quite unfair and untrue to say that the National Party when in office had not felt some of the same impulses and urgency. They had; and the considerable rate of investment achieved and their initiatives in regard to markets and trade treaties show they had responded. But harsh necessity and the Labour Government coincided. By the time the external pressures lifted, at least the higher strata of the Labour Party had received a fresh impress. The 1960 defeat of this party, whose positive programme could be summed up as 'industrialize', revealed that the remoulding had stopped well short of the sometime Labour voters.

This is not so suprprising when it is remembered that the compulsion to alter was inherently undramatic and technical and took time to register. When Parliament met in June 1958, with prospects black, import controls operating and the Budget to come, Labour's mover and seconder of the Address in Reply showed where doctrine had been. The former conjured up the shades of 1938 by saying: 'There is no doubt that there are signs of a depression or recession . . . in many leading countries. Our policy of import restrictions is a start along the lines of insulation.' The latter speaker mistook his future by adding: 'In New Zealand we have only a small market. Our manufacturing costs a unit will almost inevitably be higher than those for comparable industries overseas which have markets, in many cases, several hundred times the size of ours . . . We must use our capital resources to produce more, rather than use our capital to introduce more machines and build more plant.'

Yet the very month after these two speeches, the milk of the 1960 word could be heard from another Labour backbencher, Mr. Kitts, the Mayor of Wellington.

We have reached the stage where we should give the strongest consideration to the establishment of basic industries in New Zealand. We should set about the production of iron and steel, light metals, plastics, and chemicals because they would provide the raw materials and the bases for the establishment of the multiplicity of industries that could be built up from them. No country that has ever developed a high standard of living has been able to maintain it with an agrarian economy.

The gulf between Mr. Kitts's attitude and the views of Labour's opening speakers gradually closed as the theory of 'manufacturing in depth' acquired publicity, the sponsorship of Labour's leaders and, finally, a name which separated it clearly from the first Labour Government's general benevolence towards secondary industry and 'building a nation'.

Outside the House, however, what was proceeding was a debate rather than a conversion. At the elementary level the debate became the occasion for more intemperate expression of the long conflict between country and town in its economic guise of lower costs of primary production and freer trade versus trade union conditions and plentiful jobs. At a more sophisticated level of discussion, the need for a reshaping of New Zealand's economy was accepted by both sides instead of being neglected by both. Professor Condliffe, a New Zealander who had distinguished himself as an economic historian, first in his homeland and then in the United States, revisited New Zealand in 1957. In widely reported lectures and subsequently in a book (1959) he argued a case for concentration upon a few naturally strong industries capable of competing on favourable terms in overseas markets. Timber, pulp and paper, fisheries, woollen manufactures, the processing of fruit and vegetables, and tourism should be helped on a scale accorded in the past to butter, cheese, meat and wool. With these new and all the old arrows in its quiver, New Zealand would storm its way on to the world markets of the future as it had once captured a large share in the shops of Britain.

On the other side of the debate, the principal figure was another widely experienced economic historian of New Zealand, Dr. W. B. Sutch, a civil servant. His evolving analysis received its fullest expression in the Industrial Development Conference of June 1960, a grand inquest by 230 delegates into the problems of national growth. Dr. Sutch and others argued that primary industries could not alone carry the burden of preserving and adding to the standard of living. Furthermore, farming had reached a ceiling in the numbers employed even while farmers continued to expand production. Therefore manufacture and services must provide jobs, and imports earned by primary exports must be made to go farther. There must be more consumer goods per import, not less imports. This could be done by using funds to buy materials as near to the raw, unprocessed state as possible. Aluminium, for instance, could come in as ingots instead of as rods and sheets, or, in the future, as alumina or possibly even as the original bauxite. Then New Zealand's labour and fostered skills would build up the semi-finished and finished products without having to draw down foreign exchange for them. With mills for working up light and heavy metals from home scrap and imported ingots, with its own oil refinery and chemical plants, New Zealand could add jobs not only at this basic level but also at each further stage of manufacture. New Zealand's wealth enlarged its size as a market. Invention was making small plants economic and the country might yet yield iron, gas and oil. This conception of 'manufacturing in depth' did not directly counter Professor Condliffe's vision of 'naturally strong' industries. It added to the raw materials already produced here such raw materials as could be earned, and it aimed to process both.

The Industrial Conference of 1960 certainly did not reach an agreement of experts on the debate, but it made clear the two principal positions on economic growth and advertised the commitment of the Labour Party to one of them. The normal polarizing process of two-party politics might be expected now, if not before, to cause the Opposition to feature the views of Professor Condliffe. This did not occur, for several reasons. In the first place the National Party is a party of the city as well as of the country, collecting votes, subscriptions and advice from manufacturers as well as from importers and farmers. Then, too, the National Government had presided over much manufacturing development, the oil search and the hope of steel, while the origins of the Sutch analysis itself went back beyond the change of regime. The National Party may tacitly have recognized that, whichever concept of growth proved eventually to be the wiser, it would have to be administered in a bipartisan spirit. Certainly that was the opinion of the Labour Minister of Industries and Commerce, the Hon. P. N. Holloway. In July, 1959, he said: 'we are trying to evolve an industrial development policy based, not on a political idea, or on any person's whim, but on what industrial processes must be followed . . . whether I or any other Minister holds this portfolio.' Lastly, since they were in opposition, the Nationalists were not compelled to decide. Being certain that they had a simple, winning issue in the Budget, they could shrewdly steer clear of the heady and statistical explanations on which Labour embarked in the campaign of 1960.

National Perfects its Tactics: Scarifying the Wound

Of the reasons here advanced for the National Party's decision to preserve a watchful quiet on these large matters—a silence complained of by the Press in 1958 and 1959—undoubtedly the most persuasive was the party's conviction that the 1960 election was already won on other issues. This assessment rested on two bases: the Hamilton by-election result of 2 May 1959, and the reports of a public opinion polling organization which privately confirmed that the Hamilton particular was indeed general. During the first weeks of the parliamentary session of 1959, as the Labour Minister of Housing said in discomfiture, 'Opposition members mentioned the Hamilton by-election all the time, and it is true that the result of that by-election was an expression of dissatisfaction . . . with the increased taxation'. Then he added the numerically accurate but dangerous conclusion, 'but it is not so much a vote in favour of the Tory Party. The Tory vote went up to only a small extent'. He was to find in 1960 that National did not need to rise; Labour had only to stay down to be out.

Paying attention only to the voters who turned out and cast formal votes, the change added up to a $7\frac{1}{2}$ per cent swing from Labour to National.[2] If the Hamilton trend was sustained until 1960 and then appeared all over New Zealand, seven or eight Labour candidates would be unseated and the National Party would be firmly back in power. This hope was checked by an opinion survey which informed National Party headquarters, according to one report, that Labour's general loss might go as

---

[2] The actual situation was much more complicated than this 'swing' indicates. Non-voting went up from 7·49 per cent in 1957 to 21·60 per cent at the by-election. This was the major feature since those who stayed away from each party because it was just a by-election were joined, in the case of Labour, by those abstaining in protest. Labour's share of the qualified vote declined 12 per cent; National and Social Credit lost 1 per cent each. The National figure, in turn, presumably conceals minor gains made by National from Labour which were offset and turned into a slight net loss by the by-election apathy of National regulars.

high as 9 per cent. All that remained to be done, therefore, was to avoid blunders or rash, unpopular commitments and by 'scarifying the wound of taxation', to use a National organizer's apt description, prevent Labour's potential loss diminishing along with the memory of 1958.

The scarification process involved three years of conscientious, unremitting repetition in the House and at meetings by Mr. Holyoake and his team. They carried forward from the 1957 election campaign the theme that Labour could not and would not perform its many promises. Prior to the 1958 Budget they asked why the whole programme was not already set before the House and, in debate, linked the overseas funds crisis to the cost of fulfilling the rebate promise. Once the Budget came down, the team moved simply but surely to connect afresh in the public mind high taxation and promises. This required a subtle shift of emphasis. It was held that the cost of fulfilling promises produced the taxation at the same time as the existence of the 'black Budget' itself became the main breach of promise.

Mr. Nash twice unintentionally helped the process along. Before he was installed as Prime Minister he was asked by the Press about how Labour intended the small taxpayers to deal with their old income tax demands. His austerely correct advice was to pay up and collect the rebate when granted. He added that he regularly paid before Christmas himself. A future Labour Minister in Dunedin dealt with the same question quite otherwise: 'Burn them? Of course you can.' Pursued, Mr. Nash gave details about the technical difficulties of summoning a session and legislating the rebate before 7 February when tax became due, though penalties accrued only from 7 March. It took a week before it became obvious that those with a tax demand under £100 could safely risk using their tax savings. By then the public had begun to wonder about the dates from which other promises would operate. Letters asking whether textbooks would be free for the 1958 school year flowed in to editors. Labour eventually worked out a formula to cover the completion of the entire election programme: 'within the Government's three-year term of office.' It seems unlikely that all doubt and impatience was settled by this phrase and many must have smiled wryly at the cartoon by Minhinnick which depicted Mr. Nash holding out for christening a baby labelled 'Child Benefit'. As the young parents look on, the Prime Minister-elect is saying to the vicar: 'We want to call it Kathleen Mavourneen.'

Tactically, the second Labour Government had been placed on the defensive from the start. Cabinet hurried to get schemes operating by regulations and acts which might well have been held over to fill the rather empty sessions of 1959 and 1960. Three per cent loans, the rebate, the increased child benefit, easing of the means test, raising of the universal superannuation, abolition of compulsory military training and capitalization of the family benefit were all enacted or commenced within fifteen months. If it could well be argued that it was unwise, when export prices were descending, for any party to issue such a list or for the public to vote for such a programme, it could equally well be contended that it was imprudent for the public to expect or a government to accomplish the fulfilment of all main pledges in the midst of a crisis and in a matter of months.

The Nationalists' plan of battle was in some danger of mis-carrying as point after point of Labour policy was ticked off. Again it was to the pronouncements of Mr. Nash that they turned. In the Budget debate on 16 July 1958 the Hon. J. R. Hanan recalled—on the basis of a private recording—certain sentences from Mr. Nash's half-hour broadcast on the night before the 1957 election. ' "Finance: We do not propose to change the basis of taxation from that set out in the Income Tax Assessment Act as passed during the last [1957] session of Parliament, and the amounts to be collected will be on the basis of the schedules in the Act. Those schedules are based on the deduction of 25 per cent from the amount assessed. Those tables will not be changed if the Government is a Labour Government." '

A week later another National member, Mr. Aderman, turned the same text into a question as to why Mr. Nash had 'not kept his undertaking'. The Prime Minister admitted that he did not believe he had said such a thing until he played over the National Broadcasting Service's record of his speech. Now he agreed '. . . I did make the statement quoted by the honourable member. I would also draw his attention to my concluding paragraph of the section dealing with Finance and PAYE. legislation in the same speech: "Given normal circumstances all the finance necessary to run the country will be available next year without any altera-tions in the rates of tax provided by the present legislation." At the time I believed this could be achieved but the economic circumstances facing the Government this year could not remotely be termed "normal".'

Instead of continuing, in 1958 the 1957 tax rates were being scrapped. But circumstances had undoubtedly altered cases. Unfortunately for Mr. Nash's argument, circumstances were becoming abnormal the year before he chose to notice the fact. Unfortunately for the Nationalists' case, they could not make this apparent, because the National Government not only must have known the relevant economic trends earlier than Labour, but it was also the party responsible for acting in 1957 if trends were bad. So instead, the Nationalists utilized the implication in Mr. Nash's reply that 1957 had been normal as an admission that they had left all in order. Both sides were resolutely avoiding the fact that, in the last half of 1957, the National Government, the Labour Party, and the public all in some degree had been hoping to get by with something for nothing.

Moreover, both sides were assuming too much when they argued as though New Zealand's electoral decision had hung on Mr. Nash's last address, the exact phrasing of it, or his qualifying statement about 'normal circumstances'. Psephological research and common sense suggest that electoral decisions are made over months and years, not hours. Public speakers know the average audience are not textual critics. They take the tone and drift of an argument, not its detail. Nor was the 1957 election result so close in votes that it was likely to have been won by a last-minute sentence to an audience sated with radio speeches.

Nevertheless, the Nationalists pressed the point until the harried Prime Minister exclaimed that 'he could make a mistake the same as anyone else . . . All members would be in a peculiar position if everything wrong that they said was referred to by 41 members continuously throughout a three-weeks debate.' By 1959 the phrase 'another mistake' was nearly as common in Nationalist speeches as the words 'pledge on taxation'. For the Hamilton campaign and its results confirmed that National had found Labour's exposed nerve. Mr. Gotz duly exacerbated it: 'Of course they [Labour's supporters] did not vote . . . for the simple reason that they were disgusted by Labour's broken promises, excessive taxation, and higher cost of living.'

Austerity Continued, Concluded, and Reversed

If such was the case, a second and conspicuously emollient Labour Budget might ease the smarts left by the first. But to this there were certain barriers. One was a matter of attitude. The Prime Minister, when addressing the annual conference of his party in May 1959, viewed Hamilton as 'only the first test in the battle of ideas between good economy versus political expediency.' Of the 1958 Budget he said in January 1959, 'I am satisfied that it had to be done.' Next month Mr. Nordmeyer was still musing on New Zealand's need for realism and on the slim margin available for more, not less, taxation. To Labour's leaders the policies of 1958 were not only necessary and effective, they had become a matter of morality. To reverse them consciously, before the fundamental imbalances in the economy had been corrected, would throw doubt on the leaders' earlier assessment of the situation and offend their thorough-going, almost Crippsian satisfaction in their restorative work.

The second barrier to large concessions was found in the figures for trade. Prices for exports and the overseas balances were picking up, but not so far as to justify, in Mr. Nordmeyer's opinion, an open-handed approach to the Budget. Ironically, the terms of trade—which are determined, of course, outside New Zealand—had started to improve from the very month in which the 1958 Budget was issued. Taking 1957 as 100, the terms went up four points to 85 in the third quarter of 1958, four points to 89 for the October–December period, and another three points to 92 for the first quarter of 1959. They were still climbing while the 1959 Budget was being decided. Had he known what was to happen in May 1958, it is unlikely that Labour's Minister of Finance would then have been quite so severe. On the other hand, the limited improvement subsequently had not banished the dilemma. Would export prices go on getting better and restore matters to their 1957 footing? In the light of what had happened to external funds, was 1957 a safe footing anyway? Overseas assets stood at £85 million in April 1959, tens of millions short of the safety point recommended by the Monetary Commission in 1956. Also sobering was the reflection that the level of £85 million had been attained with the aid of £45 million of foreign borrowing.

Mr. Nordmeyer concluded that he would have to ride out the Hamilton squall more or less under bare poles. Petrol, beer and tobacco taxes, which had caused most of the 5 per cent sag in the effective wage rate, continued undiminished in the 1959 Budget. There were concessions in income tax rates, particularly for the single, calculated to total '£17 million in a full year.' That rate, however, was to be arrived at in two stages. The first reduction was to operate from 1 October 1959 and was a cut limited to a maximum of £30. The second reduction, to levels which 'will approximate fairly closely those fixed by the 1957 Budget', was to commence only on 1 April 1960. By then the electorate would have been paying for eighteen months at stiffer rates.

There were other large policy decisions underlying the 1959 Budget. The first was to continue restraining consumption internally rather than go on borrowing overseas. The second decision was that redistributive social security benefits could not come down to provide tax remissions. The third was that Government investment must remain heavy to sustain production and the new manufactures whilst taking up any slack in private investment, which was being directed and inhibited by the control of capital issues. Lastly, the 1959 Budget was not planned to expend by concessions the surplus which had been compulsorily saved by the 1958 rates, for the effect of such a surplus is disinflationary and the Minister of Finance hoped to keep the cost of living at the point where it had stabilized in September 1958.

One might judge from the Budget that austerity marched alone. Yet a patient listener could detect at a distance the soft footfalls of relaxation approaching. For the period December 1958 to May 1959, private imports, rigorously controlled, were proceeding at a very low annual rate of £193 million compared with £251 million the year before. Then on 13 April 1959 Mr. Boord, the Minister for Customs, announced an easing of licences to raise the provision for the year to £210 million. Export prices continued upwards and an additional provision of £20 million was made on 6 June. This was not yet permission for a boom. But, if relaxation had not been allowed to unlock the front door of the Budget, it was patently fumbling with the import control latch at the back.

Then the Court of Arbitration awarded a general increase which brought real wages to within a fraction of the pre-Budget figure by the end of 1959. Butter prices, encouraged by a European drought, reached the dizzy heights of 410s. a hundredweight that Christmas, though the terms of trade, affected by many more factors, stood merely at 106. In November 1959 Labour candidates at the municipal elections were evicted in job lots. Producing the equivalent of a surprise supplementary Budget, Mr. Nordmeyer in November and December reduced taxes on petrol, beer and cigarettes. The economy had plainly recovered. The March 1960 retail turnover was higher than in any previous March. The index of real national income per head[3] after going from 108 to 107, was up to 111 for the year ended March 1960. In June 1960 overseas funds were at £119 million, a better June figure than any since 1954. Mr. Nordmeyer and Mr. Nash were answered by prosperity and yet left with two great questions: Was recovery enough for the electors? and could they refrain from the triennial spree?

Only the general election could settle the former question. The latter question, also, was not quite such a matter of will as it seemed—as Mr. Watts had discovered three years before. A very little relaxation proved to go a very long way under conditions of full employment, heavy welfare contributions to purchasing power, large State investment in housing and works, and expansive confidence in the private sector. A newspaper article, significantly labelled 'Boom Period Is On Threshold', by a university economist, J. W. Rowe, made this point clearly in August 1960: 'in the previous year unsatisfied demand was probably quite small because fiscal policy was then really effective. It follows that it could be more dangerous to relax import controls now . . . in spite of the rise in net overseas assets in the intervening period.' Selling was being rendered automatic. Primary as well as secondary industries wanted the materials to go on pushing up production. Every licence issued would be used and overdrafts were increasingly available.

In his 1960 Budget Mr. Nordmeyer walked carefully round this pile of tinder, dropping no matches, but throwing on one or two dry branches. Considering that he was the Finance Minister of a party rendered sensitive on the tax issue and wanting an election-winning Budget, Mr. Nordmeyer was most restrained.

---

[3] The base for this index is 1949–50 = 100. The Estimates are in constant prices.

The cost of works and welfare, which produced an internal deficit in 1959–60, tended to enforce restraint and a glance at the downward trend of export prices must have reinforced resolution. Nevertheless, the capital programme for 1960–1 was increased by £11·5 million. There were tiny adjustments in benefits to catch up past price rises, while earnings and capital barriers to the receipt of benefits were again reduced. Having provided £143 million for welfare, the Minister declared 'any major change in the next few years is unlikely.' Income tax rates were left where they arrived in March 1960, in accordance with the previous Budget. As for indirect taxation, most of the reduction had been given just before Christmas, but a shade more was now removed while sales tax on cars descended from 40 to 33 per cent.

The pre-1958 position in taxation had been almost recovered by instalments, with the 1958 gains in benefits preserved as well. Yet the piecemeal fashion in which this had been accomplished, leaving the least to the last, probably reduced its impression on the electors to a minimum. Moreover, the sheer complexity of the four changes in tax tables over three years proved baffling to electors. Their puzzlement prepared the way for contradictory assertions in the campaign and for a quite misleading concentration by Labour's critics on the figures for gross tax collected, without correction for the steady depreciation of money or for the enlarging population bearing the taxes. People plainly retired into the recent past which was comfortingly simple and memorable. When a board of review was provided for appeals on taxation questions in September 1960, a cartoonist showed the average man appearing before the Board with Mr. Nordmeyer perched on his back. Said the citizen: 'I'm appealing against the way he's sitting.'

The electors could not mistake the importance which the Government attached to development in 1960, whether they found it personally relevant or not. At the Industrial Conference it was trumpeted forth that, since 1958, £73 million of new capital had been projected for investment in manufacturing. By 1960's end, copper, scrap iron, aluminium, wire rope, oil, and cotton processing plants were in prospect. This emphasis appeared in the Budget as the virtual abolition of capital issues control, extra depreciation allowances and more exemptions from the

6

excess retention tax on profits. At the individual level, the incomes of working husbands and wives were no longer to be aggregated for taxation and, to encourage small savings, certain exemptions were enlarged and there was a scheme for development bonds. The aim was to accelerate growth.

As a natural consequence, more imports would be required. The references to imports in the Budget were studiously general. Despite the 1959 relaxations in licensing, tightened conditions had kept private imports to £217 million for the year to March 1960. The previously announced 1960 schedule 'provides for an increased issue of licences,' said Mr. Nordmeyer. 'Some further relaxation . . . may be possible,' he added, 'if export prices are maintained and if the outlook for wool is favourable.' Export prices, unfortunately, were not maintained. Wool declined slowly then steeply in the second half of the year. By March, butter had descended 120s. from its untenable December position. It rose to 310s. in June but was back at 290s. in September and was going on down. Lamb sank, but not mutton.

The similarity to the slide of 1957 was unmistakable though the incline was not so steep. The mid September news of the trend in overseas assets must have unsettled anyone who looked back at 1954 and 1957. Notwithstanding all this, in September the Minister of Customs announced the new Import Licensing Schedule for 1961. It was rendered singularly hard to compare with 1960 for which the target was about £240 million of imports. Nominally the new target was the same. Certain past licences, however, were said to have been not taken up in full, so these 'savings' were to be transferred to other headings. 'Replacement' and 'automatic' licences were increased. In mid October the election year pattern in foreign exchange was still showing up, if not in such lurid colours as at the two previous elections. The The New Zealand Herald of 28 October carried twelve column inches of an announcement by the Reserve Bank that there had been a '£10·1 Million Deficit [on] Transactions in September.' Yet on 6 November Mr. Boord told the Press that, 'the Customs Department will consider applications for additional licences from importers who can establish that their 1957 imports were higher than for 1956, the year now used as the basis . . .' There were eighty-three items affected, ranging from cigars to vitamins.

Possibly there was some inexcusable gap in liaison. Reserve

ratio brakes on the increase of overdrafts were certainly not gripping either. It seems clear that a store of unused licences existed in the hands of importers, which confused planning and opened the way for a surge of orders. Boom conditions in the internal economy expressed themselves in the face of contrary trends in export prices. Gallup Poll reports of voter preferences indicated that the National Party would soon be the Government, with new, but one would have thought, hardly more severe import policies. Yet however one seeks to explain the pre-election run down, the decisions of September and November to increase licences remain inexplicable. They were certainly not going to help much in winning the election, since goods brought in on them would arrive long after election day, while all the importers in New Zealand, if gathered together, would not suffice to swing, say, Remuera to Labour. Altogether the value of merchandise imported in the year ended December 1960 was £279 million, £47 million more than the year before. Overseas funds ran down £63 million to December compared with £70 million in 1957.

The explanation of election-year sprees must be sought in decisions taken much earlier in the year; optimistic, general decisions about permissible economic growth, expenditure and concessions. The country is import-prone at these times fundamentally because governments are afraid of what the electors will do to them if governments do not take optimistic views and uncalculated risks. Parties can take the courage of despair from their failure to preserve themselves thus. There ought to be consolation, too, in the fact that it is the whole history of a government's term which is judged and this judgement is coloured by many more issues than the level of imports on polling day.

Most of those issues and much of that history will be built from material concerns. This chapter has been focussed accordingly. For that reason also, Mr. Nordmeyer has been enlisted to play Hamlet in this semi-moral drama of less and more. Considering his experience in such matters and his daily and decisive involvement in House and Cabinet, the Prime Minister has been a trifle unfairly set to one side. Mr. Nash was frequently away overseas, however, and his prime concern was undoubtedly external affairs.

A Prime Minister's Policy Abroad and at Home

Each year the Prime Minister, as Minister for External Affairs, undertook extensive tours. He met nearly every figure of importance in the direction of world affairs at that time and appeared at annual meetings of all the principal organizations which include New Zealand, from the Economic Commission for Asia and the Far East to the Conference of Commonwealth Prime Ministers. Indefatigably he travelled and commented, broadcasting his lively impressions when he returned. He desired passionately to penetrate his countrymen's amiable indifference towards foreign affairs and, to an extent, he probably did. For that indifference is, in reality, more a sense of powerlessness to affect issues than any lack of goodwill, interest or even knowledge.

So far as his party went, these concerns of Mr. Nash added to his general popularity, as the annual conferences showed. New Zealand Labour Party members are wont to feel and express their long tradition of internationalism. The Prime Minister's constant pleas that international problems be referred to the United Nations or that U.N. resolutions should be vigorously executed were reminiscent of the first Labour Government's faith in an active League and collective security. When he flew to New York, two months before the 1960 election, in order to speak in defence of Mr. Hammarskjöld and against the U.S.S.R.'s proposals, Mr. Nash eloquently expressed his image of the U.N. as an impartial administrative entity, a potential source of law and order against naked power between nations. It was an ideal, liberal vision but obviously the product of a small state existing in a world shaped outside of the U.N. by great powers.

Mr. Nash believed that the small states, by taking thought, could 'give a lead'. He argued for steps towards controlled nuclear disarmament without waiting for agreement to the Western 'disarmament package'. He urged the necessity of a meeting at the Summit, consultations of the Big Three over Lebanon, and U.N. action and neutralization for Laos. Considering the great powers' intermittent sensitivity to the articulate minority who constitute world opinion, Mr. Nash's voice must occasionally have been heard to good effect. It could not, in the nature of the case, be shown to have been heeded.

Instead of credit for activity, the Prime Minister attracted much Press and Opposition criticism for inactivity, because he left unfilled major posts in New Zealand's foreign service. The Washington and U.N. posts stayed vacant after September 1958, London was managed by an Acting High Commissioner, and so on. With a majority of one, senior Labour politicians could not be removed to higher things, so leaving behind them the risk of a lost by-election. New Zealand's first Maori diplomat was sent as the High Commissioner to Malaya and one retired M.P. and ex-Minister was found for Canberra, but the Prime Minister would adventure no further. Mr. Nash repeated that the career officers who ran affairs ran them well. He pointed to the rapid creation and filling of commercial posts to facilitate the trade drive—an equivalent to the creation of diplomatic posts in World War II. But he gave no satisfactory reason for not promoting, and thus assisting the work of, those to whom he entrusted the 'vacant' posts.

There was another fundamental limitation to the initiative and drama which the Prime Minister could publicly introduce into the conduct of external affairs. For Mr. Nash and the great majority of his party agreed with the basic design of the complex structure of treaty and other relationships already shaping New Zealand's role in the world. Prior commitments left small room for colourful gestures. Moreover, Mr. Dulles or Mr. Macmillan would hear the Prime Minister more attentively precisely because New Zealand was a responsible if junior partner. In consequence certain things could not be done and said. The Prime Minister was opposed to nuclear testing and there was widespread feeling in the community with him in that, yet New Zealand sent naval ships to assist a test with their observations. A persistent group in the Labour Party wanted to follow the U.K. rather than the U.S.A. about recognizing China. Mr. Nash made several carefully qualified statements over the years revealing that he was disposed by the reasoning to agree, if only he could move his patrons. He could not, so New Zealand supported the *status quo* at U.N. When in opposition, Mr. Nash had been dubious about aspects of the South East Asia Treaty Organization. In office he praised it unreservedly, limiting his efforts to an emphasis on the organization's very subordinate function of 'raising living standards, economic and social welfare work'.

He triumphed notably over these inherent limitations when the Antarctic was neutralized. As early as January 1956 Mr. Nash advocated a United Nations regime for Antarctica. The idea was not popular across the Tasman Sea nor was America initially inclined to agree. The International Geophysical Year showed what co-operation could achieve and offered Mr. Nash fresh arguments and opportunities. As soon as he became Prime Minister, he pressed the case to Mr. Macmillan in Wellington in January 1958, and to Mr. Dulles in Manila in March. What other prompting or what additional factors weighed with President Eisenhower we cannot know, but the fact remains that, on 3 May 1958, the President proposed to the countries working in Antarctica an international treaty according freedom of scientific investigation and, in effect, neutralization or demilitarization of Antarctica. Territorial claims, including New Zealand's, were to be kept in abeyance and the international regime would have, as Mr. Nash once put it, 'the blessing of the United Nations.' The Conference met on 15 October 1959, and the Treaty was signed on 1 December 1959.

Behind orthodox foreign policy lies force. Antarctica did not require it, but it was required by New Zealand's presence in the Commonwealth Strategic Reserve in Malaya and her obligations to S.E.A.T.O. and A.N.Z.U.S. Labour abolished compulsory military training in 1958, in accordance with their 1957 platform. The Opposition, the Returned Services Association and a large body of retired senior officers regarded this as a failure to live up to treaty commitments. The Labour Government issued a Review of Defence in 1958 which rested their decision heavily on the United Kingdom White Paper of 1957 and lightly on the National Government's own Review of the same year. In an age of brush fire wars and hydrogen missiles the real need, ran the argument, was for professionals and equipment. The compulsory training intake had grown too large to be well trained or employed usefully. Yet New Zealand stood committed to a battalion in Malaya and a division in wartime. So the decision was made to maintain 8100 regulars, including a brigade group which could service Malaya, and to recruit a volunteer territorial force of 7000 to help meet the larger obligation. Behind the organized forces there would be for some years a reserve pool of men already compulsorily trained. Although this was one of the major changes effected by the Labour

Government, New Zealand at large accepted it peacefully enough. Such interest as there was can only be described as fierce, but it came mainly from within the upper ranks past and present.

A much more sustained and mingled uproar greeted the New Zealand Rugby Football Union's decision to exclude Maori players from selection for the representative 'All-Black' team to tour South Africa. Before the controversy died away in mid 1960, the oft-expressed adherence of the Prime Minister, the parties and New Zealanders generally to the ideal of racial equality and non-discrimination was severely questioned and tested. The Rugby Union took the stand that they were protecting Maori players from possible insult. The Citizens' Association, whose branches sprang up in all the main centres, believed that to exclude Maoris would be to practise racial discrimination within New Zealand, to render the team unrepresentative, and to misrepresent and dishonour New Zealand abroad. Their slogan, 'No Maoris, No Tour', decorated protest meetings attended by thousands. At the same time hundreds of letters poured in to the papers, the great majority opposing the Rugby Union's position.

Convinced that greater issues than a sporting tour and its receipts were at stake, the opponents of the Rugby Union began to look to the Prime Minister and the parties for assistance in budging the Union. As Minister for Maori Affairs and guardian of New Zealand's reputation overseas, Mr. Nash was expected to help, at least with his approval. From the first the Prime Minister disclaimed the right to interfere with a private body. A pall of silence descended on both parties and the State radio service. Meanwhile protests continued and a petition gathered 153,000 signatures. Finally, after nine months of mounting agitation, Mr. Nash and the Hon. J. R. Marshall for the National Party, met a large and unusually distinguished deputation on 26 February 1960. The deputation did not ask for legislation or the use of executive powers. Instead it requested that M.P.s should be freed to express their opinion, that the political leaders, especially Mr. Nash, exercise their influence and provide moral backing, and, lastly, that there should be 'a plain and solemn declaration at to what is New Zealand's racial policy.'

Its reception gravely disappointed the deputation. Thenceforth, however, a few M.P.s and even two Ministers began to speak out—on both sides of the controversy. Eventually on

5 April 1960, just after the tragedy at Sharpeville in South Africa, the Prime Minister made a long statement which left no doubt as to his whole position.

I am satisfied that they [the Citizens' Association] miss the main issue of concern to New Zealand—that it would be an act of the greatest folly and cruelty to the Maori race to allow their representatives to visit a country where colour is considered to be a mark of inferiority . . . I am satisfied that the Rugby Union has acted from the highest motives, and as true friends of the Maori people . . . As for the demand that the tour be completely abandoned, I can well understand the feelings which prompt it. But it is not the place of the Government to interfere in the affairs of a sports body . . . I am sure that the Rugby Union, in its final deliberations, can be trusted to keep uppermost our welfare and national unity—a unity of which we are proud, and which has not always been easy to achieve over the last 100 years.

Mr. Nash concluded by affirming that the fundamental principle of New Zealand's racial policy was: 'There are no inherently superior people.'

Compared with a general election, many fewer were involved in the tour controversy, but it stirred far more profound principles and feelings and lasted a dozen times as long. The belief that they were opposing racial discrimination united the Churches and touched the young people of the Dominion as nothing else had done in the postwar era. Professional men were mixed with trade unionists on the Association's committees which included many supporters of both major parties, though Labour's sympathizers were more numerous.

While Maoris were initially reluctant to protest, as the issues became clearer they united in a quite new way to preserve the concept expressed by 'Tatau, tatau', literally 'we and you', with the connotation of 'together', but translated by the late Dr. Winiata as 'We are all one people'. An idea of the kind of difficulties created for the Government can be had from the *Auckland Star* of 13 June 1960, reporting the attitudes of the Maori delegates at Labour's Annual Conference. 'The chairman of the Maori policy committee, Mr. P. T. Watene (who has been nominated for the Eastern Maori seat) said that although the committee remained loyal to the principles of Labour, "blind loyalty, in the face of so much frustration, must reap its own reward." '

The 'reward' in the Maori seats would come at the election.

For most electors, however, the half-year which intervened before the campaign sufficed to divert their thoughts back to more familiar, if more shallow channels. The last session of Parliament rang with the cries of faction. The authorization of a railway for Nelson held the headlines. For the second time the Crimes Bill was abandoned unpassed. Finally a rushed revision of the liquor laws produced just ten licences to sell wine with meals for the whole Dominion. The truth was that the Government had acted decisively and legislated compendiously at the start of its term and would so be judged. Since then it had administered and adjusted while coming slowly to the conviction that it had found a new and sustaining principle in the promotion of economic growth and the changeover to manufacture in depth. On that Labour rested its case.

PART TWO

THE CAMPAIGN

IV

PARTY ORGANIZATION AND THE ELECTION

EACH stage of a party's organization has some specific task at a general election, whether it be deciding the policy of the party or expounding it to the elector on his doorstep; planning the movements of Ministers or taking the voter to the poll. Naturally all these tasks are not equally important. There are two leading roles in the electoral drama: those of the party head office, concerned with planning policy, propaganda and the campaign, and of the professional party staff whose function it is to guide, supplement and supervise the activities of the mass of volunteer helpers on whom both parties ultimately depend.

The efficiency of these two units depends on many factors, imagination, enthusiasm and energy being but a few of them. Beyond such personal factors there lies a more basic requirement. The size of a party's professional staff, the number of functions its head office is able to perform, and the scope of the campaign it is able to wage, all depend ultimately on the size of its income and its campaign funds. This does not mean that the richest party is inevitably the most successful, but simply that a sizeable and regular income is essential to a modern political party. Without one it will find the greatest difficulty in winning friends and influencing voters. Indeed, with each campaign need for money increases as the electorate grows, as Press and pamphlet propaganda become more expensive, and as New Zealand politics begin to enter the age of professionalism.[1]

Any study of the organizational side of an election campaign must therefore begin at the financial grass-roots even though the parties have shown an obsessive concern with shrouding their finances in secrecy. National publishes no accounts and resents questions, Labour publishes generalized accounts to conference but is only slightly more open. Only the Communist Party, accused by the others of being engaged in a conspiracy to subvert

---

[1] The cost in postage alone of distributing one campaign pamphlet to the 600,000 homes in New Zealand is £2,500.

democracy, is completely frank about the financial side of its campaign. If exaggerated popular views prevail and academic discussion is depressingly tentative, the parties have only themselves to blame.

It is clear that the National Party is much better equipped financially than its main rival. Its income from subscriptions is larger than that of any other party, amounting to nearly £30,000 a year. This is supplemented by donations and contributions which, though voluntary, do in fact flow in steadily enough since the party has created an efficient machinery for soliciting them. Like so much else in the National Party the exact arrangements vary from division to division, but the general outline is that every organizer, besides acting as party agent in his area, is also, in fact mainly, concerned with raising money, his efforts being supplemented by other fund raisers, some employed full time, others working on a commission basis. Much of this work is carried out in the electorates through visiting of householders, farmers, business and professional people and firms, but some is also done through the divisions, particularly if large firms are involved. In the case of the largest firms, those providing the bulk of the income, the approach is sometimes made by senior party office-holders who can make a friendly personal approach which paid party servants might be unable to achieve.

The electorates, the basic unit for fund-raising, cover their own expenses and also pay a fixed levy to the division which in turn pays a levy to the Dominion headquarters. Total party income from all these sources is difficult to gauge. Normally it is higher when the party is in opposition than when in power, so that it was probably higher in 1960 than before the previous election. Any total figure given would be purely guess work, though a figure rising to ten times the income from individual subscriptions is a possible estimate.

Labour has a more marked division between local and national fund-raising. Nationally the party bases its finances on the income from affiliations together with that proportion of membership dues which is paid to the head office: an average of £13,500 a year to the central funds over the last five years before the election.[2]

---

[2] As in the case of the National Party, membership rises steeply in an election year, when this income is as high as £16–17,000, equal to just under 180,000 members.

Much of this income is needed for regular expenditure but the party also builds up a national campaign fund over the three-year period, a fund which amounted in 1957 to £28,000 and in 1960 to £25,000. The L.R.C.s make donations to this fund once their own local needs have been met, though many show a marked reluctance to part with hard-earned funds and N.E.C. pleas for more generous contributions have been a regular feature at conferences. More important to the fund are the trade union donations which are often substantial. In 1960 the Federation of Labour itself donated £2500 and the Seamen's Union £2000, with other unions contributing smaller sums.

National M.P.s expressed the fear that Labour's funds would benefit greatly from the passage in the session before the election of legislation to allow unions to apply funds to political objectives with the consent of only a majority of the members voting, instead of that of the majority of the total membership previously necessary. In fact no increase in trade union contributions took place, though a decline which normally occurs when the party is in office may have been checked. Trade union donations have not, however, increased very much since the 1930s. On the other hand there was an increase in contributions from another source: individuals and firms. Manufacturers had never supported Labour as liberally as they did in the 1960 election; some contributions were as large as those of trade unions, and collectively they may have totalled as much as a third of the £19,700 donated to the campaign fund. This increase came in spite of the fact that the party had no regular machinery for reminding such supporters that their gratitude to the Government for its policies could take concrete forms. With proper encouragement a higher total might have been reached and, more important, the party might have been better able to forecast the amount of money it could budget for. Lacking such a forecast Labour found itself in the last week of the election with more money in the campaign fund than had been estimated, and at a time when it was too late to spend the surplus to good effect. A regular machinery for inviting contributions and securing members is one of the more obvious needs of the Labour Party.

Regular funds of any kind are one of the most pressing needs of the Social Credit Political League. Receiving few large contributions, the League has to depend for the bulk of its income on the membership subscriptions of 5s., on members' donations, and on such fund-raising activities as the electorates are able to organize. Headquarters and campaign expenditure are financed by an annual levy of £250 on each electorate but this is a moral obligation only and one which some electorates are unable to fulfil, having enough difficulty in raising money for their own local campaign. Rather more manage to pay a proportion of the levy, and a minority pay in full. Faced with these financial difficulties Social Credit can draw consolation only from the fact that the Communist Party is in an even worse position. Though its regular financial arrangements are obscure, the party carries on its financial preparation for the election quite openly. This it has to do since the entire election fund is raised by a public appeal for donations. The target in 1960 was set as £2000, candidates being limited to an expenditure of £40 each, with the rest of the sum being allocated to central expenses and particularly to the distribution of a special edition of the *People's Voice*. By the end of the campaign the initial target had been exceeded by £700, but with expenses also exceeding estimate nearly all the surplus was anticipated. With 2423 votes in the final result the party spent £1 for each one.

A larger income makes possible better physical amenities and these National has. A newly completed Dominion headquarters, was opened in August 1960, in a completely reconditioned building which also houses on its three floors a National club, the Wellington division, *Freedom*, the party weekly (now monthly), and the research department. In addition to the headquarters staff, each division of the party has its own offices and a small office staff, seven in the case of Wellington, under the full-time divisional secretary. Some of the electorates also own, either individually or jointly, an office or a room. Some centres have National clubs, though the social side of party activities has never been as intensely developed in New Zealand as it has by the Conservative Party in Britain. By contrast Labour is badly equipped at the centre where it has only a small office suite to accommodate its headquarters and in the electorates where the party can rise to the dignity of a room or office, situated usually in the Trades Hall, in but a few centres. Social Credit works from an even smaller central office, which also houses the *New Zealand Guardian*.

A larger income also supports a larger professional staff.

Centrally National has a full-time general director, a publicity director, a research director and the necessary office staffs, a marked contrast with Labour's central staff of four, including the national secretary and the research officer, and Social Credit's of one, the national secretary. In the electorates National's advantage is even more marked, for the divisions have their own paid organizers, Wellington having sixteen, Otago-Southland seven, and the divisions of intermediate size, an intermediate number. Though numerous this professional staff probably fails to be as completely effective as it could be because it has not yet been brought up to the standards of overseas staffs. Most of the organizers are men in their fifties, some retired from other occupations, and the career is not markedly attractive to young men, partly because there is no integrated system of promotion 'from the ranks', partly because salary is not high, though it can be supplemented by taking on extra duties as electorate secretary with the consequent honorarium. A central training scheme is also lacking so that standards and efficiency, as well as pay, vary between the divisions. Naturally, too, there are the inevitable personal variations of attitude. 'I'm a proper bloody dictator', one organizer commented on his relations with his branch and electorate committees, while others held the contrary view that guidance and influence should be unobtrusive and that 'the best organizer is one who organizes himself out of a job'. Yet even though the system is capable of improvement, the existence of a professional staff of organizers does give to the National Party a considerable advantage over its rivals. Since many of the electorates either have an organizer of their own or share one, the voluntary workers can be supervised and guided towards that higher degree of efficiency which characterized National's local campaign.

Earlier in the fifties Labour had four or five able organizers each covering several electorates and fulfilling more of an executive role than National's, though without a correspondingly superior salary. The post attracted rising young men anxious to break into politics, or, as the critics put it, to 'organize themselves into Parliament'. This they had done with such success in 1954 and 1957 that by 1960 Labour had only one full-time organizer, and he a new appointee, covering the Auckland area. The secretary of one L.R.C. was also full-time but only because he was also a trade union secretary. His fellows were either retired men or fulfilled their duties in their spare time, some of them receiving an honorarium for this. Labour had, in fact, fewer paid organizers than the Communist Party which, as well as a full-time national secretary, also had three organizers in the Auckland area, though their duties were not primarily electoral. Lack of professional organizers undoubtedly weakened Labour in 1960. In the numerous electorates he had to cover, the Auckland organizer could do spot checks to ensure the efficiency of canvassing or pamphlet delivery, supplement the work of lazy or incompetent officials, and generally see that the party machinery was running as smoothly as its design permitted. Elsewhere even these safeguards were impossible.

Labour was further handicapped by a failure to tighten up the party organization before the campaign began. In 1957 the organization had reached a peak of efficiency, but since that year there had been a decline in both efficiency and enthusiasm. Organizational decline is a complaint which often afflicts a party in power, though the Conservative Party in Britain and the Liberals in Australia have proved comparatively immune to it. Labour's resistance was slight because of the smallness of its professional staff, because of lack of interest on the part of the leaders and because of concentration on the parliamentary struggle. Early in 1960 a small sub-committee consisting mainly of M.P.s had discussed organizational questions and reported to the N.E.C. but no action resulted from its report. Little else interrupted the gradual relaxation of efficiency.

National by contrast had been preparing for 1960 ever since its 1957 defeat. This defeat had not led to any drastic overhaul of the organization. It had stimulated a quiet and continuous improvement which was combined with long-term planning for the next election. This began in 1958 when it was believed that the Labour Government would call a snap election early in the year. In readiness for such an eventuality the 1957 manifesto had been completely revised before the June Budget removed any likelihood of electioneering. Preparations resumed in November 1959, when the policy committee again began to meet, continuing its deliberations throughout 1960 and devoting the equivalent of fourteen full days and nights to the task. As a result the bulk of the National Party manifesto was ready well before the campaign. Though some planks, such as the commitment to voluntary unionism, were only nailed in during October, the fact that the bulk of the policy preparation had been done in advance, freed energies for other necessary tasks.

Labour Party policy preparation was carried out later and more hastily, being delayed by Mr. Nash's decision to visit the United Nations in late September and early October. This trip set policy preparation back into October, and the implications of some items were worked out only during the campaign itself. Late preparation removed any possibility of a carefully worked out and original manifesto and even ruled out an attractive and clear presentation such as was found in the National Party document.

National also carried out corresponding long-term preparations in other fields. Early in 1960 a small seven-week advertising campaign had been initiated to keep the 'tax and promises' themes in the public mind, and in April 266,000 copies of a pamphlet on taxation had been distributed to householders in marginal electorates. This was merely a minor part of the full-scale campaign, the main lines of which had been worked out by the publicity director as early as November 1959. In planning the campaign, the director worked with a large publicity committee and its small Wellington executive on which sat the deputy leader. Early preparation was supplemented by full consultation of expert opinion. Labour's Press publicity and propaganda committee of four gave to the party's advertising agency the advertisements and pamphlets required and then chose between the proofs which were submitted. National maintained much closer contact by employing two agencies which were represented, together with other professional experts, on the publicity committee. From its early stages the National campaign was professionally supervised.

In terms of volume there was little to choose between the pamphleteering campaigns of the two parties. The actual figures were:

Labour

Abridged Manifesto	650,000
'Everyone is Better-Off Under Labour'	350,000
'Check the Facts and Nail their Lies'	277,000
Housing Pamphlet	125,000
Industrial Development Pamphlet	100,000
Total	1,502,000

National

'A Three Years Wiser Vote'	650,000
'A Policy for Young Voters'	300,000
'The Essential Differences between National and Labour'	300,000
'What They Said and What They Did'	200,000
Total	1,450,000

National closed the gap revealed in this table by issuing 100,000 copies of each of six 'Information Sheets' produced cheaply and designed to press home one or two points. At the other extreme the party also produced a small quantity of two glossy pamphlets, one directed at young voters and one dealing with the Nelson railway. There was also a special Maori pamphlet, similar in format to those for the European electorates.

National made more use of newspaper advertising than Labour. It could better afford to. The party placed advertisements in two union periodicals, the rest refusing space, and in a series of weeklies and monthlies, most of which carried appeals to different sectional groups. The number of newspapers used was reduced slightly as compared with 1957 by a decision not to use the smaller circulation papers. In most of the fifty-six newspapers it did use, National took some 900 inches distributed in a series of 'block-busters' of 60 inches and 90 inches respectively.[3] Labour used rather more newspapers but fewer periodicals. Its advertisements were as numerous as National's but were smaller, totalling only some 500 inches. Labour's largest advertisement was only the same size as National's smallest with the inevitable result that Labour Party advertisements failed to catch the eye in the same way. In each party local advertising was additional to the campaigns which were arranged nationally.

Both parties used the cinema screens, and also the hoardings. National taking twenty major hoardings each chosen with a view to traffic density, and issuing 2000 each of a series of three smaller posters which appeared like a rash in some North Island electorates but were completely absent elsewhere. Labour made similar use of the medium, taking hoardings and turning out 5500 each of a series of 20 inches by 30 inches posters.

[3] An approximate cost is about £7,500 for National's campaign in the four main-centre papers (morning and evening) and just over £4,000 for Labour's.

Adding verbal to visual persuasion both parties arranged speakers' tours through head office; touring Labour M.P.s, for example, addressing nearly two hundred evening meetings. There was little to choose between the efficiency of the parties in shunting ministerial or would-be ministerial talent across the country. Where there was a difference was in outlining arrangements to be followed by local organizations. While National gave specific instructions so detailed as to cover the presentation of sprays to Mrs. Holyoake, Labour laid down no such precise routines with the result that local arrangements fluctuated markedly from place to place.

The National Party's financial advantage over Labour enabled it to carry on a more intensive propaganda campaign. This was inevitable, but National improved its lead even further because its propaganda was markedly superior in presentation and impact. To some extent this was attributable to the public relations advice available to the party, but it was also a product of greater awareness on the part of National Party officials of the importance of modern political techniques. One instance is the despatch by the Wellington division of its secretary, Mr. C. L. Cleal, to Britain to study the methods used by the Conservative Party in its 1959 victory. Cleal's report had stressed the importance of 'image building' techniques, an importance also emphasized by Australian contacts. Yet these 'image building' techniques amounted in fact to little more than efficient advertising, and in previous campaigns National advertising had usually been more effective than Labour's so that there was no need to depart drastically from precedents.

The contrast between the two party campaigns was marked. Where Labour pamphlets concentrated on detailed summaries of the manifesto, or on tax tables with their psychologically depressing overtones, National's were designed with a view to 'eye appeal' as well as content. Where Labour's propaganda was packed with facts and details of the Government's record, National's pamphlets and advertisements concentrated only on driving home one point at a time with the maximum possible impact. Where Labour's was a defensive campaign, National's was one of attack, and attack by assertion. Assertion, whether about 'honest government', the 1958 budget, socialism or private enterprise, served to drive Labour further on to the defensive. In short Labour was fighting in 1960 a political campaign of a traditional type and appealing to a possibly mythical 'rational voter'. National was carrying on an advertising campaign tailored specifically to fit the medium and to create, by assertion, favourable images of National and un-favourable images of its opponent.

In waging this campaign the National Party was in a better position than Labour to know which themes to stress, since it had extensive information on the public mood, provided by public opinion surveys carried out before 1960, during the course of that year and in the campaign itself. While Labour was relying on a curious blend of occasional conversations with the 'man in the street' (or the pub) and an assumed insight into the mind of 'the people', National was dealing with deliberately collected data and since it was provided by the same firm which carried out the successful newspaper Gallup Polls, this information can be assumed to have been reasonably reliable. This investment in polls paid double dividends. National had a clear idea of which issues it could effectively stress in the campaign and which issues were better left alone. It was also abreast of the tide of public opinion and could chart the eddies during the actual campaign. When, therefore, Mr. Holyoake stated after the election that he had known before the poll the result would be victory, just as he had known before the 1957 election that it would lead to defeat, in neither case did he have to rely on his own unaided intuition. Such knowledge, properly used, could have made possible correc-tive action to profit from the trend of events, and the leader's attempt on 23 November to woo the Social Credit vote may not have been unrelated to the fact that the polls pointed to Social Credit as the only party actually gaining ground during the campaign.

Prior to the 1957 elections the Labour party had been offered the services of Public Opinion and Gallup Polls Ltd., the firm used by National and the Press. The offer had been refused. Prior to the 1960 election the N.E.C. had decided to appoint a public relations officer. Nothing was done to implement the decision. Even Social Credit was more active in both these fields than was Labour, for the League employed a public relations consultant whose advice was largely instrumental in shifting the main emphasis in the 1960 campaign from technicalities to benefits, in securing the production of a full policy manifesto and in organizing propaganda themes. Through this consultant the League also financed a public opinion survey in which 7,509 people were interviewed by Social Crediters in all eighty electorates, the results being used mainly to provide ammunition for party propaganda, but also as a guide on where campaign emphasis should be placed. In the implementation of political techniques used in other countries Labour was not only lagging well behind its main rival, but was behind the third party as well.

Important as propaganda is, party headquarters in an election campaign are also concerned with more detailed organizational work, and particularly with the supervision and control of the local campaign. This is something for which both parties make very similar arrangements, concentrating on the marginal electorates where a disproportionate crop of seats is waiting to be harvested. Labour worked with a list of sixteen marginal seats, most of which were visited by the national secretary in August and September and which all got a full selection of the nationally issued pamphlets, though at their own expense. As a result of his visit to the electorates the national secretary had declared himself satisfied with the organization in most of them, but as a final security organizers were asked to send reports in to head office during the campaign itself.

Characteristically the National Party preparations were more elaborate, being based on a longer list of twenty-three marginal seats, mostly those with a majority of up to 2000 for Labour or up to 1000 for National, and on a further schedule covering ten key electorates to which even more particular attention was paid. Most of the electorates on the lists were visited by the general director in the course of a three-week tour in September. Normally the director spent less than a day in each individual electorate but his tour, like that of his Labour counterpart, was beneficial in revealing any deficiencies in local organization, and, perhaps more important, in convincing local workers that an active interest was being taken in their work. This conviction must have been reinforced by the amount of paper work demanded from marginal electorates, for regular reports were required from June onwards and a series of forms was provided, with questions relating to most aspects of the local scene. This volume of paper moving in to the centre was outweighed by the bulk moving outwards, for key electorates received, free of charge, a full coverage of National Party pamphlets.

Provision of pamphlets amounted to a concealed subsidy, but neither party attempted to divert any further central funds to the marginal seats in spite of their disproportionate importance. Wellington and South Auckland divisions of the National Party joined to form a marginal seats committee to encourage mutual support, and in two cases, divisions made trifling sums available to key seats. Occasionally extra organizers were provided in marginal seats so that Gisborne, for example, had the services of two National Party organizers during the campaign, but all this was done through divisions not head office. Neither party, it would seem, concentrates on the marginal seats to the maximum possible extent.

Propaganda campaign launched, and marginal seats prepared, the functions of a party head office during the actual campaign period are confined to the less important spheres of supervision and co-ordination. In the Labour Party these tasks were performed by the Press publicity and propaganda committee of four which met twice a week. Between meetings, and in the absences of committee members from Wellington, the tasks of co-ordinating reports, dealing with requests and enquiries, and supervising the machinery fell on to the shoulders of the national secretary. A slight disruption was caused towards the end of the campaign when this official was called for some days of jury service, and had to carry out his party work in the evening. Coupled with the smallness of the central staff, this distraction reduced the degree of central control and co-ordination which could be maintained by the Labour Party.

The National Party's campaign was controlled by a campaign planning committee set up by the Dominion Council at the end of October. Initially including eight people, the committee was in practice reduced to five since the leader, the deputy leader and the president of the party were away from Wellington most of the time. This committee met twice a week during the campaign, its main tasks being to review progress, deal with local problems, and supervise strategy. To guide it, basic information was forthcoming in the forms returned by electorate secretaries at regular intervals and covering the progress of the local campaign, attendance at meetings, issues being raised and other topics. This outline was filled in by telegram and telephone and colour was added by specially arranged reports of what leading figures on the Government side were saying. With such extensive information at its disposal the committee was able to form an overall picture of the campaign, a picture shared with organizers, candidates and secretaries all over the country through a regular series of bulletins which included suggestions on topics to be emphasized and information on organizational questions. This degree of centralization, in a party which boasts of its decentralization, helps to bring into contrast Labour's more haphazard and informal arrangements.

Most of the sections of this chapter have had a common refrain of National Party superiority in the particular field examined. In respect of both professional staff and central organization the National Party demonstrated a marked superiority over Labour in the 1960 election, a superiority which had its basis in financial strength but which was also attributable to greater receptiveness to specialist advice and new ideas, and to more painstaking planning. Yet though the superiority is undeniable it would be a mistake to assume that it was the reason for the National Party victory. Organization does not win elections. The best propaganda and the best organization can only amplify very slightly an existing advantage, cushion very slightly a predestined defeat. Organization, advertising, and image-building are not akin to witchcraft, much as the defeated party might like to attribute its defeat to such alchemy. The National Party's own public opinion surveys demonstrated quite clearly that with all its advantages in these fields it gained no ground in the months before the election.

V

THE CAMPAIGN AND THE ISSUES

A SYSTEM of triennial elections robs the New Zealand campaign of any real element of surprise. With a maximum of three years to work in, Prime Ministers very rarely anticipate disaster or realize on windfall popularity by a snap election. Nor do they manoeuvre far from the November of the third year as the time for trial by ballot, so the dates are as familiar as the process. Tradition further prescribes a short campaign, beginning in 1960 on 31 October, three days after the dissolution of Parliament, and ending with the election on Saturday, 26 November. Such a regular pattern gives no help to politicians in their efforts to grip the national imagination and in 1960 the normal impression of monotonous regularity was heightened by the quiet nature of the campaign itself. The campaign lacked issues such as the dramatic strike of 1951, the surprise Social Credit intervention of 1954, or the policy proposals of 1957. The comment of a shopkeeper in Wanganui who, asked by a reporter who he thought would win the election replied absently, 'Kennedy I suppose', helps to illustrate the absence of obsessive concern with the electoral struggle in the Dominion.

Lack of drama reflected absence of policy. The debate concentrated on the previous three years of Labour government and particularly on 1958. The parties busied themselves with the history of a bungle. They differed only as to what the bungle was, 1957–8 crisis, or 1958 Budget. Social Credit simply added 'Amen' to both.

The few diversions from this three-year-old debate were the new policies brought forward for the election. Most of these were urged by National. Traditionally it is the task of the Opposition to present new policies while the Government rests on its laurels and points, with a satisfaction real or assumed, to its record. The 1960 election was no exception, and the National Party began its allotted task early so that after revision at the end of March and the beginning of April 1960, a large part of the manifesto was ready for release well before a November election and in reserve against any surprise poll before the mid-year Budget.

This early preparation enabled Mr. Holyoake to begin a 'Meet the People' tour in May. He visited marginal electorates in several parts of the country releasing different aspects of policy in each place, but combining them everywhere with the same general critique of the Labour Government. At Palmerston North early in May he announced policy for industry and commerce including a proposed abolition of capital issues control, and the establishment of a Ministry of Overseas Trade to encourage exports, aided by an Export-Import Advisory Council and a Tariff and Development Board which would replace the Board of Trade. While condemning Labour's blanket import control, Mr. Holyoake announced that import licensing would be retained for a time. It would, however, be removed from manufacturers' raw materials and gradually replaced by 'adequate protective duties', as the Tariff and Development Board advised. Two further items in this section of policy were a promise to repeal the Trade Practices Act 'as it now stands', and also to sell Government-owned shares in trading corporations in small amounts so as to encourage widespread investment.

Agricultural policy announced at Kaikohe included little of interest beyond a pledge to remove the clause much criticized by Federated Farmers in the Land Settlement Act of 1959 which provided that people developing new land had to live on it. An anxious Nelson audience was told that National would secure the necessary facts before making any decision on the Nelson railway, while Gisborne merited a review of external affairs and a pledge to fill the two vacant diplomatic posts in London and Washington 'immediately'. Policy on delinquency announced at St. Kilda provided for an extension of the penalties for car conversion, and a promise of assistance to youth welfare organizations. This was combined with constitutional policy and the promise to create an appeal authority like the Scandinavian Ombudsman to whom citizens could appeal against administrative decisions. Christchurch was chosen for health and for social security, benefits for which, announced Mr. Holyoake, would not be increased immediately though all except the family benefit would be supplemented as national income rose. Education was for Taupo, while Whakatane was brought up to date on housing policy. This included a promise to provide loans of up to 100 per cent with a £2700 maximum on the cost of a new house where a suitable section was owned, and a further promise of 'making finance available by second mortgage or the guarantee thereof' for the older and larger houses which were declining in value because the Labour Government had made finance so readily and exclusively available for new houses. A final return to Dunedin on 7 June produced another major item, a pledge to 'progressively reduce the rates of both personal and indirect taxation', which evidently superseded a promise already made at Wanganui in April to reduce taxes to their 1957 level. Dunedin was also told that death duties would be reduced, gift duties would be 'reviewed', and donations out of income to charitable, educational and welfare organizations would be made deductible for tax purposes.

The Leader of the Opposition ended his extensive tour just before the opening of the parliamentary session on 22 June. About four-fifths of the National Party's election policy had been released in a refreshing departure from the traditional fetish of maintaining strict secrecy about policy until the formal unveiling at the beginning of a campaign. However great the initiative, its results were unspectacular. In spite of the wide publicity it had received the policy could hardly be said to have made a marked impact. Attacks on Labour and promises to reduce taxation had been received with enthusiasm by the audiences of party supporters. These same audiences had accorded the other policies little more than a perfunctory welcome. Few of the trial balloons had soared skywards.

Something more was necessary if National's opponents were not to be allowed to portray it as a party without a policy. On the other hand National could not afford too wide a range of policy since this might distract attention from 1958 and the taxation issue. The next few months saw the achievement of a judicious, though possibly accidental, balance between these conflicting needs. More policy was announced in the parliamentary session. In September a vague idea of National's obviously incomplete television policy was given when Mr. Holyoake proposed an independent controlling commission to lay down programme standards, allot viewing time, and allow some share to private enterprise. More momentous than these shaky outlines was the brief announcement on 13 September that National would continue the capitalization of the family benefit and the 3 per cent loans for house purchase. Coming after National's opposition to the passage of these measures and the party's continued criticisms of their operation, the announcement excited some derision among Labour M.P.s. It should have stimulated a different reaction. Many Labour strategists had expected their opponents to continue opposition to these measures, so allowing Labour to fight on advantageous ground. Now this ground was gone. A quiet unobtrusive announcement had removed social security advances from the scope of the debate.

The remaining aspects of National Party election policy were revealed only with the opening of the campaign. Then Mr. Holyoake proposed a Monetary and Economic Commission to advise the Government on economic questions and improve popular knowledge of economics. A decision was announced to link the power systems of the Dominion by making surplus power from the South Island available in the North through a Cook Strait cable, a proposal on which the Labour Government had been reluctant to commit itself. Television policy reached a final, though still vague, form in a proposal to establish a broadcasting commission 'composed of citizens' and independent of Government, to control the medium. This body was to have the assistance of an advisory committee widely representative of the community, and the power to allow private enterprise to provide programmes. A concession, received with scant gratitude, was made to the Constitutional Society's Right-wing point of view, by a proposal to introduce a written Bill of Rights. Another pressure group, the Returned Services' Association, had been urging a return to the system of compulsory military training abandoned by the Labour Government. National did not, however, take up this policy. It adopted instead a 'wait and see' policy of instituting a full enquiry into defence and then taking the 'steps necessary to re-establish the defence of the country on a sound basis'. This facilitated fierce criticism of Labour's defence record but entailed no definite commitment. The manifesto was completed by its two major innovations. Caution on the Nelson railway was replaced by condemnation: work was to be stopped immediately. National could therefore pursue the question more vigorously than its policy of five months before would have allowed, although it was still felt necessary to soften the blow to Nelson by the subsequent promise of a paper mill. Finally voluntary unionism, abolished by Labour in 1936, was to be restored. All workers were to have the right to choose whether or not they would join a union.

Attractively presented in a bulky full statement, and summarized in party pamphlets, the National manifesto betrayed from some points of view the appearance of an interesting collection of ideas and items. Yet viewed as a whole it had three main aspects. It prevented opponents depicting National as an enemy to the welfare state. At the same time a sustained effort had been made to give substance to the traditional image of National as the party of freedom, by innovations such as voluntary unionism and by the checks to the power of the State provided in the Ombudsman, the Broadcasting Commission, and the Bill of Rights. The third element was the inevitable blend of concessions to supporters and vote-winning promises. Concessions were extended to farmers in the promise to free road transport of livestock from restrictions and the pledge to revoke the compulsory residence clause which had been criticized by Federated Farmers. Business too was promised minor gains such as the removal of capital issues control, while an appeal was extended to the entire electorate through the major pledge of 1960: to reduce taxation 'given normal circumstances'.

By contrast with National's effort, Labour Party policy preparation was tardy. A few indications of new developments were given in April 1960 by the Minister of Finance. At St. Kilda Mr. Nordmeyer announced a decision to introduce an entirely new tariff and to revise tariff cover for industry so as to ensure a reasonable measure of protection until such time as import control would no longer apply. He also unveiled a proposal to encourage industrial development in those areas which were developing slowly by erecting Government factories which could be rented to industry. However this brief and early initiative was not followed up. The party conference in June, though intended as a 'policy conference', urged only one major development: the inclusion of dental and optical benefits under the Social Security Act. With this exception, which was not in any case adopted by the policy committee, conference provided that body with very little basis for its deliberations. The Budget, expected by many to produce some large vote-winning rabbit from the hat, turned out to be a very conservative and restrained document and presaged an unspectacular election policy.

Many commentators still assumed that major vote-winning promises would be produced at the last minute. Only the announce-

ment on 10 October by the president of the party that there
would be 'no gimmicks, no spectacular policy and no vote-
catching in the Labour campaign', and the release of the actual
manifesto served to dispel these expectations. It was then seen
that Labour Party policy for the election of 1960 was built on the
twin bases of achievements in office and industrial development.
The party, which ever since the 1930s had urged economic
diversification, now placed the major part of its electoral eggs in
this basket. A case for industrial development was presented and
justified by the need to economize on overseas funds by manufacturing at home, and by the necessity to provide employment
for the rising population and the rapidly increasing numbers of
young people coming on to the labour market. Details were
given of projects already initiated and of those being considered
by the Government for the next three years, and due emphasis
was placed on the means of development, import licensing, tariff
reforms, a development council, and an industrial finance corporation to provide funds for development and administer the rental
factories.

Other policies were few. Too many social security advances
had been promised in 1957 and implemented since for many
further developments to be immediately forthcoming in that
field. Possibly none were wanted for there was a school of thought
in the party half ashamed of the wide ranging appeals of 1957
and urging that Labour should not again lay itself open to the
accusation of promising its way into power. More important, the
economic climate necessitated restraint. As a result practical but
unspectacular proposals such as a postal clearing system for
cheques through the post office, and a promise to provide gymnasia
free to schools, with a subsidy for local gymnasia set the restrained
tone for Labour's manifesto. An increase in the basic war
pension, and an increase in payments to doctors so as to secure a
system of medical treatment completely free to the patient were
pledged, but lacked mass appeal. Finally there came Labour's
major promise of 1960: to raise the personal tax exemption in the
next parliamentary term to £10 a week for single tax-payers and
£15 for the married. This slim list of promises pacified the purists,
ensured that there would be no accusations of 'bribery' and yet
placed the party at a considerable electoral disadvantage. There
was little to catch the enthusiasm of voters and party workers;

nothing to draw attention away from taxation and the 1958 Budget.

When the manifestos of both major parties were announced it was clear that the steady trend to convergence of Left and Right seen in the affluent fifties had combined with the circumstances of 1960 to produce an even greater degree of similarity. Both parties were sensitive to this, and each strove to differentiate itself from the other, National making particularly strenuous efforts, for the party president outlined ten points of difference at the 1960 conference and a special pamphlet on these 'essential differences' was distributed just before the campaign. Such efforts could not disguise a mutual choice of unspectacular policies, and a whole range of actual concurrence. Both parties promised a veterinary school, a decimal currency, equal pay for women, a review of tariffs, and an intensified land settlement policy with increasing opportunity for civilians to settle land. Both would co-ordinate road and rail transport, Labour through a transport council, National through a Ministry of Transport; both would encourage industry through provision of bulk power and through tax concessions on reserves for development. Revision of the licensing laws through the traditional cautious and piecemeal efforts was featured in both manifestos and finally both parties chose to make their main bid with the same policy: reduction of taxation. Broad acres of common ground meant that the actual battlefield was all the more restricted. Debate concentrated the more heavily on the few issues actually at stake.

Amongst the other parties, Social Credit had worked out its policy well in advance through a series of policy committees, though the immediate platform for the election was not released until the leader's opening speech. The policy put forward was a much broader one than at previous elections, for the League and its public relations consultant were anxious to break away from the image of Social Credit as a party of one idea. Each aspect of national affairs was covered in a policy which embraced an unusual collection of good ideas, odd ones, and local particularisms. Thus health policy promised an increase in the family allowance to parents of mentally defective children, housing policy allowed for starting with a small housing unit and enlarging it gradually with the family, and harbour policy included the maintenance of Greymouth Harbour to accommodate ships of up to 5000 tons.

The escape from the 'one idea image' was not achieved because the hard core of the policy was inevitably the implementation of Social Credit through the creation of a national credit authority to control the issue of credit and create money for Government purposes interest free, and where circumstances warranted, debt free.

This credit substructure was to support the planks of the platform, planks which consisted mainly of a list of tax concessions. The party pledged to abolish direct taxation up to the first £520, death duties on sums up to £20,000, and gift duties on sums up to £1000 a year. Petrol tax was to be reduced and beer and tobacco tax brought down to 1957 levels. At the same time as taxation was reduced expenditure was to be increased. Parents of children attending private schools were to be allowed a taxation refund of £10 a year, all pensions were to be increased by 10s. a week, and subsidies were to be introduced on meat, fish, footwear and clothing. The League clearly had considerable faith in its ability to make Major Douglas's theories work.

Though nineteen candidates were fielded, Communist Party policy made little impact. The main proposals were a new trading policy which would develop New Zealand's trade with the socialist countries and particularly with Russia and China. Monopoly was to be fought at home by the nationalization of key industries such as the freezing companies, the stock and station agents, the banks and insurance companies, and coastal shipping. Prices, profits and rents were to be pegged, pensions and benefits increased along with taxation on the wealthy, and a minimum wage of £16 was to be guaranteed for a forty-hour week. Evidently if the major parties were not anxious to indulge in promises in the 1960 election, the minor ones were quite prepared to fill the gap.

The campaign itself was opened by Mr. Nash for the Labour Party at Auckland on 31 October. With the accumulated pressure of campaign preparations, the visit to New York and a hectic session, the Prime Minister appeared tired, a tiredness which gave a slightly flat atmosphere to the meeting. Auckland was followed by nineteen other major meetings as well as occasional morning and afternoon addresses to workers. So tired did Mr. Nash appear at earlier meetings that a Labour M.P. at one of them pleaded with his leader to take a weekend's rest. Mr. Nash, proud of his staying power, managed without. By the third week he had thrown off fatigue but he rarely achieved on his tour the form which had characterized his performance in 1957. With warm, friendly, and respectful audiences, most of the meetings lacked either exhilarating enthusiasm or the stimulus of opposition and heckling. Veneration was no substitute for producing an atmosphere conducive to platform artistry. Government business, omnipresent in suitcases of papers, constant telegrams and frequent discussions with delegations, provided a further restraint. In 1957 the Labour leader had carried on a very active campaign, visiting schools and factories and meeting party workers during the day as well as speaking at night. In 1960 an equally hard-working leader had to confine most of his activity to the less conspicuous official sphere. Combined with initial fatigue, and the absence of exhilaration or opposition, this prevented the recreation of the dynamic image of 1957.

The speeches used during the campaign were written for the Prime Minister by his Press secretary, Mr. R. E. Coury. Though there were local variations and Mr. Nash ad-libbed frequently, especially at his more successful meetings, the basic outline was usually the same. The basic range of subjects included the 1957–8 crisis and what Labour had achieved in spite of this setback, not only positively by introducing the social security advances pledged in 1957 and expanding the housing programme, but also negatively by avoiding the unemployment which had hit America, the United Kingdom and Canada during the period. This was followed by replies to National accusations such as the frequently repeated claim on taxation: 'I'll guarantee that anyone with an income of less than £1000 is paying less tax than under National'. Finally there came policy for the future with especial emphasis on industrial development, the need to create 330,000 new jobs by 1970 and the £180–£200 million of overseas capital which would be drawn into the Dominion in the next five years by projects such as the Southland aluminium smelting plant announced on 19 November. Embellished with frequent quotation of financial statistics the basic theme emerged as: 'You've never been so well-off in New Zealand as you are today. You wouldn't have been so well-off if we had not taken the measures we did in 1958.' It was a message of which audiences clearly approved even though it did not rouse them to enthusiasm. It was also a message repeated with different emphases by the other Cabinet Ministers touring the country.

Mr. Holyoake opened the National campaign at Palmerston North, the first time the party had gone outside the main centres for its opening meeting. He followed up with practically the same number of meetings as Mr. Nash, using, like the Prime Minister, the same basic speech, prepared in this case by Mr. Webber, public relations expert and a former editor of *Truth*. Once again the great majority of the audiences were the party faithful. They were a slightly more enthusiastic flock than Labour's but not all the goats had been removed, for Mr. Holyoake met with more opposition than Mr. Nash. At the second meeting in Auckland heckling amounted almost to a barrage, it was strong again at Napier the next night, and absent from only a few meetings. This caused fears that Mr. Holyoake, attempting to talk down the opposition, might lose his voice as he had in 1957. After an initial wavering the voice rallied and stood up to its ordeal remarkably well, and for the most part the heckling was an unmitigated gain. It provided just the whetstone which Mr. Nash lacked, keeping audience and speaker on the alert, and allowing Mr. Holyoake to demonstrate his considerable skill at scoring off interjections.

Inevitably Mr. Holyoake dealt with party policy, emphasizing freedom, choice and enterprise, but inevitably, too, this was subordinated to the main theme of the speeches: the attack on Labour. With claims such as 'people must be able to depend on trust, and have complete faith in their public men' this was in part an attack by inference which tied in well with one theme of the party's advertising campaign. In the main it was a direct attack which also tied in with the remainder of the advertising campaign, an attack on 1957 'bribes', on 1958 Budget, and on taxation, a tactic as one commentator put it of 'jumping up and down on the exposed nerve'. Mr. Holyoake saw Labour's record as one of high taxation, slight unemployment, increased bankruptcies and closure of small factories, and contrasted this unfavourably with the previous eight years of National Party tax reductions and economic expansion. The whole case was argued with vigour and energy. Three years had greatly improved Mr. Holyoake's platform manner and his performance in 1960 was a vital one. True it did not improve towards the end of the campaign in the way that

Mr. Nash's did. This was unimportant since Mr. Holyoake successfully achieved all that was necessary: a maintenance of the initial vigour and drive.

Mr. Matthews, speaking at Wanganui, opened the campaign of the Political League on 2 November. After a dynamic listing of the platform proposals he tailed off into a rambling dissertation which could not be redeemed since the Social Credit leader held only a few other major meetings outside his electorate. In the speeches he did make he concentrated in the main on the theme that 'there is no difference between Labour and National' and on the tax concessions offered by Social Credit. In explaining these concessions the leader, like most of the candidates, placed the main emphasis on their effect in stimulating the economy and so expanding remaining revenue. Deeper technicalities of Social Credit theory were not emphasized. The raft of promises floated mainly on credence.

The trends of the campaign were clearly set with the opening meetings and the announcement of the manifestos. Very few of the policy proposals in these manifestos excited much discussion or attention. One of the few that did, and that belatedly, was the question of voluntary unionism. Early trade union reaction was mild, radical trade unionists approving the measures as freeing them from the restraint imposed by a mass of reluctant unionists, most secretaries warning that the trade union movement generally would be weakened. For his part Mr. Walsh, the president of the Federation of Labour, simply stated: 'I am not losing any sleep over the threat.' While he slept National Party speakers continued to advance the stock arguments that voluntary unionism would restore freedom of choice and strengthen the unions by reviving interest on the part of the now uncoerced workers and vigour on the part of a union secretariat more dependent on the goodwill of its members. On the Labour side speakers warned of industrial discord and stressed the unfairness of the non-unionist receiving the wage increases and benefits for which union members alone had worked and paid. Not until 11 November was Mr. Walsh's sleep interrupted. Then he announced: 'Trade unionists should know that the National Party's attack on compulsory unionism is a frontal attack on the workers of New Zealand' since it would weaken the trade union movement generally and reduce its strength. Voluntary unionism, the statement urged, would be a severe blow to the weak unions, but would only serve to strengthen the already strong unions, who by strike action and picketing would be able to drive wages up. Industrial discord was inevitable. On this issue the employers appeared to be in agreement with the Federation of Labour for on 8 November Mr. P. J. Luxford, secretary to the Employers' Federation, publicly defended the existing system of compulsory unionism. Yet these items of ammunition were little used by Labour. After the intervention of employers and employees, debate on voluntary unionism returned to the stock platitudes, probably because there was no kindling of public interest to keep the fire alive.

For a brief period in the campaign it appeared as though new policy proposals might be introduced which would concentrate debate on fundamental differences of attitude between the parties. Mr. Nordmeyer, speaking to cargo workers in Auckland, appeared to hint at a State shipping service by saying: 'It may be possible, I hope it will be, that we will have some ships of our own so that we can counteract the interests of the powerful shipping lines.' It also appeared that National might take its defence of private enterprise to the logical conclusion of returning State-owned enterprise to private hands, when Mr. Marshall on 22 November and Mr. McAlpine the following day, mentioned the National Airways and the Bank of New Zealand as possible enterprises in which the public should be allowed to buy shares of small denomination. These twin beginnings of what might have been a fundamental debate over the virtues of nationalization and private enterprise simply dropped into a stony tomb of silence. The dirty, because electorally unpopular, linen of theoretical difference was not to be washed in public.

If the major parties could not provide policy proposals which would grip public attention, neither could the minor parties. Social Credit had made a valiant effort with its wide-reaching policy, but this excited little interest. Attention was paid to Social Credit during the campaign not so much because of the League's policy, as because of National's attempt to win over the Social Credit vote. At this very first meeting Mr. Holyoake emphasized that a vote for Social Credit was a vote wasted, and pointed out that Social Credit and National had much in common, particularly a shared faith in private enterprise. This initial effort was reinforced less than a fortnight later with the release of a letter from Mr. Owen, leader of the League in the two previous elections, to Mr. Gotz, National M.P. for Manukau. This letter emphasized that believers in the need for monetary reform, whatever they called themselves, should 'work within the framework of the National Party'. Finally in Mr. Holyoake's broadcast on 23 November he made a determined play for Social Credit votes, stating: 'We've got to move along the road in monetary reform as in other reforms . . . I do not disagree with the Social Credit candidates who say that their policy is very close to ours . . . I have noticed that in many ways the fundamental proposal, the money reform proposal, by Social Credit is much the same as National . . . to those who are considering voting Social Credit, I say that if you vote National you'll be voting for your own policy.' The net was spread.

Since the policy proposals put forward by the parties had failed to excite interest the way was clear for outside bodies and events to bring influence to bear on the campaign. An attempt to exploit this opportunity was made by a group of bank employees, anxious about Labour's Reserve Bank Amendment Act, the Land and Income Tax Amendment Bill, and most important of all, the postal cheque clearing system, which would have brought the State into direct competition with the banks. To counter these 'threats' the Banks' Staff Action Movement was organized in Wellington by bank employees working independently. Formed at the beginning of the campaign the movement was taken up by contacts in other centres, and issued a statement on 4 November claiming that 'the Nationalization of the bank industry by stealth is perfectly possible under existing legislation and is a real danger to free competitive enterprise'. Government influence, it was inferred, was a constant restriction on the free operations of the banks and one which was preventing them from expanding their services to customers. This first and widely publicized statement was followed by others in the course of the campaign and supplemented by questions at meetings and letters to the Press. Some 3 per cent of all the election letters published in the main-centre papers dealt with this question. National went a considerable way to meeting the demands of the movement with a statement by Mr. Shand that the National Party had rejected the postal clearing system when in power, and would not go ahead with it if it took office again. Labour remained unrepentant.

State aid for church schools provoked another outside intervention. Roman Catholic groups had always been concerned about this issue. Now their concern was amplified as rising numbers in church schools and the growing burden of costs threatened financial crisis. Having appointed a commission on education, Labour's policy was to stonewall until its recommendations were made. When, therefore, on 4 November Mr. Nash was asked to address the Home and School Association of Hawera Convent School, he took his main stand on the need for full consideration of State aid by the commission. National took a similar, though more flexible stand. Though also awaiting the commission report, it announced that the promise to exempt donations for charitable and educational purposes from tax would be extended to cover school fees. At the same time a few National candidates promised, like Mr. Riddiford in Wellington Central, to support State aid as individuals if elected, and others made sympathetic though noncommittal noises. Labour caught up with this situation only in the last week of the campaign when, after urgings by candidates in marginal seats, there was a series of announcements that the similar Labour promise to free donations from tax could be construed in the same way as National's.

The sensitivity of both parties appeared justified when what had previously been a little publicized movement reached the newspapers in the last week of the campaign. On 22 November the Auckland Diocesan Federation of Catholic Parent, Teacher, Friends' Associations and a Catholic lay body, the Holy Name Society, held a meeting in Auckland attended by some two hundred and fifty representatives of Roman Catholic educational and lay associations in the Auckland Diocese. At the meeting the replies of the party leaders to questions on State aid were read out, and though the replies of both Mr. Holyoake and Mr. Nash were similar in import, the reply of the former was considered to be rather more favourable in tone. Mr. W. S. Otto, the national president of the Holy Name Society, called on Catholics to 'cast aside political affiliations on election day and vote for the man', and asked them to 'look for the man with principles and integrity who would see the justice of the cause of State aid for private schools'. Though widely reported, the importance of address and meeting was greatly exaggerated. If they aimed at opportunistic action by Roman Catholic voters as local candidates and their attitudes dicated, the effect could be felt only over the long term. Lifetime political ties could certainly not be broken by a delegate meeting and a few words from a layman immediately before the poll.

A last minute influence loomed up suddenly on 20 November. Dissatisfied with a pay increase awarded by the industrial tribunal the Wellington and Palmerston North branches of the Engine Drivers, Firemen and Cleaners' Association announced that they would strike from midnight on 21 November, while their Auckland colleagues would work to rule. This would have been the first strike by the union for thirty years, and one which would have stopped rail traffic in the Wellington area and seriously delayed it in Auckland. The threat was soon withdrawn. On 21 November Mr. Nash, Mr. Nordmeyer, and Mr. Moohan, the Minister of Railways, met the council of the Association. After two hours of discussion in which the Government representatives insisted that no consideration could be given to the wage demands until the strike was abandoned, the union informed the general manager of the railways that the strike notice had been withdrawn. The effect of threat and withdrawal on the election is impossible to assess. Any harm to Labour's chances was of the very slightest order, though it would be difficult to go further and say that success in securing the withdrawal of the threat actually helped that party.

The electorate in 1960 showed little interest in the comparatively short list of policy proposals laid before it. It was not gripped by other important topics such as foreign affairs for the parties tended to fight shy of such questions and they were in any case rendered dull by the extent of bipartisan agreement. Outside interventions and influences had proved comparatively minor. Inevitably the parties filled the vacuum by restaging the debate of the previous three years. Discussion concentrated on what some saw as a garbled secular litany of father, son and holy ghost: the means used by Labour to secure office in 1957, the 1958 Budget, and the 1957–8 crisis.

In replaying the long-playing records of the last three years Mr. Holyoake began with the bribes. Right at the beginning of the campaign he accused Labour of having 'fooled and tricked' the people in 1957 with their glittering 'bribes'. To this attack Mr. Nash responded the next day with a saddened defence of his integrity, and, on 9 November, a criticism of his opponent for claiming that Labour had 'deliberately deceived the public'. This criticism Mr. Holyoake brushed off next day with the comment that 'Mr. Nash might be angry at my saying he deceived the people, but that is nothing to the anger of the people who have been deceived'. Since many of Labour's promises of 1957 had been accepted by the National Party in 1960, the 'chief bribes' to which that party directed its attack were the £100 tax rebate coupled with Mr. Nash's promise not to increase taxation. The rebate, claimed Mr. Holyoake, was an attempt to buy the people's votes with their own money, and one costing £21 million, part of which had had to come from reserves prudently built up by National. The Prime Minister and the Minister of Finance replied to this with a collection of arguments. The first was to point out that the rebate had also been promised by Labour in 1954 but had not then carried the party to victory. In any case the National Party in the 1957 Budget had provided for a tax rebate of 25 per cent, with a maximum of £75, so that Labour was not the only briber if bribery there had been. The final argument was to point out that National had not intended to collect one year's social security tax from the self-employed until those owing it died or left the country. This scheme of 'pay it when you're dead' (a joke repeated from the 1957 campaign), had been cancelled by Labour, and collection of the charge had brought in £15,200,000. This had in large part covered the cost of the tax rebate.

National claimed that the 1958 Budget represented the 'bill' for the 'bribes' of the year before. Labour on the other hand defended the Budget as having been necessary to deal with the situation left by National. Debate moved in this way on to the 1957-8 crisis. Labour's case was relatively straightforward. In December 1957 when Labour took over, argued Mr. Nash, overseas reserves had amounted to only £45,500,000 'the sharpest trade crisis since the early thirties'. 'Tough measures' and increased taxation had been necessary to deal with this situation. Stock charge produced stock reaction. Mr. Holyoake claimed that on election day, 1957, there had been £58,500,000 in overseas funds as well as reserves of £19,200,000 in the defence fund, £3,200,000 in the reserve fund, £3,100,000 in the earthquake fund, all invested in London. He thus reached a total of £84,000,000 though the means used to get there were described as unfair by Mr. Nash who argued that the investments were set aside for specific purposes and were not part of normal reserves. The Leader of the Opposition did not deny that there had been a run on the overseas funds. He stated in Wellington on 7 November: 'I said so from this platform in 1957 and was the only public man to say so.' The cause of this rundown was fear of import controls if Labour should get into power. Labour knew what the situation was and yet had seen fit neither to mention any crisis during the campaign nor to moderate their promises. In any case at the time of the election 'The position was completely satisfactory. For anyone to say "panic stations" with such reserves was just silly.' National would have been able to deal calmly with the situation just as they had dealt with the similar problem in 1954. Labour on the other hand 'panicked after the general elections. Labour is a crisis party.'

Quotation of official figures, instead of clarifying the issue, merely served to confuse it further. This fact emerged in the third week of the campaign, when the party leaders moved into the South Island. In Dunedin, in reply to an interjector who quoted 'Wally's' claim that overseas reserves had been £45,500,000 at the end of 1957, Mr. Holyoake replied: 'The figure Mr. Nash quoted was correct but it was the figure existing in March 1958.' The next night in Oamaru the Prime Minister quoted from the latest *Abstract of Statistics* which gave overseas reserves in December 1957, the month Labour took office, as £45,500,000, the lowest figure since the war (a claim he frequently reinforced by showing a poster from the *Dominion* for 11 December 1957, bearing this legend). Mr. Nash promised to post a copy of the *Abstract* to his challenger to provide him with accurate statistics. In Christchurch, working from his own copy, Mr. Holyoake promptly replied: 'My statements about overseas funds are proved to the hilt by official publications. The Prime Minister's have been partial, garbled and incorrect . . . It is simply not true,' he went on, 'that at the date of the election in November 1957 overseas assets totalled £45,474,000.' In fact they were £84 million, the lower figure being reached only at the end of December. At this point debate deadlocked into joint reiteration of previous claims. This reorchestration of the theme music of the previous three years carried on into the fourth week of the campaign.

Towards the end of the campaign Mr. Holyoake suddenly discovered yet another crisis, this time in the current overseas funds, a situation he pointed out, for which Labour could blame nobody but themselves. The overseas funds he stated, had dropped in October 1960 by £12,200,000, a much larger drop than that of £11,500,000 which had taken place in October 1957. Though briefly mentioned, this new and inconvenient crisis was quickly dropped by both parties. Possibly this was because some economists were already advocating increased taxation to deal with the situation by reducing demands for imports, while the parties themselves were broadcasting tax reductions throughout the land. In any case National, the only party which could have used the current decline in the overseas funds to its advantage, may have been reluctant to do so because of its own commitment to remove import controls from manufacturers' raw materials and equipment not made in New Zealand, and from books, as well as the indirect promise made in Dunedin by Mr. Holyoake to end the accumulated shortage of cars which Labour's import restrictions had built up. Another overseas fund crisis would automatically invalidate all these promises.

One of the quietest election campaigns for many years closed on 25 November with the final speeches and messages of the party leaders. Mr. Matthews added little beyond a renewed emphasis on the lack of difference between the major parties, and a further stress on taxation. Mr. Holyoake picked out what he saw as being the dominant question of the campaign, 'Can a political party promise its way into office undertaking solemnly not to raise taxes and then within eight months raise taxes to undreamt of heights and escape the wrath of the electors?' Mr. Nash for his part was still concentrating on the Government's record and on the 1957 crisis, 'the most serious economic situation New Zealand has faced since the depression of the 1930s.' As in the previous few months he appeared to be viewing the election as a very evenly balanced contest which Labour could win by holding its own seats and possibly winning one or two of the marginal seats held by its opponents.

The confused nature of the campaign made prediction of the result extremely difficult. *Truth*, predicting a National victory and a 43–37 majority made one of the few definite predictions, though the political column syndicated in several newspapers such as the *Otago Daily Times* stated cautiously, 'the result is not a foregone conclusion either way, but National must be given at least a

50–50 chance of changing the Government'. Most papers were less sure even than this, the *Auckland Star* stating: 'only one thing is clear: Labour is almost certain to win Manukau', and the *Evening Post* concluding: 'The result of tomorrow's general election is so wide open that any forecast could be well wide of the mark.' The public appeared to share this puzzlement.

Nevertheless on 26 November in uniformly fine weather a clear verdict was delivered by the electorate. The prognosticators had made the mistake of looking to the campaign for indications of victory or defeat. A quiet unspectacular campaign had provided none and probably did little to influence an issue which had been determined by long-term trends. The basic question had been the relative weight of the fading memories of 1958 and 'hard times' as opposed to the increasingly rosy glow of 1960 and 'happy days'. In the campaign National had pointed to the first, and Labour had attempted to point to the second, though, bogged down in explanations, it had also pointed backward. It was, however, the relative influence of the two trends rather than the campaign itself which had determined the result. The very slight influence of the campaign is revealed by the Gallup Poll. An analysis of the answers to the question 'Which Party do you favour at present?' reveals the following trends.

Date of publication	National	Labour	Social Credit	Undecided
13 September 1960	47%	44%	6%	3%
18 October 1960	49%	43%	6%	2%
22 November 1960	46%	43%	9%	2%
Actual Vote	48%	43%	9%	

After a four-week campaign in which National had taken the initiative from the first, Labour had fought on the defensive, and Social Credit had attracted little attention, only Social Credit had gained. Experts have long since reached the conclusion that campaigns have but a slight influence in deciding election results. The 1960 New Zealand election campaign would appear to have been even less influential than most.

VI

BROADCASTING AND THE ELECTION

BROADCASTING played a dual role in the 1960 election constituting both an issue and a factor. New Zealand has never had a Royal commission on broadcasting and the result has been the slow, haphazard development of a service which no one has attempted to view comprehensively. Accordingly, when in 1960 the long-awaited advent of television forced attention on the constitution of the service, the response of the parties was to treat it as an election issue, and formulate party planks in unseemly haste. Labour championed the application of the existing system to television: a Government department originally set up by that party in 1936. National espoused the vague ideal of control by a corporation 'like the B.B.C.'. Neither party appears to have seriously considered the implications of their policies.

The second role, that of a factor in the election, is the immediate concern of this chapter because of the large numbers of people who heard something of the campaign through its auspices. There is little audience research in New Zealand but the *Auckland Star* Gallup Poll asked its sample of 1000 before the election 'How often do you think you will listen to campaign broadcasts?'; 23 per cent said 'regularly', 40 per cent 'occasionally', and 37 per cent 'practically never'. The Dunedin survey in chapter X shows that in fact more people actually listened than these figures would indicate, a conclusion corroborated by the Social Credit poll. When asked 'Do you listen to election broadcasts?' 5753 of their sample said 'yes' and only 1737 said 'no'.

This enormous potential was hardly tapped as effectively as it might have been because the parties approached the use of broadcasting as they approached the question of its organization, without fundamental thought and with an over-cautious adherence to traditional methods. New Zealand has a developed pattern of local broadcasting which would be the envy of B.B.C. planners, but the parties were reluctant to use the available radio facilities for a series of broadcasts by local candidates even though the major New Zealand foci are often the local ones. In spite of all the modern methods of presenting politicians to the public, the New Zealand parties adhered to the traditional device of inordinately long nation-wide harangues from broadcast public meetings, supplemented by one-man studio talks. In Britain in the 1959 election there were twelve broadcasts on television and thirteen on sound, the longest of which lasted thirty minutes, the shortest ten minutes. In New Zealand in 1960 the public were treated to thirty-five party political broadcasts, ten of which were scheduled to last two hours, three half an hour and the rest fifteen minutes. This total has in fact been increased since 1951 when there were only twenty-two broadcasts, eight of them for two hours, and since 1954 when there were thirty-one broadcasts, of which eleven were marathons.

Broadcasting time is allocated on the responsibility of the Government after informal discussion between the two main parties. This is a very *ad hoc* arrangement compared with the 1949 'Party Agreement' in Britain, possibly too much so, for before the 1960 election even the usual arrangements were made in an atmosphere of haste and indecision. A preliminary meeting was held in Parliament on 29 September 1960, to which, representatives of both the National Party and the Social Credit Political League were invited. At this meeting, the Social Credit representatives allege, Mr. Boord, Minister of Broadcasting, stated that all three parties would discuss the allocation at a meeting to be held when the Prime Minister returned from overseas. Nothing more was heard until 19 October (the campaign was due to open on 31 October) when representatives of the parties were called to Parliament again, given the allocations and informed that this was 'the decision of the Government'. To the Social Credit representatives, Mr. Boord said that there had been no three-party discussion because he could find no precedent for it. Oddly enough, no one, not even those who stood to gain from it, seemed to be able to remember clearly what had taken place before the 1957 election. In the event the decision about the allocation came so late as to cause considerable difficulties in the arrangement of venues, and the New Zealand Broadcasting Service, because of this uncertainty, had to set aside four evenings in the first week of the campaign for the first three two-hour speeches.

This informal system, followed in 1954, 1957 and 1960, is obviously satisfactory to the two main parties, but the minor parties have less reason to be happy about it. In 1954 the Social Credit Political League, fielding a full complement of eighty candidates, was given only one broadcast, though it was treated to a barrage of broadcast criticisms by the major parties. In 1957 it fared better, receiving seven broadcasts, or a total of five and a half hours compared with the ten and three-quarters devoted to each major party, and this precedent was followed in 1960. Even so, it was accepted only under protest. A minor party relies heavily on broadcasting to make an impact and though it is questionable whether, without electing a single M.P. over three elections, Social Credit should have equal radio time with major parties, it could, by virtue of the number of its candidates, justly claim a larger share. In Social Credit's own poll, 7056 of 7509 people interviewed thought that the three parties should have equal radio time.

Treatment of the Communist Party appears not only unfair but also illogical. This party has been consistently banned from the air by both Labour and National governments and in past elections it might have been pleaded justifiably that it hardly had enough candidates in the field. But in 1960 with nineteen candidates it might well have been considered entitled to broadcasting time. If, for example, the British criterion of fifty candidates out of 625 were adopted—that is, roughly seven out of eighty in New Zealand—there could be no grounds for refusing time. If the Communist Party is allowed to exist as a legally constituted party then it is unjust to berate it over the air, as all three parties did in 1960, and then refuse it the right to reply. In 1935 the British Ullswater Committee set a positive lead when it stated '[that the B.B.C.] while recognizing in the allotment of time, according to correct parliamentary practice, the preponderating position of the main political parties, should allow expression to minority views *however unpopular*'. New Zealand democracy has still not recognized this principle.

Traditional allocations were used in the traditional unimaginative manner. The campaign was launched by three two-hour speeches on successive nights by the three party leaders, followed by another series of three two-hour broadcasts also from election meetings addressed by senior party members, interspersed with studio broadcasts of which the major parties had nine each, Social Credit four. National and Labour each had a two-hour live broadcast in the last week and on election eve each of the three party leaders delivered a thirty-minute summing up. Two-hour broadcasts are largely monopolized by senior party members and following traditional emphasis on the leader, National devoted four and a half hours to Mr. Holyoake. Mr. Nash spoke only for the first two-hour broadcast and the final half hour, his fellow leaders taking the remaining Labour two-hour speeches. The only surprise was National's allocation of a two-hour broadcast to Mr. Leon Gotz, M.P. for Manukau, an accomplished radio speaker representing a very marginal constituency. Social Credit had few problems of allocation. With only two long broadcasts at their disposal these were allocated to the leader and the deputy-leader.

With the quarter-hour broadcasts, several factors had to be taken into consideration. Seniority and specialization played a part, the Labour panel including several Ministers speaking on departmental policy, for example, the Hon. P. G. Connolly on defence and police; the Hon. Mabel Howard on social security and the Hon. W. A. Fox on housing and State advances. Then, speakers for all three parties were selected from the marginal constituency of Hastings, despite the fact that only the Labour candidate was really effective as a broadcaster. Another factor was the usefulness of broadcasting for gathering in the far-flung electorates. The Labour Party, for example, selected Mr. Kirk to speak for Lyttelton, an electorate which includes the Chatham Islands, and Mr. Nash twice referred to the Chathams in his last thirty minute speech. Similarly, it was obviously considered wise to include a Maori speaker where possible. Both Sir Eruera Tirikatene (Labour) and Mr. Pei Te Hurunui Jones (National) delivered part of their addresses in Maori.

The National Party having been out of office for the previous three years, and with a competent planning team, was able to display greater flexibility. Its panel included some likely ministerial candidates as well as younger up-and-coming men such as Mr. B. E. Talboys, whose talk was directed specifically to the younger voter. This greater flexibility, however, was not extended to an undue concentration on the marginal seats. Out of twenty-three seats considered by the National Party to be marginal, three were allotted broadcasts, though not necessarily for that reason alone. The Labour Party by contrast allotted six broadcasts to these twenty-three 'marginal' constituencies.

Social Credit might be thought to have had even greater scope, since in 1957 their candidates were not serious contenders in any of the marginal seats. This was offset somewhat by the smaller number of broadcasts allotted to them, but nevertheless they made an earnest attempt to plan their programmes. All candidates were asked to provide tape recordings of speeches for vetting by the campaign committee and the most successful speakers could thus be selected on a basis of presentation and content as well as other factors. It was unfortunate that so few of the Social Credit candidates availed themselves of the opportunity and that the party campaign failed to live up to its initial promise. Heavy siege was laid to Wanganui where the party received its largest tally of votes in the 1957 election. The campaign was opened from there by the leader with a two-hour broadcast public meeting and the local candidate contributed the first of their fifteen-minute broadcasts. Different considerations obtained with the selection of Mr. T. H. Greenwood to give the third Social Credit fifteen-minute broadcast. Mr. Greenwood's chances at St. Kilda looked slim from the outset, but his position as a bank manager eminently qualified him to assure people that Social Credit's monetary policy was essentially 'sound banking practice'. In Hobson, the party had the triple advantage of a good speaker who was a public accountant speaking from a sympathetic electorate. Despite the attempt at planning, Social Credit broadcasts in practice showed quite clearly that the allocation of radio time is not an unmixed blessing as, generally speaking, Social Credit speakers showed up in a poor light.

Only the National Party succeeded in making a worthwhile effort in planning the broadcast campaign. All the parliamentary party were voice-tested, all were required to write their own material and they were carefully judged for audience appeal. This must have done much to boost the confidence of the selected speakers. Moreover all speakers had some training with a tape-recorder and specific problems of broadcasting, speed and pauses, were explained. In all this the party was influenced by current party practice overseas, particularly that of the Australian Liberals. The result was important. Although the best broadcasters of the party, Messrs. Gotz, Shand and Algie, stood out because they are accomplished speakers anyway, training at least helped to ensure that there were no bad speakers. Unfortunately there was

9

no attempt to follow up these efforts by audience research and there was little real attempt to combat assertions made by the other parties, and of course, the two-hour marathons remained. The lack of attempt to combat assertions was, however, the product of National Party policy, whilst that of the Labour Party was due to sheer neglect.

The campaign opened formally throughout New Zealand with the broadcast of a speech by the Prime Minister, the Rt. Hon. Walter Nash, relayed from the Civic Theatre, Auckland. At the outset it appeared likely that this would develop into a gala occasion. The bagpipes heralding Mr. Nash into the theatre, a brass band, the singing of 'For he's a jolly good fellow' and the National Anthem, all gave to the meeting something of the air of a mass rally. Yet despite the enthusiastic bursts of applause in the early stages—usually at the mention of earlier Labour leaders, especially Michael Joseph Savage which constituted a 'hurrah' word for Labour audiences—the speech itself was restrained. By contrast, Mr. Holyoake, more tub-thumping and extroverted, had fewer props, no brass bands, no bagpipes or singing of 'For he's a jolly good fellow'. In some ways this was rather an odd reversal of political protocol as one would expect the party which embodies the leadership principle most clearly to start with just such a libation.

Despite the differences in introduction, in both cases length and apportionment of material made the speeches a test of the listener's concentration. If Mr. Nash used the second hour mainly for restating in more detail points made in the first hour, Mr. Holyoake devoted so much of the first hour to attacking the Labour Party that it began to sound as if there would be very little policy to announce. This was a particularly unfortunate impression to convey since, when he eventually came to discuss policy one and a quarter hours after the start of the speech, he had so much to deal with that he was unable to treat it properly in the time available. The result was a hurried scrambling through material with constant references to the shortage of time. The speech rapidly degenerated into a catalogue of headings—'My next note is on a nature conservancy . . .'. At 9.50 Mr. Holyoake announced that he had insufficient time to talk about twenty or thirty other topics which he was putting aside for later meetings. Although this might have given the impression that the National Party cornucopia was so overflowing that two hours were sadly inadequate to explain it all, it failed to give a clear idea of that policy. In the closing minutes of his speech, however, Mr. Holyoake resorted to a well-prepared peroration and with the introduction of a rather clumsy ex-Social Credit slogan, 'We need a New Zeal for New Zealand', the speech ended in a fighting climax.

The next night's address by Mr. P. H. Matthews, leader of the Social Credit Political League, provided an interesting contrast with that of Mr. Holyoake. Whereas Mr. Holyoake's speech got under way slowly, the opening of the Social Credit campaign was almost breathtaking. At the outset Mr. Matthews announced amidst enthusiastic applause that his speech would be 'different from the established pattern of political broadcasts'. The intended difference appeared to lie in reading out congratulatory telegrams and then launching into an extraordinary list of tax concessions and subsidies, before formally opening the campaign and congratulating the local candidates. Judged in terms of presentation rather than content, the opening twenty minutes of the speech were very effective though spiced with some unintentional humour. For example, Mr. Matthews announced in ringing tones that: 'Social Credit will abolish all direct taxation!' (storm of applause) —'up to £520 per annum including social security!' (silence).

Throughout the speech, in addition to criticizing the allocation of broadcasting time, Mr. Matthews made constant references to the time available that evening. Yet twenty minutes before the scheduled conclusion of the broadcast, after a long pause and a hurried consultation with the chairman of the meeting, Mr. Matthews announced that he had *more* time than he expected. An observer in the hall noted that Mr. Matthews, having seemed nervous and uneasy throughout the speech and having played continuously with his notes, at this point began to turn furiously through them, holding them in front of his face. It appears that he had lost two pages of this important speech. As a result the last fifteen minutes of the address consisted of an embarrassing and obvious filling-in of time, punctuated by longish pauses before the speaker finished with a slight rally at 9.54—four minutes early.

The main differences between the speeches are to be found in the emphases placed on certain topics. Mr. Nash, with his humanistic approach, put the main stress on the family. Even the complex economic position was interpreted at one point in terms of housekeeping accounts. This theme, asserted as 'the basis of any country is a good home', 'the family is the basis of society', 'the building of a good home is essential'; was woven into the more general, watered-down version of 'you've never had it so good'. The emphasis was put on Labour's past record and trust in the party for the future rather than on any specific policy. The general presentation, which was not without its quiet humour, made up in character what it lacked in preparation. Thus at one point Mr. Nash remarked—'Forgive me for using some millions, but it wouldn't be me if I didn't use some millions!'

Mr. Holyoake by contrast was more urbane and impersonal. Not unnaturally he devoted far more time to attacking his opponents, but he also demonstrated a marked shift in emphasis compared with Mr. Nash. 'Farming', said Mr. Holyoake, 'is the basis of all economic life in New Zealand.' Social security and the duty to to look after the poor and aged came farther down his list and a much greater stress was placed on the role of voluntary organizations. This difference of emphasis was important, for it enabled Mr. Holyoake to point forward to future development and policy.

The older people, 'senior citizens' as he preferred to call them, were not forgotten by Mr. Matthews who put the stress, in his occasional patches of benignity, on 'brotherly love' and 'deeds not words'. This speech, however, was a much more histrionic performance, snarls and smiles following one another in rapid succession.

In considering the three opening speeches, one is forced to the conclusion that few people would have bothered to hear all or indeed any of them throughout, for after the live audience's enthusiasms had worn thin, the tendency to repetition became marked. Indeed, though Mr. Holyoake's speech was probably the best of the three, all of them suffered from either inadequate preparation for broadcasting or a failure to adhere to plan. In the case of Mr. Nash this was undoubtedly due in large part to pressure of Government business, which naturally continues throughout the campaign. Fortunately, however, Mr. Nash's natural platform ability compensated somewhat for his lack of acquaintance with his notes.

Generally speaking, the problem of boredom became even more noticeable with the other two-hour speeches. It might be posed more clearly by considering the speeches of Mr. Skinner, Deputy

Prime Minister, Mr. Nordmeyer, Minister of Finance, and the final two-hour speech of Mr. Holyoake. Mr. Skinner at Invercargill deliberately set out to talk down the few interjections which he met. The result was that his speech developed into a long harangue containing little new material. By contrast Mr. Holyoake in the final two-hour speech for the National Party had an audience which gave vent to unbounded enthusiasm even before he began. It even appeared that one staunch supporter in the front of the hall had equipped himself with a large chunk of timber with which he pounded the floor vigorously at appropriate moments in order to manifest his 'solid' support for the party. One felt as soon as the broadcast began that the scent of victory was in the nostrils of this particular audience at least. Mr. Holyoake successfully captured this spirit and his speech, though using almost the same material as that used in the opening speech of the campaign, had a much more rousing character. The wind-up speech for the Labour Party given, not by the Prime Minister, but by Mr. A. H. Nordmeyer, Minister of Finance, was the most successful listening of the whole campaign. Faced in the marginal electorate of St. Kilda with an extremely rowdy audience and insistent heckling, Mr. Nordmeyer rose to the occasion and took advantage of the opportunity to exhibit a ready and lively wit. Opening his speech with a slashing attack on the National Party and its policy, Mr. Nordmeyer immediately ran into heavy opposition from a section of the audience. At first it seemed that he would adopt Mr. Skinner's tactics and talk down the opposition. At one stage he advised an interjector: 'Don't waste your breath sir, I will only talk louder . . .' But as the interjections continued, he met them fairly and squarely and, indeed, deliberately provoked them. For example, he taunted the most persistent interjectors with such phrases as: 'All right sir, here is what your "good old Keith" said . . .' or, 'Looking at our friend, I should say that he would be very interested in the price of beer'. With a good-humoured and largely loyal audience, Mr. Nordmeyer showed up to advantage and the first half of his speech smacked of the old-time hustings. There was little attempt in the first hour to give a thorough appraisal of policy but he dealt with the charges and countercharges of the campaign, a treatment which proved both useful and entertaining. The second hour, though lively in parts, was taken up with policy points and was much quieter. The whole speech was a model of what a live broadcast speech should be—informative and entertaining—and yet at the same time it illustrates the extent to which the speaker is dependent upon having a lively audience.

Nevertheless, the overall value to the parties of the numerous two-hour speeches is highly questionable. There appear to be good grounds for believing that the opening addresses by the party leaders are valuable in giving the campaign throughout the country an initial impetus. This impetus might have been more effective, however, if the speeches had been drastically shortened. The same might be said of the closing two-hour speeches. It is difficult to find anything in favour of the intermediate full-evening speeches being broadcast throughout the whole country. The speeches delivered by Messrs. Gotz and Marshall for the National Party, Mr. O'Brien for the Social Credit Political League, and Messrs. Skinner and Watt for the Labour Party, contributed little of national importance. After the opening campaign speeches only Mr. O'Brien and Messrs. Gotz and Holyoake introduced any new policy material. Mr. O'Brien in a melodramatic speech introduced a Social Credit Party pledge to resign after two years *if* they were returned as the Government and failed to implement their promises—a device used in a previous election. Mr. Holyoake, in a move foreshadowed in the speech of Mr. Gotz, sought to woo the Social Credit vote and promised monetary reform. Generally, however, the secondary two-hour broadcasts were superfluous, if not harmful. Perhaps the most noteworthy incident was the cutting off of Mr. Gotz by the N.Z.B.S. Mr. Gotz had promised interjectors to shorten his address so that questions and answers could be broadcast. As soon as he did so, he was cut off. Another National speaker, Mr. Marshall, also finished early—deliberately. All these speeches in the form that they took would have been better left to the hustings.

A broadcast speech makes considerable demands on listeners' concentration and, since alternative programmes are always seductively close at hand, it is clear that if anything is to be expected of a broadcast by the party organizers, one should at least be able to listen to a speaker comfortably. This was not always the case with the fifteen-minute talks which were much nearer an effective broadcasting length but were treated and prepared by the parties more lightly than the marathon addresses.

In the matter of telling a speaker how to use a microphone there appeared to be a lack of co-operation between the New Zealand Broadcasting Service and the party organizers, or a failure of both to guide the speakers. One cannot expect the broadcasting service to accept responsibility for a candidate's speech, and although it can, and does, offer its facilities, the onus is on the political speaker to ask for the expert help available. To judge from the results, such help was all too rarely sought, speaker after speaker dutifully and painfully laboured his way through an all too obviously prepared speech and one speaker gave the impression that he did not even understand what he was reading.

The themes of the broadcasts, which are exclusively the preserve of the party organizations, displayed marked divergences in approach. Undoubtedly the National Party again scored handsomely here in angling their broadcasts to catch the attention of certain specific sections of the audience, for example, the younger voters and the women of New Zealand. By contrast the Labour Party series was haphazard and lacking any real continuity or progression. Out of nine Labour Party talks, five dealt, in whole or part, with the 1957–8 balance of payments crisis, a topic also covered at length in Labour's two-hour speeches. The Social Credit Political League was equally culpable. Four out of five Social Credit talks concentrated on the theme of 'Where the money is to come from'.

Similar criticisms were applicable to the three important thirty-minute broadcasts on the eve of the poll. Mr. Matthews again complained about the allocation of broadcasting time, which was 'a breach of faith', and went on to launch a lively attack on Mr. Holyoake's attempts to woo the Social Credit vote in his Wednesday night wind-up broadcast, as well as dealing with some general points of Social Credit policy. After a bright speech, Mr. Matthews bowed out with a blessing.

Mr. Holyoake, starting off at a rapid pace, evinced less ebullience than usual, though the note of confidence was still marked. Suggesting that a vote for either the Communists or Social Credit was a wasted vote, he nevertheless distinguished between the two, staking claim to the Social Credit vote and ostentatiously telling the Labour Party that they were welcome to the votes of the Communists. The hoary old question of what was implied when Communists were told to vote for Labour candidates in the absence of one of their own, had been raised again during the election. A comparison of the records of the previous Labour and National governments followed, then a discussion of the 1957 crisis and world affairs. It is particularly noteworthy that considerable emphasis was given to the latter, the last seven minutes of the broadcast only being reserved for more detailed points of policy. Mr. Holyoake unfortunately found it necessary in the broadcast to use jokes and asides he had used in earlier efforts.

Mr. Nash, after an excursion into electoral technicalities to explain why the system was weighted against Labour, went on to deal with what he called some of the 'signposts' of Labour Party policy: taxation, help for house builders, farmers, manufacturers, and retailers. Almost all of this was taken up with the record of past achievements. After a defence of the principles of the welfare state and the claim that Labour had succeeded in reconciling redistribution and increased production, Mr. Nash again criticized the existing voting system and asserted that the National Party was responsible for the 1957-8 crisis. The choice lay for him between following the chosen path to bountiful opportunity or National opportunism. Returning to the subject of taxation, Mr. Nash asserted that there was nothing fearsome about it and proceeded to give another outline of Labour's policies under the headings of development, taxation, finance, housing, licensing reform, and external affairs. With time nearly running out Mr. Nash was reading at speed, almost garbling the speech. However, he went on to 'Have a word with Maori friends and citizens' and yet another 'word' to the Chatham Islands. These in turn were followed by what may best be described as a succession of sentences about gymnasia, social security, and a further attack on National. Then, 'One or two points of the real facts of what has been done'; this consisted mainly of a quotation from the *Canberra Times*, and, at last, the conclusion. The last eight minutes of the speech lost all effectiveness by being hurried and confused. The Prime Minister eventually concluded the election series having exceeded his allotted time, and leaving the listener breathless and bewildered.

The thirty-minute addresses certainly summarized some of the issues of the campaign, but again, the full possibilities were not exploited. If the content and presentation of the addresses left much to be desired, the size of the audience must be a matter of some doubt, for though probably larger than for most of the other broadcasts, they did coincide—7.30 to 9 p.m.—with the peak weekly shopping time in New Zealand and this could not be without effect.

This may not have been the only evening upon which a maximum possible listening audience was not tapped, for a feature of the broadcast campaign was the bad advertising accorded it. True, the main speeches were quite well indicated in advance by both Press and radio and there was some paid advertising in the Press for the broadcast speeches of party leaders, but, for the fifteen-minute broadcasts, it was deemed adequate to announce the names of the speakers at intervals on the day before the broadcast. Until half-way through the campaign, no indication of either speaker or party could be gained from the programme weekly, *The N.Z. Listener,* and most of the newspapers simply left a blank in the programme timetables for the time of the election broadcasts. The commercial stations were used simply to carry 'spot' paid advertisements giving the times and speakers at local meetings. Hence it follows that much more could, and should, have been done to arouse interest by drawing attention to the speeches arranged, and providing background items in the *Listener* and on the air.

It has been aptly remarked that the party meeting is a transient phenomenon, that its rise and most of its fall is already history, and that persuasion must today be steadily directed into other channels. Broadcasting is one of these channels and, like the newspapers, it has its own requirements and techniques. It is not the fault of the party organizers that these needs do not blend harmoniously with the old type of campaign methods, but it is their fault that they have not assessed the role of broadcasting rather more carefully, and persuaded the politicians to exploit it to the best advantage.

It is no secret, for example, that campaigns formerly were fought on the basis of a 'sham fight'. A candidate could concede nothing to an opponent and had to counter all arguments. Newspapers have lent themselves to this exaggerated style of debate because news value rather than the value of the news is their criterion. The political speaker is accustomed to make his points at length, broadcasting requires him to be short and succinct. The quietly reasonable and persuasive methods of the studio contrast strikingly with the techniques of debate, and, in particular, of the political platform. The speaker has not the close atmosphere of Parliament, nor in most instances the emotional charge of a mass meeting, and even where such conditions do obtain, in the case of the two-hour broadcasts, only rarely does the listener receive an accurate idea of the 'feeling of the meeting'. Moreover, it must not be forgotten that the audience is listening at home with all the attendant distractions.

The introduction of television throughout the country is hardly likely to help this. Before the next election, with the establishment of television in the four main centres of population, the political parties will obviously have to reconsider their whole approach to broadcasting. There is every probability that 1960 will be the last of the 'old style' elections as far as broadcasting is concerned. The limitations and stratagems of television require more, rather than less, technique, so that the rough-and-ready amateur shows up even more to his disadvantage. Television must bring new techniques to New Zealand as it has to other countries and these techniques may be belatedly transferred to radio. Press conference techniques, in the questioning of leaders about important aspects of the campaign, panels and discussion, in which views are discussed reasonably and fully, could be used with advantage. This would help to obviate the confusing and useless practice of the two main parties constantly reiterating conflicting statements, for example, quoting different sets of figures concerning the 1957–8 crisis without any attempt to reconcile them. The juxtaposed figures in the 1960 election were so confusing that the average elector must have emerged more, rather than less, puzzled. It is perhaps significant that the most interesting broadcast of the whole campaign was a Voice of America production of one of the television 'debates' between Vice-President Nixon and Senator Kennedy. Nothing could have served better to illustrate by contrast the out-of-date character of the New Zealand election broadcasts.

VII

THE PRESS AND THE ELECTION

FOUR widely separated main centres and a score of secondary centres make a national Press impossible in New Zealand. There is instead a series of country and small-town newspapers, eclipsed in size and in volume of circulation by the morning and evening newspapers in the four main centres. These four cities contain two-fifths of New Zealand's population, and over half of the rural homes in the Dominion also receive one of these eight newspapers.

The circulation of the 'big eight' varies in proportion to the size of the cities they serve, ranging from the two Auckland papers, the *New Zealand Herald* and the *Auckland Star* with circulations of 200,000 and 130,000 respectively, to the two Dunedin papers, the *Otago Daily Times,* circulation 39,000 and the *Evening Star* selling some 28,000 copies. Yet multiplicity of papers does not mean diversity, for the New Zealand newspapers share the services of the New Zealand Press Association which relays both internal and external news so that there is a fair uniformity of content. They also share a common adherence to sober journalism and high standards, for lack of competition has removed one of the main stimuli leading to sensationalism. A staidly presented sensationalism is left to *Truth,* a weekly, which, however, devoted little attention to the election beyond a minor flickering of its old feud with Mr. Holloway, the retiring Minister of Industries and Commerce.

The Press is conservative in attitudes as well as standards. Only one newspaper, the *Grey River Argus,* published in Greymouth and having a circulation of only just over 4000, supports the Labour Party. An earlier Labour venture, the *Southern Cross* of Wellington, succumbed to a declining circulation in 1951. Within the prevailing conservatism, however, the evening papers are slightly less to the Right, and certainly less strident in their political sentiments, than are the morning papers. This may be due to the fact that the evening papers came into being after their morning rivals were both established and conservative. It is also due in part to the fact that the morning papers circulate more widely in the conservative rural areas, the evening papers more intensively in the cities to industrial and city workers.[1]

Yet whatever the cause, the difference between morning and evening papers is slight. All the papers are pro-National. 'Newspapers are telling the opposition story all the time and members opposite could almost remain silent and still have their policy stated,' claimed a Labour M.P. just before the elections. This long-standing Labour suspicion of the Press produced remits at the 1959 party conference demanding the creation of 'community newspaper boards', and provision 'to exercise supervision of the public press'. Even the cautious remit committee, while not endorsing these specific demands, was driven to recommend that the N.E.C. should 'investigate the question of alternate means of offsetting the press propaganda'.

Though exaggerated, Labour's suspicion of the Press is in part justified. National Party views are more prominently and consistently stated than are Labour views, and any division or controversy in Labour ranks is emphasized by a Press which plays down National Party disagreements. The essential problem posed by an examination of the Press and the election is, therefore, to discover whether the Press's commitment to the National Party and its bias, however slight this is judged to be, influenced its treatment of the election.

One accusation of bias can be immediately dismissed. Some Labour M.P.s claimed that the Press deliberately played down the election in order to encourage apathy and a consequent lower poll, a tactic which a former cabinet minister described as 'devilishly clever'. Certainly the election could hardly be said to have dominated the papers. Few gave it more than 7000 square inches in the period up to the poll, a very small proportion of total space, and it was not normally front page news, reaching the front page in the *New Zealand Herald* only twice as many times up to polling day as the American election. This did not reflect any plot. Rather did it represent the election itself, quiet, undramatic and with no great news value.

[1] As an example, the *Christchurch Star* sells 83 per cent of its 60,000 circulation in the Christchurch urban area; the morning paper, *The Press*, only 60 per cent of its similar circulation. Market research has indicated that nearly twice as many people in Christchurch have the *Star* delivered to their homes as take *The Press*. This difference in circulation between morning and evening papers may, incidentally, have hastened the demise of Labour's *Southern Cross*, which was a morning paper.

It could, on the contrary, be argued that if the newspapers had devoted space to the election on the basis of public interest in it, they would have allocated less than they did. In giving quantities of valuable space to the three-yearly party battle, and in their conscientious efforts to give full coverage to the campaign both local and national, the Press showed a considerable sense of responsibility. The arrangements for covering local candidates were particularly conscientious. All the newspapers gave to the candidates of the three main parties in their circulation area one report of a certain stipulated length, ranging from 500 words in the *Dominion* and the *Auckland Star* to a whole column in the Dunedin papers, as well as covering other meetings often on a rotation basis and featuring columns of 'pars' or pithy and pointed comments from candidates.

Some details of the different forms taken by the allocation of space are given in the following table which measures space in square inches and the number of meetings covered.[2]

The papers tried to give the major parties equal treatment and the table shows that, for all practical purposes, most of them succeeded. The exact amount of space devoted to major party leaders and candidates varied. Contrary to expectation it was often larger in the evening papers than the morning, even though the news was no longer as fresh. Just as surprising is the fact that it tended to be larger in the southern papers than in the northern ones even though the latter had more candidates to cover. A few papers gave much more space to Mr. Holyoake than to Mr. Nash, possibly because Mr. Holyoake was introducing rather more changes into his 'stock' speech. With both leaders valiant efforts were made to present their much-repeated comments as news, though reporters were clearly longing for both to say something new by the end of the campaign. Thus during the campaign

[2] The initials of each paper are given and the table covers the period from 1 November to 25 November inclusive. It includes only reports of meetings so that, for example, reports of Mr Moohan's journeyings, Mr Nordmeyer's announcement of the credit squeeze, and comments on Mr Nash's Khrushchev–Semple remarks are not included. The only exceptions to this concentration on meetings are the inclusion of the space devoted to the manifestos (which may account for Mr Holyoake's slight lead in some papers since the National manifesto was longer), to the three final messages and the items in 'What the candidates say', these being counted as meetings. The 'other national Leaders' include those M.P.s who toured, and also reports of leading party figures from their home electorates where these were outside the paper's circulation area. For both parties, speeches of leading figures in their own electorates where these are in the circulation area are counted as local candidates.

several papers announced that Mr. Holyoake 'revealed yesterday' that before the 1957 election he had asked his party caucus whether they should attempt to match Labour's 'bribes', and had met with a unanimous refusal. This would have been an interesting revelation had it not been for the fact that Mr. Holyoake had already 'revealed' it during his 'Meet the People Tour' earlier in the year. In all but one paper the second rank of Labour leaders received more space than their National counterparts, this being inevitable since they were doing more travelling. In fact the amount of space allocated to them was comparatively small when it is remembered that some Labour leaders such as Mr. Nordmeyer changed their speeches more often and more interestingly than did Mr. Nash.

	Morning Papers				*Evening Papers*			
Local Candidates	O.D.T.	P.	D.	N.Z.H.	E.S.	C.S.	E.P.	A.S.
Labour Space	1050	890	660	360	660	810	420	880
Number	(72)	(37)	(26)	(32)	(34)	(32)	(18)	(46)
National Space	1050	860	740	400	670	880	390	850
Number	(78)	(39)	(37)	(36)	(38)	(34)	(20)	(45)
Social Credit Space	540	790	400	50	460	720	200	500
Number	(37)	(34)	(20)	(8)	(21)	(26)	(11)	(23)
Communist Space	30	140	40	—	20	—	70	—
Number	(1)	(6)	(2)	—	(2)	—	(4)	—
Independent Space	70	30	28	—	50	20	—	(30)
Number	(3)	(1)	(2)	—	(4)	(1)	—	(1)
Leaders								
Mr Nash	680	610	550	490	750	990	710	800
Mr Holyoake	610	620	760	600	780	975	1050	940
Mr Matthews and								
Mr O'Brien	150	220	120	100	240	300	260	260
Other Labour	160	250	120	280	120	190	120	390
Other National	150	140	30	180	140	160	60	200

Press treatment of the minor parties varied. Most papers gave Social Credit less than half the space allocated to the major parties. The League's candidates, like the other minor candidates, were not holding anything like as many meetings as their major rivals, and Mr. Matthews and Mr. O'Brien were doing very little touring. Yet with due allowance made, only the *Evening Post* gave the Social Credit leader's campaign opening the same amount of space as it had devoted to the major parties, while the *Herald* did not even bother to print the final message from Mr. Matthews, a message to which the other papers gave equal, or nearly equal, prominence with those of the other two leaders. Social Credit had made strenuous efforts in 1960 to improve its Press treatment. Social Crediters in all parts of the country monitored Press reports so that it was clear which papers were not providing satisfactory treatment. In addition copy was circulated direct to the newspapers so as to bypass the Press Association, and Social Crediters approached, and on occasions reproached, editors all over the Dominion in an effort to secure fair space allocations. Possibly as a result of these efforts the League was better satisfied with its treatment at the hands of the Press in 1960, than it had been in previous elections. The general complaint remained that the improvement still had some way to go.

The Communist Party had more to complain of. The *Herald* and the *Christchurch Star* and *Auckland Star* gave no space at all to Communists, one of the Auckland papers also refusing their advertisements, so that the tender minds of the citizens of Auckland were well shielded. Only disorder could draw the attention of some other papers to Communist meetings. *The Press* alone gave the Communist Party a treatment which verged on fair, and it was the only paper to allow space to Communist candidates in the columns of 'What the candidates say'. Most papers demonstrated that their ears were not closed to minor candidates by devoting space to Independents. In some cases these candidates secured more space than did the more numerous Communist candidates.

Mere adding up of inches does nothing to indicate the tenor of the reports. So far as local meetings were concerned these were nearly always fair. Mistakes, when they existed, arose from carelessness or bad journalism not from wilful distortion. Complaint was heard in Christchurch when the *Star* featured the views of the Labour member in marginal St. Albans on the touchy State-aid question as 'Private schools get sufficient State Aid now', a report which the candidate claimed was misleading. Yet few such complaints were heard from candidates, who were in any case frequently consulted as to which points they wished to emphasize. Bias was also unusual in the treatment of the leaders, though there were some welcome attempts to describe the performance of the party leaders. Several papers asked after

Mr. Nash's opening meeting 'Where was the old-style Nash magic?', commented next day 'Dynamic Holyoake wins first round', and summed up again during the campaign, by which time Mr. Nash was stated to be 'back to his tireless campaign best'. There can be no criticism of such attempts to convey the atmosphere of a meeting provided they are honest and objective. Occasionally a report did depart from objectivity as when one reporter dealing with a meeting addressed by Mr. Nash stated 'He still apologises for having to borrow overseas, yet he made it plain in the North Island that more overseas borrowing was likely for capital development' and 'He repeatedly quotes the case of a woman in a tailoring business [over equal pay], apparently forgetting that there is no tailoring in the public service'.

Like biased treatment, other efforts to influence the voter were very rare. The *Dominion* towards the end of the campaign published on its editorial page a feature article accusing Labour of trying to bribe electors by paying the increase in universal superannuation benefits in a lump sum just before the election. The paper was firmly rebuked the next day by the Minister for Social Security who demolished most of the arguments used, though the rebuttal was not accorded quite the same prominence as the original. The only other example occurred in St. Albans and concerned a declaration of support for the National Party issued by the 1957 Labour nominee in the electorate, a nominee who had been forced to withdraw at the last minute through illness. This declaration was read out at a National Party meeting on 14 November, but it was not published in the papers until a moment of greater impact, Wednesday, 23 November. Then it appeared as a front page item of some nineteen column inches in the *Star* with the heading 'Ex-Labour Nominee in support of Nationalists'. Next day it was repeated as a small item in *The Press* and other papers. Probably this represented a well-timed release to the Press, yet the first reading of the letter should have attracted newspaper attention to an item of such interest.

'Comment is free: facts are sacred' runs the adage, and comment in the editorials was certainly free, for most papers devoted about a quarter to a third of their editorials in the campaign period to the election, while some, such as the *Otago Daily Times* and the *Auckland Star*, took nearly half. Whatever the space the comments were for the most part surprisingly similar. The attitude to

Labour's manifesto for example was almost uniformly subdued and restrained. The *Otago Daily Times* commented 'The election manifesto . . . announced at Auckland last night contains excellent points: that cannot be denied', as though denial would have taken place if at all possible. Most of the papers echoed the verdict of the *Herald* that Labour's was 'A policy of quite surprising moderation . . . the most sober that the party has ever presented to the New Zealand electorate', and 'an interesting and ingenious policy which deserves consideration on its merits'. Only the *Dominion* was really critical, classifying the manifesto as 'drab' and 'uninspiring'.

Where faint praise characterized the reception of the Labour manifesto, enthusiasm was inevitably felt for National's. 'A blue-print for solid progress' enthused the *Evening Post,* and the general verdict was that the manifesto was 'sound' and 'realistic'. The undertaking to reduce taxation was uniformly welcomed. No paper raised the question of how it was to be achieved in view of the welfare commitments National had taken on. This question had been almost automatically raised with Labour's similar promise, and the *Otago Daily Times* had then pointed out that 'more money will be required for defence, for education, for roading, for the development of the South Island . . . and for the other promised objects of government expenditure'. The same nagging doubts were nowhere raised about National's promise which was accepted on its face value.

Having praised both policies, Labour's faintly and National's enthusiastically, the editors were clearly aware of the fact that there were similarities between the two. The *Otago Daily Times* headlined its article on the comparison 'Who Cribbed?', while the *Herald* pointed out that 'in many ways the two parties have come closer together. There are passages which could be lifted at random from either manifesto, and the casual reader would find it difficult to identify the source.' Most of the papers accepted this similarity, but classified it 'superficial', and were at pains to point out to their readers that there were real differences. In doing this they looked either to the past, 'the election will be fought on records rather than promises' asserted the *Evening Star,* or to differences of approach and principle, 'basic differences of approach remain' said the *Herald.* In nearly every case the conclusion was that 'there is figuratively and literally a wealth of

10

difference between Labour and National', to quote the *Dominion*.

The *Herald* saw taxation as being the main difference, and the *Christchurch Star* asserted: 'that is one of the few vestiges of true socialism to be discerned in Labour's present attitude . . . the urge to spend the people's money better than they can themselves is irresistible'. Comparison of the tax records of the two parties was enough to satisfy most papers. While pointing a collective finger at taxation as the main difference, several also thought that Labour was still a socialist party, and both the *Christchurch Star* and the *Evening Post* asserted in similar terms that 'Mr. Nash was at such pains to soft-peddle socialism that his words . . . cannot be equated with the actions of a Labour Party once it attains power'. No specific socialistic policies were pointed to in the last three years, but the assertion that the party was socialist enabled a dependent assertion to be made: that the main issue in the election was between 'socialism and individual freedom'. 'On the one hand,' claimed the *Otago Daily Times*, 'Labour seeks an extension of the Socialistic-Communistic doctrine of state intrusion into, and control over, every aspect of the national life; on the other the National Party would give to the people themselves greater freedom to control their own affairs', for National could see that 'being bundled about by bureaucrats, enchained in the listless over-taxed mediocrity of socialist serfdom, is a destiny too drab for the New Zealand people'.

Two papers, the *Evening Star* and the *Herald,* saw the differences mainly in terms of honesty and integrity. As the *Herald* put it, the difference was between 'lollies or leadership' with Labour handing out the lollies. Most papers followed up this theme by taking the retrospective opportunity to castigate Labour's 'promises' or 'bribes' of 1957, *The Press* for example criticizing the party for 'misleading electors into believing that its policy could be put into effect without heavy taxation increases'. When the 1958 increase in taxation was mentioned it was seen as a result, not of a crisis in 1957–8, but of Labour's election promises. Only three papers dissented from this verdict, one was the *Evening Post* which criticized National for turning a blind eye to the gathering storm in 1957, though thinking that Labour had been 'perhaps too drastic' the year after. Another was the *Otago Daily Times* which denied the existence of an overseas funds crisis, stating that 'the only crisis arose when Labour began to collect the price of its promises' and a third, the *Christchurch Star*, which simply declined to discuss a subject people were tired of.

Other comments on the manifestos and the campaign were few. Five papers made a ritualistic denunciation of Social Credit which could have been reprinted word for word from 1957 editorials or the Monetary Commission Report. There were also comments on the leaders, and four papers criticized Mr. Nash for his 'I don't want to tell you' remark which tended to become a peg on which to hang a personal criticism. The *Herald* was particularly severe on the Labour leader, painting him as the 'veteran political trouper, eagerly seeking the limelight at home and abroad, to the detriment of his real duties'. By contrast Mr. Holyoake was an 'assured campaigner' who deserved to be Prime Minister because of the impact he had made on the country. Understandably Mr. Nash's performance attracted neither the same attention nor the same admiration that it had in 1957.

Most of the remaining editorials were devoted to reviewing, item by item, the planks of the National Party manifesto and attaching to them the seal of Press approval. Labour policy was more rarely commented on, though three papers went out of their way to condemn the Nelson railway. Prepared to criticize National on occasions between elections, the papers were loath to admit that the party could have faults just before the poll. The rare criticisms which did appear were mostly mild. *The Press* pointed out that neither party had a concrete idea on how to tackle 'New Zealand's chief social problem, the declining status of the Maori'; the *Christchurch Star* said neither party had a good defence policy; and the *Evening Star* thought both demonstrated lack of courage in regard to the International Monetary Fund. The *Auckland Star* admitted at the beginning of the campaign that 'National will need to clarify some of its other planks during the next few weeks'. Among these 'other planks' were the proposed television commission which was vague and the Ombudsman on which the party did not appear to have 'fully thought out the implications of its proposal'. The *Star* also thought more information was necessary on the proposal for voluntary unionism, though later, without the extra information, it decided that the voluntary system was 'worth a trial'.

One paper alone made more fundamental criticisms. The *Evening Post* opposed voluntary unionism, pointing out that the existing system 'has contributed towards the relatively happy and satisfactory operation of our industrial system', and that voluntary unionism would mean disputes over closed shops. It also claimed that National had no right to criticize Labour as a 'crisis party', and considered little would be achieved by the proposed Bill of Rights. The *Post* still plumped heavily for National, but pointed out that 'most people will have found points in the policy of each party with which they do not agree'. This degree of realism did not influence the approach of the other papers to National Party policy.

Some of the papers regarded an election as a fit opportunity to urge local views and needs, though generally speaking parochialism varied in inverse ratio to the circulation of the paper, being much stronger in Dunedin than in Auckland. The Christchurch and Dunedin papers were inclined intermittently to ride local hobbyhorses. For one paper, the *Otago Daily Times*, the ride became a headlong gallop. The *Times* was carrying on its very own personal crusade against Labour for holding back the progress of Dunedin and Otago. With the *Evening Star* puffing in its rear it hounded the city's four 'sleepy' Labour M.P.s who had, it was claimed, been backward in urging Dunedin's claims. Their failure was 'the greatest single factor in delaying this city's entry into the general current of expansion'. Even worse was the fact that the Labour Party had a positive and unexplained hatred for Dunedin. The 'single retarding factor' (though the second to be so-called), to Otago's development was 'the socialist government which insists that this region should send its people and its resources elsewhere.' In passing, the *Times* had to chide the National Party over its proposal for a Cook Strait cable, but this did not prevent the paper from urging that 'Every vote cast for Labour on the election day is a vote deliberately cast against Dunedin'. This was not quite as obvious to all the northern papers, for the *Herald* went so far as to claim that Labour was 'wooing' the South Island with 'artificial development', and showing a 'geographical pre-occupation completely at variance with the hard facts of population trends and industrial expansion.' Not supported in the North, the *Times* also attracted sarcasm from ungrateful readers, one of whom cried 'God Bless the O.D.T.—God's own paper', and from a senior National M.P. who suggested privately afterwards that the paper might have helped National more had it supported Labour with the same unbalanced vigour. No sarcasm could check the violence with which the *Times* worked the parish pump.

Just in case any reader should still be in doubt as to which party ticket should be endorsed on election day, most papers summed up the reasons for voting National on the Thursday or Friday before the poll. At this stage many of them agreed with the *Christchurch Star* that 'this has been the quietest election for many years', and that 'What has really happened is that the 1957 election has been fought over again in retrospect', yet some were also sure that the situation was quiet because the electorate had already made up its mind. All that remained was for the papers to appeal for a high poll and remind readers of their democratic duty to vote.

The reaction to the actual result was inevitably one of rejoicing, though this was subdued in Dunedin because of the city's mistake in electing four Labour M.P.s and thus excluding itself from the Government and reducing its pull on the pork barrel. Most of the Press echoed the moral drawn by the *Herald*, 'Public resentment had endured against the means employed by Labour to gain office in 1957. The people then were beguiled by Labour promises and seven months later they were presented with the bill. With justice they felt they had been tricked.' This being the case *The Press* saw that the verdict was 'less a vote for National than a vote against Labour', but some of the other papers hastened to point out with the *Dominion* that 'it was certainly not that alone which secured National's victory', and with the *Herald* that the electorate had also passed 'a vote of confidence in Mr. Holyoake and the National Party'. Moderate as ever, the *Evening Post* was alone in stating that, though the electorate had shown 'their desire for a change of direction . . . that does not mean that they want to discard overnight as it were all that the Labour government had done or had in contemplation'.

Other sections of the papers added little of interest to the election. About a third of the correspondence columns was devoted to it, though there were wide variations in the number of letters printed, the *Otago Daily Times* publishing 150 bearing on the election, the *Auckland Star* under a score. Except for the *Dominion*, whose columns were weighted to National, most papers maintained a rough balance between the major parties. For the most part this famous democratic safety valve performed its natural function and released a lot of hot air. It also gave the parties the opening for driving home more propaganda by manufacturing letters, and National certainly encouraged its officials to do so. The news columns added infrequent items of relevance to the election as well as accounts of Mr. Moohan's peregrinations opening public buildings. Occasionally a news item was unjustifiably played down: some papers failed to give Mr. Walsh's condemnation of voluntary unionism the prominence it deserved but again this was rare.

The weekly, *Truth*, and several of the newspapers featured constituency surveys giving details of issues, candidates and electorates all over the country, but most of these enormously overstressed the possible importance of local issues and of the personalities of candidates and heavily hedged any bets made. The few clear predictions, for example that Manukau would fall to Labour, were usually wrong. The only other interesting developments were the Gallup Poll carried by two papers but turned down by others, the summaries of the manifestos in the *Christchurch Star*, and the questions on foreign affairs posed to the two main leaders by the *Evening Star*. For the rest ingenuity and originality were not characteristics which could be associated with Press treatment of the election.

To sum up, Labour had little to complain of in its Press treatment beyond the customary, almost ritualistic, drubbing from the editorials. Several Labour leaders when interviewed did in fact express surprise at the fair treatment they had received and the party could probably have improved its Press treatment still further by making the same extensive effort over Press relations that the Nationalists did. Social Credit and the Communists had more complaints, for the sense of duty which prompted the full coverage given to the election seems to have weakened in respect of these two parties. With this reservation a comforting if unoriginal conclusion seems to be indicated: Press treatment was reasonably fair and its influence on the result probably slight. Yet one essential reservation to this obvious conclusion needs to be remembered. Most people make up their minds well before the actual campaign period, and a blatantly one-sided Press treatment of the campaign could hardly influence the result, and might even repel voters from the side thus favoured. If there is a Press influence on opinion formation it must come in the important long-term period with which this chapter is not concerned. Such an influence would be exercised through the emphasis on the virtues of private enterprise, and the weaknesses of socialism and State-owned industries, through according greater weight to pro-National publicity than to that which is pro-Labour, through failure to explain the economic background to Labour policies and through singling out Labour motes while ignoring National beams. Any real assessment of the Press influence on opinion formulation and hence on elections, must be carried out over a period of many years and an examination of four brief weeks can provide only the barest of indications of the correct conclusions. By November 1960 the damage, if damage there was, had already been done.

PART THREE

THE ELECTORATES

VIII

THE CANDIDATES

COMPARATIVELY speaking, in contrast with their nineteenth-century predecessors, the candidates in a modern general election are unimportant figures. Their personalities, their occupations, their educational backgrounds, their ages and even their abilities mean little when compared with one all-important fact: their party colours. The Labour voter in a British election was only describing in extreme terms a situation which also applies in New Zealand when he said 'I'd vote for a pig if my party put one up'. Yet even though personal characteristics of candidates have only a slight influence on the result, they are worth looking at, for their own interest, for what they tell us about the parties that put up the candidates, and because it is of importance to discover what sort of man does secure election and become that much-abused figure, a Member of Parliament.

The odds are against such election so far as most candidates are concerned, for only eighty of them can win a seat. Revolution alone could dislodge many members in safe seats and only ten or twenty major party candidates fighting marginal seats can have realistic hopes of displacing a sitting member. Yet this prospect has not deterred an increasing number of candidates from offering themselves for election in recent years. In 1960 there were 269 candidates, which was eleven more than 1957 and seventeen more than in 1954. With such a large number of candidates most seats saw a three-cornered fight, since Labour, National and Social Credit contested every seat just as they have done at every election since 1951.[1] There were, however, twenty-seven seats which were contested by four candidates, and one, the Hutt, where four other candidates competed against a well-entrenched Prime Minister. The majority of these fourth candidates were put up by the Communist Party which contested nineteen seats. This meant fourteen more lost deposits than it had suffered in 1957. The

---

[1] In 1954 National did not contest the solidly Labour Westland seat. It was, however, contested by an Independent with Nationalist support and he has been counted as a Nationalist.

remainder were the ten independent candidates who included among their number men bearing a whole series of exotic titles such as Independent Maori Movement, Kauhanganui, People's Progressive Independent, and United New Zealand Political Movement. The magnificent plumage did not prevent the bird from dying, nor did these titles enable the independents as a body to gain more than 0·15 per cent of the qualified vote.

Only a minority of the candidates were entirely new to the facts of electoral life: twenty-six Labour, thirty-five National and thirty-six Social Credit candidates were fighting their first election, and for the most part their young hopes were doomed to disappointment since only nine of them, six National and three Labour, were successful. Many of the remaining candidates, those with experience, were sitting members, since only nine of the members of the last Parliament, five National and four Labour, did not offer themselves for re-election. A few of the experienced candidates were former M.P.s, four of whom attempted to return to the Elysian fields, though only two succeeded in the attempt, and they had taken the precaution of securing nomination for safer seats than the ones in which they had earlier been defeated. The remaining candidates with experience of the hustings were those who had made the attempt to enter Parliament before and were hopefully trying again. Of these, Mr. T. G. Santon, who had been defeated five times as Labour candidate in the Bay of Plenty electorate, had fought the record number of unsuccessful contests. He maintained his record in 1960.

An examination of the date of first candidature shows that many of the 1960 candidates had made their first entry into politics at a time when the political scene bore a very different complexion from that of today.

Seven of the candidates for example, all but one of them sitting members, had first stood for Parliament in 1931 or earlier at times when the three-party system was either still existent or merger was incomplete. The record for the earliest first candidature was shared by Mr. Mason, the outgoing Minister of Justice, and Mr. F. Langstone, now a Social Crediter but formerly a Minister in the first Labour Government, both of whom had first stood for Parliament in 1919. Nine others had fought their first campaign in other elections during the thirties, and forty-one in the forties. The remainder, the bulk of whom were Social Crediters, had

TABLE I

Date of First Candidature*

| | National | | Labour | | Social | Com- |
	Elected	Defeated	Elected	Defeated	Credit	munist
1931 or earlier	2	—	4	—	1	—
1935	—	—	3	—	—	—
1938	3	1	3	—	—	—
1943	7	—	3	1	—	—
1946	4	—	5	2	—	1
1949	5	—	2	5	1	4
1951	1	1	6	1	—	—
1954	12	—	4	6	21	1
1957	6	3	1	8	21	3
Totals	40	5	31	23	44	9

* Candidates standing at by-elections are included in the number
for the *previous* general election

strutted and fretted on the political stage in the course of the affluent fifties.

If fighting previous contests is the measure of political experience, then Labour offered the most experienced team of candidates in 1960. It had fewer new candidates, three more sitting members, and a body of members in safe seats who had sat for rather longer than the National M.P.s in a similarly happy position. Paradoxically this more experienced team was also a younger one on balance, for the average age of Labour candidates was lower than for the candidates of any other party. The ages of its candidates, where known, averaged out at 47·5 years, those of the Communists at 48·1, the Social Crediters 49·5, and the highest average age of all was that of the National Party candidates at 49·6 years. The volume of complaints that Labour was a 'party of old men' was obviously not justified if it referred to the whole party as opposed to the leadership. Yet because the National Party was winning seats and bringing young men into Parliament while Labour lost several of its younger members who had first been elected in 1954 and 1957, the National M.P.s after the election had a lower average age at 52·8 years than the Labour M.P.s at 54·8 years; a reversal of the situation in the previous Parliament. Details of the age spread of the candidates are given in Table II.

TABLE II

Age Groups of Candidates

	National		Labour		Social	Com-
	Elected	Defeated	Elected	Defeated	Credit	munist
21–9	—	4	—	4	1	—
30–9	3	7	5	16	15	1
40–9	19	8	7	11	16	7
50–9	11	9	8	10	21	5
60–9	10	3	11	2	11	—
70–9	3	1	3	—	2	—
Not Known	—	2	—	3	14	6
Totals	46	34	34	46	80	19

This demonstrates quite clearly that it is a young man's prerogative to be defeated in parliamentary elections while old M.P.s never die: they go on being returned. Labour, incidentally, provided both the oldest candidate, the Prime Minister who was seventy-eight, and the youngest, Mr. B. S. Gustafson at twenty-two, as well as the youngest M.P. actually elected, Mr. J. G. Edwards, the Labour M.P. for Napier who had also been the youngest member of the previous Parliament.

Merely fighting parliamentary elections is not the only nor possibly the most desirable means of securing political experience. For many, the road to Parliament and to political experience lies through the various local government bodies. With such a multiplicity of local authorities in New Zealand, 981 at the latest count, it is inevitable that a fairly high proportion of the candidates should have served in local government of some kind, and Table III gives details of this service.

TABLE III

Local Government Experience

	National		Labour	
	Elected	Defeated	Elected	Defeated
Boards	6	2	4	5
County Councils	7	1	—	1
City and Borough Councils	9	7	17	10

In this table local government is divided up into boards, county councils, and city and borough councils. County councils are counted as being more important than boards, and city and urban councils as more important than either, so that where a candidate served on more than one he is counted only under the most important. In this aspect of experience there was little to choose between the parties. Though more Labour candidates had served on city and borough councils and more National candidates on county councils, the proportion of elected members of the two parties with local government experience was roughly the same, about half of each party. Only a very small proportion, about a tenth, of the Social Credit candidates had had local government experience and very few of the Communists and Independents.

Experience can also be acquired by would-be politicians through holding office in societies and organizations. In fact, for some aspiring politicians such office is part of the main road into politics, since it at once provides contacts and experience and helps to make the individual better known. If three leading organizations are considered as an illustration, it is found that seventeen National members, (nearly all of them elected) and five Labour candidates (all defeated) had held office in the Federated Farmers, seven National candidates had held office in chambers of commerce, and twenty-five Labour candidates, nearly a third of the team, but only two National candidates, had held office in trade unions. Clearly, though the candidates of the two parties go in for rather different types of organizational experience, a reasonable proportion of both has had experience in different sectional economic organizations.

Even though the National and Labour teams differed little in respect of experience in previous elections, local government, or economic organizations, they naturally differed in other respects, for to some extent candidates are the embodiment of a party and differences between parties are found not only in policy and organization but also in the type of person each puts up for Parliament. The differences between Labour and National candidates in 1960, just as in previous elections, centred most clearly on their occupations, or to interpret occupation another way, on the social grouping of the candidates. A leading National M.P. boasted in the course of the campaign that 'Our candidates are from every walk of life. We are spread over all sections of the community, and we are no particular man's party.' A descent from these realms of electoral fiction makes it clear that neither the National nor the Labour Party could make such a claim. An examination of the occupations of the candidates shows that National candidates were drawn mainly from the top of the social and occupational scale, from farming, business and the better-paid professions, while the Labour candidates, although rather more evenly spread between occupational groups, were concentrated lower down the scale. Skilled and unskilled workers formed the largest single category among Labour's candidates, though they were not the majority since the party also drew several candidates from the professions, particularly teaching, and from business. Neither in respect of its candidates nor of its M.P.s can the Labour Party claim to be predominantly a 'workers' party', though it can claim to be the party of the 'less well-off', whether they be working people, professional people or in business. This difference between the parties is exaggerated if one considers only those candidates who eventually secured election, for many of the candidates who were out of line with the general occupational trend in their party were, significantly, fighting hopeless seats. Thus the National Party's two white-collar workers were both beaten, as were the majority of the Labour Party's farmers. A candidate anxious to secure election as a National M.P. would be well advised to be a farmer, in the Labour Party a trade union secretary.

All this is illustrated in Table IV in which an attempt has been made to allocate the candidates to their occupation on selection, even though a certain amount of arbitrariness about the allocations is inevitable. Professional politicians have been allocated to their previous occupations, and retired people to their occupations before retirement. Besides the light which it sheds on the composition of the two main parties, the table also shows that Social Credit has a wide distribution of candidates among the occupational groups. Though farmers and business men are the main element in the party it also includes a sizeable proportion of both blue- and white-collar workers so that it alone is really entitled to make the claim that its team of candidates represents all sections of the community. The remaining party, the Communist Party, would certainly not want to make such a claim. So far as its candidates are concerned it is solidly proletarian and it is almost certainly proud of the fact.

Another difference follows from this basic social difference.

TABLE IV

Occupations of Candidates

	National Elected	National Defeated	Labour Elected	Labour Defeated	Social Credit	Communist
Farming	23	9	3	9	30	—
Company director	3	5	1	—	10	—
Business	3	8	3	2	5	—
Small business	2	1	1	4	7	2
Civil service	—	1	2	4	—	1
Law	6	1	1	1	—	—
Medicine	1	2	—	—	3	—
Min. of religion	1	—	2	—	—	—
Accountancy	5	2	—	—	1	—
Teaching	1	1	1	5	2	—
Engineering	—	—	1	—	1	—
Party Officials	—	—	2	2	—	4
Journalists	—	—	2	—	—	—
Armed forces and police	—	—	—	3	—	—
T.U. secretaries	—	—	6	—	—	—
White collar	—	2	1	5	7	—
Blue collar	—	—	7	10	11	12
Housewife	1	2	—	1	3	—
No information	—	—	1	—	—	—
Totals	46	34	34	46	80	19

National candidates had, on the average, a higher level of education than their Labour counterparts. Of the National candidates 42 per cent had been to university, usually to pursue professional studies, and only 5 per cent had finished their formal education at the primary level. Of those Labour candidates whose educational background is known, only 29 per cent had been to university and 20 per cent had, like so many of the workers earlier in the century, not continued their formal education beyond the primary school.

In respect of education the differences noticeable when all the candidates are taken as a body are not quite as clear if only the elected members are considered. It is, however, still a fact that the general rise in educational levels in New Zealand has been reflected more slowly among Labour M.P.s than among National M.P.s. The term 'education' can cover a multitude of sins and

TABLE V

Educational Levels

	National Elected	National Defeated	Labour Elected	Labour Defeated	Social Credit	Communist
Primary	4	—	8	6	6	3
Post Primary	21	19	19	18	36	5
University	19	13	6	12	11	3
No information	2	2	1	10	27	8

schoolings, but while it is impossible to assess the benefits derived by M.P.s or candidates from their schooling, closer examination does reveal that there is yet another educational difference between the candidates of the two main parties, a difference once more caused by the basic social consideration. Thirteen of the National candidates were educated at the better-known private fee-paying schools—Christ's College, King's College, and Wanganui Collegiate School—which would thus seem to produce more political aspirants than could be expected solely on numerical grounds. Only one of the Labour candidates was so educated, while fifteen of his fellows were educated at public technical colleges and only four of the National candidates. The educational differences found in the British House of Commons, between public and private school and between the academic and the non-academic State schools, is also found in New Zealand. It is less marked in extent but its very existence is surprising in view of the New Zealand educational system.

It might be expected that in New Zealand as in some other countries, such as Britain, another difference between the parties would be that the party of the Right, the more conservative party, would contain the higher proportion of candidates who are related to each other or to former M.P.s. In fact, however, it is the Labour Party which contains the highest proportion of such candidates, eight in all as opposed to the five in the National Party. It was also the Labour Party which put up the only titled candidate in 1960, Sir Basil Arthur, though he democratically insisted on being called 'Mr.', an insistence the Press most exactly fulfilled.

There were, however, two other differences between Labour and National candidates which did conform to the patterns visible in Britain. One was that women were more likely to secure election standing for Labour than for National. Each party put up five women candidates, Social Credit put up four, the Communist Party two, and there was one woman standing as an Independent. Only four of this minor regiment of women secured election, and three of these were Labour candidates, leaving only one woman to be spokeswoman for her sex in the governing National Party caucus. Similarly, religious affiliation did provide a difference between the two main sets of candidates. Information on this topic is difficult to secure because most candidates do not mention their religion in published biographical details, while some even resent being asked to give details when written to. The figures are necessarily incomplete, therefore, but they do show that while Labour, National and Social Credit all drew the majority of thier candidates from the Anglican and Presbyterian churches, Labour had more Roman Catholic candidates than National. Roman Catholics made up one-tenth of the total number of Labour candidates. As might be expected, the proportion was lower among the Nationalists and only three could be identified as Roman Catholics. The Communist candidates were all atheists or agnostics though one admitted to being a 'nominal' member of the Church of England.

This examination of the candidates does add one more to the list of differences between the two main parties which could be compiled from other chapters. In respect of religion, education and occupation there are differences between the two sets of candidates. Essentially these reflect the differences between the main bodies of party supporters, but with the essential qualification that the centre of gravity among the candidates of each party is rather higher than it is among the mass of that party's supporters. Thus the National M.P.s and candidates occupy on average a slightly higher social position than do the mass of National supporters, while the Labour M.P.s include fewer working men, and more professional and business people, than is the case with the party's main voting strength. The social conflict is continued, but at least one step higher up.

It is impossible without a full-scale examination of the candidates in previous elections to say precisely how the 1960 candidates differed as a body from their counterparts in previous elections. Probably the general educational level had risen slightly, possibly the proportion of working men had declined slightly, while the contingent of farmers seemed larger than ever, but the differences are undoubtedly minor. The average candidate in 1960 was much the same as that average candidate who in previous elections had attempted to impress the electorate with his unique ability and aptitude for guiding the destinies of the nation.

Like the candidates, the means which they used to 'sell' themselves had hardly changed, depending as they did mainly on speeches, and on the candidate's own personal pamphlet or 'householder'.

Not all candidates distributed such 'householders', for both parties tended to economize on safe seats, whether their own or those of the other party, by distributing only a small selection of the nationally produced pamphlets. This was particularly true in rural electorates. Few of the Social Credit candidates could afford to distribute pamphlets of their own, but the majority of them were able to raise enough money to distribute to all householders in their electorate the special election issue of the *New Zealand Guardian* which included biographies and photographs of the majority of the party's candidates. The Communist Party also distributed a special election issue of the *People's Voice* to the householders in the electorates where its candidates were standing, and some of the candidates had biographical details printed which they then distributed strategically if not widely. In both cases the failure to use a 'householder' was an economy measure, but some candidates deliberately avoided using one, like the Labour candidate for Nelson who inserted his as an advertisement in the *Nelson Evening Mail* arguing that 'No one is likely to tear that up before they read it as they do with the leaflets'.

A few of those 'householders' which were distributed betrayed the hands of the enthusiastic amateur, bearing, as some did, odd montages of trains, dogs, and faces, or quite outrageous puns on the names of the candidates. Others suggested the smoother hands of public relations men whom both major parties encouraged their candidates to use. Many of the National candidates in the Wellington Division issued what was essentially the same pamphlet with different personal details. The four Labour M.P.s in Dunedin also shared the effort of creation. In presentation both parties came out more or less equal, with Social Credit lagging badly behind, partly through the need for economy, and partly through an attempt to cram too much solid argument into the space available.

A sample of fifty-six 'householders' was examined to discover just where the emphasis was placed by the different candidates. Half of these were issued by Labour candidates, being the only Labour householders that were collected, the other half were National pamphlets selected by thoroughly mixing those available and then taking the top twenty-eight. An analysis of this sample reveals that nearly all were similar in presentation, a four-page pamphlet with the candidate's photograph, some personal details and a brief message. One candidate placed at the top of his list of 'assets' the fact that 'He is a New Zealander born in the South Island', but with an odd exception here and there the biographical details which were introduced were very much the same. The candidate's occupation was mentioned by half of the pamphlets, his educational background by a third. About a quarter of the candidates considered their sporting interests and achievements sufficiently monumental to influence the electors, and a similar proportion, with a good deal more justification, made the same estimate of their war service. The only difference, and it was not an important one, between the candidates of the two parties was that National candidates tended to place more emphasis on wives and families. This was particularly odd when we remember that the Labour leader's appeal hovered around the family hearth. In two cases Nationalists went to the length of dragging in photographs of a political-looking family dog, perhaps in memory of Mr. Nixon's useful 'Chequers'. Half of the National candidates mentioned wives and families as opposed to a third of the Labour candidates, and a quarter of the National candidates included a photograph of the domestic cluster whereas only one of the Labour candidates did so. All the remaining candidates printed their own photograph, though some would have been better advised not to, or at least not that particular print.

Roughly a quarter of the candidates stressed the needs of their districts, and their achievements in securing, or hopes of getting, public works there. This was more common in rural electorates than in urban and the practice was more numerous among National candidates than among Labour, though Labour did distribute a special pamphlet listing its public works achievements in the Auckland area, which prominently featured both the face and the name of Mr. Watt, who had, indeed, guaranteed payment for the initial printing of this attractively produced encomium. In some cases this emphasis on local works and the needs of the electorate led to aimless wrangles as to who was originally responsible for what. While the National candidate in Invercargill busily listed all the public works completed while he had been an M.P., whatever the political complexion of the Government in power at the time, the Labour candidate demanded 'A New Deal for our City', evidently convinced that more needed to be done. In New Plymouth on the one hand, Labour issued 'A Record of Achievement', listing works Labour had carried out or was planning for the electorate. National, on the other, replied with a pamphlet, 'A Record of Bereavement', the same in format and outlay, but replacing photographs of the planned school, courthouse and station with photographs of the existing, antiquated buildings, or their empty, muddy sites. This was not only one of the most astute and amusing pieces of local electioneering in the whole campaign, but it served as well to demonstrate the futility of disputes about whether Member or Government or indeed anyone else was responsible for public works carried out or not carried out in the electorate.

Since the pamphlets were intended for local consumption and as a supplement to campaign pamphlets issued and distributed all over New Zealand, national issues were little stressed in most of the householders. When such issues were mentioned it was more frequently by Labour candidates than by Nationalists. This was partly because several National Party pamphlets concentrated on vague generalities. The National pamphlets issued in the Wellington Division, for example, made the none too noteworthy policy declaration 'that only by the recognition of moral and spiritual values and the upholding of the law can a country prosper'. The comparative absence of nation-wide issues was also due to the fact that National Party pamphlets placed more emphasis on the candidate himself than did the Labour pamphlets. Because of this difference between the parties a comparison of the general topics raised in the householders is not very useful though it does indicate the main trends in emphasis.

The topic most stressed by the Labour candidates was industrial development which was in accord with overall party strategy. National candidates placed their main stress on tax reduction, again derived from their plan of campaign. The analysis demonstrates likewise, a difference in attitude between candidates of

TABLE VI

Topics mentioned in Pamphlets

Topic	Percentage of Labour candidates	Percentage of National candidates
1. *Social:*		
Capitalization of Family Benefit	42%	8%
Education	31%	8%
Full Employment	23%	4%
Housing	46%	8%
Juvenile Delinquency	—	12%
Pensions	23%	—
Social Security and Welfare State	46%	23%
Three Per Cent Loans	42%	4%
2. *Economics:*		
Agriculture	35%	18%
Controls	4%	23%
Incentives	4%	23%
Industrial Development	65%	4%
1957 Crisis	12%	—
Socialism	—	18%
Private Enterprise	4%	13%
3. *Financial*		
Taxation	—	23%
Tax reductions	27%	31%
4. *Other:*		
Party Leader	4%	18%

the two parties. Labour candidates placed the emphasis broadly on security and welfare services. National men tended to emphasize opportunity, incentives and a removal of controls. Whatever the 'essential differences' between the parties, real or imagined, their candidates did their best to divide between putting emphasis on society and putting it on the individual, between the collective and the private.

IX

LOCAL ORGANIZATION AND
THE LOCAL CAMPAIGN

A GENERAL election is a national event. The politicians who hold the centre of the stage are national figures, the campaign is nation-wide, and the issues which dominate it are national in scope. Clearly the roles played by local party organization and the local campaign are comparatively minor, yet they are, even so, roles which have an importance of their own. Through the quality of the candidates elected, through the amount of money made available to party head office for the national campaign, and through enthusiasm in canvassing, putting the case to the electors, and getting voters to the poll, local party organizations can still exert a slight influence on the overall result, while in the four or five seats with very small percentage majorities, local organization may be decisive.

The most important single task performed by the local party organizations, and the one which gives them their greatest potential influence on the destinies of the country, is the selection of candidates. In both parties there are certain basic similarities in this procedure. Reselection of sitting members, both Labour and National, is usually automatic and unopposed; only in three cases in the 1960 election was there a nomination to oppose that of a sitting member, and in all three the influence of personal factors could be detected. In no case was the sitting member refused renomination, though Mr. Warren Freer in Mount Albert had his difficulties. Another similarity is that the remaining candidates are all selected late, usually within the few months before the election. No attempt is made in New Zealand to have a candidate nurse his electorate for a long period and make himself known by setting up a rival focus of attention to the sitting member. Both parties fear that self-advertisement by a 'prospective candidate' might serve to generate hostility. Indeed any attempt to bring selection forward to a period well before the election would certainly meet with opposition from traditionalists and from local parties who want to hang on in the hope of getting the best possible man. Possible gains through influencing and enlarging the small 'personal vote' which does exist and through reinforcing party loyalties by loyalties to a candidate are thus ignored.

The final similarity is that both parties give considerable weight to the views of the local party members in the selection of candidates, though in the National Party these local interests are preponderant, in the Labour Party they are modified by a degree of control from the centre. Labour's selections are made by a committee consisting of three representatives from the N.E.C., usually the president, the secretary, and the local area representative, together with three local representatives residing in the electorate and appointed by the L.R.C. The selection takes place before a meeting of party members in the electorate and is decided by the committee after each candidate has made a short speech. In the event of a deadlock on the committee a ballot is taken of the party members in the room, though this is merely for the guidance of the committee and is not binding on them. Should the deadlock then remain unresolved the question is in practice referred to the N.E.C. for a final decision, but this has happened only twice since the present selection procedure was first introduced in 1951. On these two occasions, one of which took place in 1960, the N.E.C. has decided once in favour of its own representatives and once in favour of the local representatives.

Such a system does reduce local control, and complaints against it on this ground are frequent. In practice, however, it works reasonably well and can be used to secure a balance between local interests and the interests of the party as a whole. Where relations are strained between a sitting member and the local organization, a situation in which the party's only lawyer M.P. has found himself on occasions, the local representatives can normally be persuaded to agree to renomination if the selection is contested. When the local representatives have no 'favourite son' candidate, they can usually be persuaded to pay due attention to the needs of the party. If they have very strong views in favour of a local candidate they usually get their way.

No similar branch complaints could be launched against the selection procedure practised by the National Party nor can the same advantages arise, for the degree of central control is minimal.

Control can in fact be exercised only at an early stage when the nominations for all the competitors are sent to the division and then to the Dominion Council for approval. Even here vetting is normally confined to checking for moral and other personal lapses, these being matters about which both parties are extremely sensitive. Where such lapses are discovered the usual course is that the nominee is informally persuaded to withdraw. Only if this fails is a nomination not approved and this has to happen only on rare occasions, though it did occur in 1960. Once approved, the nominations are passed back to the electorate selection committee made up of unpledged delegates elected either by the branch general meetings in the ratio of one delegate for twenty members, or at a general meeting of the whole electorate membership. As in the case of the Labour Party the selection is usually made in a large hall so that members not on the committee may attend, and once again the potential membership of the legislature is decided on the basis of a short speech after which the selection is made by ballot among the committee.

The National Party takes great care to ensure that the selection procedure shall be, and shall be seen to be, democratic. Lobbying may take place for certain candidates and on occasions there is a 'preferred' candidate just as there can be in the Labour Party, but undoubtedly the National system produces a greater degree of participation on the part of the average member than does that practised by Labour. This, however, brings on the counter-balancing defect that it takes no account of the interests of the party as a whole. National boasted in election pamphlets that it endeavoured to send to Parliament 'men who make up a balanced team with an even grading between experience, occupations and academic attainment'. In fact there is no means of ensuring any such grading among the candidates. Often men of long-established substance and standing in the community are preferred to other candidates. This may be why the average age of National candidates was slightly higher than that of Labour candidates; it is almost certainly the reason why the party is unduly weighted with farmers since rural electorates prefer a farmer, in some cases whatever his ability, to any other kind of candidate.

Social Credit nominations can be dealt with briefly. Selection is by the electoral branch, every member of which has the right to vote. It is therefore potentially even more democratic than the

National Party system, though a drawback arises from the difficulty of finding more than one candidate in many electorates. Candidates must all be approved by the provincial executive and the Dominion Council but, such is the reluctance on the part of these bodies to interfere with local powers, that approval is very rarely refused.

In the 1960 election the pattern of selection for all three parties differed little from that of previous years. As is usually the case with the party in opposition, National was ahead in the selection of its candidates; the first selection was made in March, and by early September, seventy-eight selections had been completed. Labour Party nominations had to be in to the head office on 14 May; some were made later, but by the same early September date there were only eleven selections still to be made. One of these, that of Mr. Freer, was kept back deliberately, but a few selections were still being made in rural electorates in October and even in November because of Labour's perennial difficulty of finding candidates in these areas. In a few rural electorates candidates had to be brought in from nearby urban centres and in an extreme case a candidate had to be imported from Wellington into Southland to put up a last-minute, hopeless fight. Social Credit nominations came in two main groups, a steady trickle through the course of the year so that some sixty had been nominated by the time of the annual conference in June, and then a last-minute rush which appeared to be, in some cases, as much a matter of finding any candidate at all as deciding between nominees. The Communist Party had decided on and announced its nineteen nominations by early September.

Once selected the candidates had to be trained, a more rigorous process for National candidates than for Labour. As early as 1959 the Wellington division of the National Party had held a public affairs discussion group, a group which, since twenty-eight of the forty people attending it were later nominated as candidates, amounted to an informal candidates' conference. This was an innovation, and there was a further new development in 1960 when two candidates' conferences were held instead of the usual one. The first was a three-day affair held in September at Paraparaumu. There, new candidates received instruction in techniques of speaking and presentation, and briefings from the leader and two former Ministers on policy, economic conditions, and political issues. This was followed in October by the major candidates' conference which was held in Wellington and was technically attended by all the candidates, M.P.s or unfledged, though some of the sitting members visited rather than attended. The main function of this conference was to discuss, amplify and explain the manifesto, to ensure that whatever the other abilities of the candidates, they did at least know the policy of their party.

The Labour Party candidates' conference was a shorter two-day event held towards the end of October, but it did take place in Parliament Buildings, a venue presumably designed to inspire new candidates to greater exertions. The emphasis here was less on overall party policy for the future, though that was discussed, than on the achievements of the Government. The bulk of the time was devoted to a series of speeches by Ministers who outlined the past policy and achievements of their departments and then dealt with questions. Topics likely to crop up during the campaign were discussed, as they had been at the National Party conference, so that candidates of both parties knew the stock answers to the stock questions. Where Labour fell down as compared with National, was in the failure to instruct new candidates fully on such technical questions as speaking, platform manner, microphone technique, and the fitting of their local presentation into the presentation of the party's case on a national scale. National candidates went into the fray somewhat better armed. They were also more amply primed with facts and documentation by the research division as the campaign progressed. Indeed the amount of documentation received by National candidates was intimidating in its proportions.

With the candidate selected and fully briefed, the local machinery to back him had still to be either created or brought into action. Characteristically this machinery is more complicated in the Labour Party than in the National Party. In the four main centres, the Labour campaign in each individual electorate is controlled by the Inter-Branch Council under the supervision of a campaign committee of the L.R.C., which keeps an eye on the whole area, but normally interferes very little in individual I.B.C. decisions. In the remaining electorates, which have their own L.R.C.s, this body appoints a campaign committee, small in number and possessing the power to co-opt. In a typical city seat, where the campaign is controlled by the Inter-Branch Council, its secretary is the key figure in the campaign, while in a one-electorate L.R.C.

the secretary to the L.R.C. normally plays the main role. These two individuals are, for the duration of the campaign, the local party's organizers, a task which they fulfil in some cases after their normal daily work is done, in other cases by taking leave for the few weeks before the election. Inevitably the efficiency of these organizers varies enormously. Some are a major driving force; others, particularly in rural electorates, are comparatively inactive. At least one candidate reported never having heard from or about the secretary to his I.B.C. for the whole duration of the campaign. In addition certain secretaries were hampered in 1960 by the fact that, as well as organizing in one electorate, they were standing as candidates in another, a practice which must make for reduced efficiency in both. These variations in individual efficiency are inevitable, but it is a major fault in Labour's election machinery that little close supervision can be maintained over the activities of local officials. During the campaign the only check available is the series of reports sent in by organizers to the head office. Often these can be suitably coloured during the campaign, since the picture emerges in black and white only with the announcement of the results.

Usually the candidate himself has to take a share in the work of organizing. In some electorates in rural areas or wealthy suburbs, where Labour Party membership is low and committees small, the candidate becomes in practice his own organizer, arranging his own meetings and Press publicity as well as carrying out his normal duties. At least one Labour candidate in such an area had to deliver most of his own pamphlets. This was exceptional, though in the majority of electorates the organizational work was shared between organizer and candidate. In such circumstances each can help the other, and in 1960 it was noteworthy that those candidates who had themselves been organizers possessed local machines which were the most efficient in the Labour Party.

The National Party's local campaign is controlled by the electorate committee, though the secretary to this body is not quite as important as his counterpart in the Labour Party, for most electorates either have a permanent full-time organizer of their own or share one with a neighbouring electorate. A complication in National Party organization arises from the fact that the candidate, can, if he wishes, create a small candidate's committee to arrange meetings, tours, publicity and propaganda. This then receives a grant of up to £500 from the electorate committee to cover those expenses which must be declared under the Electoral Act. One member, at least, of this candidate's committee is also a member of the electorate committee so as to ensure co-operation, and normally both bodies work efficiently with the professional organizer. The result is that the average National candidate is far less concerned with organizational matters than the average Labour candidate. He is correspondingly freer to carry out his tasks *qua* candidate.

The Social Credit Political League organizes its local campaign through the electorate executive, but since this body is small, and in many electorates the branch is weak, the bulk of the organizational work normally falls to the candidate himself assisted by as many friends, followers and sometimes relatives, as he can muster. Quite often in urban electorates the candidate has to do his own organizing, deliver his own pamphlets and arrange his own meetings. On top of this, some Social Credit candidates are compelled by the financial stringency of the branches to contribute to their own expenses. In 1960 some forfeited deposits were paid by the Dominion headquarters but, even with this help many candidates spent their own money on the campaign as well as losing wages when time was taken off work.

The two major parties have more efficient financial arrangements, centred on a three-year effort to build up a local fighting fund. Labour draws its finances from two main sources. Trade unions, as well as contributing on a national level, also contribute locally. These contributions can be as large as £1 a member and can amount to substantial sums in the main centres, though inevitably they are very small in rural electorates. The second main contribution is in the form of money raised by the branches mostly from bazaars, 'Housie', carnivals, and other functions. In city areas where I.B.C.s controlled the constituency campaigns, they were financed almost entirely out of such sums, since the bulk of the trade union contributions and those sizeable individual contributions which came from local manufacturers, were made to the L.R.C.s. In the case of a very few rural electorates, the head office of the party was compelled to make a grant to support at least a token campaign because insufficient money could be raised locally to do so.

National Party electorate committees raise most of their funds by the canvass for subscriptions which is carried out over the three years before the election. There is also the income from donations and voluntary subscriptions, an income which, as in the case of the Labour Party, tends to rise steeply only in the period immediately before the election when the need is obvious. Candidates can, and in some cases presumably do, make contributions themselves, without any limit being fixed as it is in the case of the British Conservative Party. The National Party is, however, so strong financially that there is no indication that ability to contribute to local funds is ever a factor in securing nomination.

The Electoral Act of 1956 limits the amount of money a candidate can spend on an election to £500. In marginal electorates both parties came close to this maximum, some as close as the £498 11s. 7d. spent by Labour in St. Kilda; in safe seats they came nowhere near the figure. It is folly for the Labour Party to spend much more than £200 on electorates which it has no hope of winning, and very few sitting members in Labour strongholds exceeded £250 either. It is equally profitless for National to spend large sums on safe Labour seats or on its own strongholds, though an average figure for personal expenditure of National candidates would almost certainly be about £100 higher than that of Labour candidates. Few Social Crediters spent more than £200, some under £50, and most of the Communist candidates and some of the Independents fought their campaigns on £40 or even less, including the inevitably lost deposit.

An analysis of the returns in sample areas shows the main single expense to be the cost of Press advertising, on which several candidates spent over £200. This is followed by the cost of printing and distributing a 'householder' pamphlet, usually about £70 for an average sized electorate. The remaining sums in most cases cover hall hires, telephone charges and calico signs. However a nation-wide analysis of the expense returns would not only be impracticable but unnecessary, since the £500 limit is by no means a reliable guide to what has actually been spent. 'We couldn't hope to run an election on £500' was a cry often heard from organizers of both parties and not just in marginal seats. Most of this extra expenditure is perfectly legal. Travelling expenses, which can be heavy, are sometime not disclosed, though in this and other matters there are wide variations of practice.

The cost of travel is indicated by the fact that the Labour candidate in Franklin travelled 3700 miles in one month, while the damage sustained by the car of the Labour candidate for Waitomo when it was charged by a bull was presumably some form of travelling expense. Nor does personal expenditure include the cost of accommodation which can also be heavy in rural electorates. The major loophole, however, is not this but the fact that the limit does not include most of the money spent by a party on its own local campaign as distinct from that of the candidate. The maintenance of offices, the payment of organizers, the expense of outside speakers, and the cost of nationally distributed literature and posters, all a major part of the cost of any campaign, are simply not included in the items which need to be declared. The meaningless nature of the returns is perhaps best demonstrated by the fact that, according to them, the National candidate in solidly Labour Mornington spent £432 on a fight which he was predestined to lose, while the National candidate in marginal St. Kilda spent only £396. Clearly such returns do not reflect the actual distribution of resources between the two electorates. The days when the candidate's expenditure was important passed with the rise of mass parties and the time has clearly come when the return should be either extended to cover expenditure of party as well as candidate, or dropped entirely. At present it has little point, and many returning officers profess little faith in it.

In the campaign proper the local party organization faces three major tasks. The first, that of arranging meetings for the candidate and visiting speakers, is straightforward. So also is the second, that of arranging for Press advertising and the printing and distribution of a 'householder' pamphlet where one is used. The third group of tasks includes making sure that the electoral rolls are complete, arranging for special votes, and canvassing to discover and encourage supporters.

The efforts of the parties to get the rolls filled were supplemented by the organization representing the licensed trade which, in 1960, set up thousands of kerb-side booths where people could check that they were on the roll and make arrangements to be included in the supplementary roll. This organization also arranged for canvasses in some areas so as to ensure a full roll. Happy in the knowledge that the work was being done for them in this way, some local party organizations were inclined to sit back and content themselves with opening a committee-room or two where voters could check that they were on the roll. In other electorates, especially the marginal seats, a more vigorous effort was made by canvassing sections of the electorate, particularly the newer parts, to ensure that everyone was registered.

In respect of sick and absentee votes the organization of the National Party was more efficient than Labour's, for several electorates appointed special votes committees to compile a register of such votes. Normally these were collected well in advance of polling day so as to save trouble at a time of particular pressure. With a handful of exceptions Labour arrangements were more casual. In some electorates the special votes became the concern of the candidate's wife, while in others the party tended to wait until it was applied to by supporters to make arrangements for such votes instead of going out looking for them. As a result, more of this work was left until the day of the election, and so Labour must have won a smaller proportion of the special votes than it might otherwise have done.

Seeing that voters were on the roll and arranging for special votes were only part of the general canvassing arrangements which again were less efficiently carried out by Labour than by National. A full coverage of an electorate by either party was rare, but National probably came nearer to it in more electorates than did Labour, while Labour failed to make any canvassing efforts at all in more electorates than did National. National had advantages which gave it a head start in this field. In many electorates the party kept street books recording the names of voters street by street and noting their political views as 'National', 'Labour' or 'doubtful' where soundings had been taken by canvassers. These books were not only retained between elections, but were kept up to date during the periodic canvasses for subscriptions. Another advantage was that, with a larger membership, National had more helpers to call on for canvassing before and during the campaign. In addition, being wealthier, it could, on occasions, employ paid canvassers such as retired people and students to cover newly developed or critical areas. In several of the marginal electorates and some others, these resources were all used to draw up a full card index system with a card for every elector or, more usually, for as many as possible, recording name, address and political sympathies. Though it was found in only a minority of the electorates in 1960, the use of the card index is likely to spread. Building up and maintaining the index may well become a focus of organizational activity between campaigns as well as in the actual election period.

Without the funds to employ paid canvassers, and with an individual membership far smaller than National's, Labour was by no means as efficient at canvassing. Without a full canvass, the party lacked the detailed knowledge necessary to build up a card index system. The national secretary encouraged electorates to use such a system but very few did so, and even then in one electorate the system was not complete through faulty canvassing. In several electorates local organizers claimed to have a rough knowledge of voters they could count on and those they could not, an estimate arrived at by consulting party members as to the views of the inhabitants of their respective streets. This 'mental card index' was at best a haphazard method, and in any case attempts to codify, organize, or even use what information it did provide were not numerous. The third party, Social Credit, made no pretence of canvassing outside isolated, individual efforts in a few electorates. Usually if its supporters were on the roll they were there thanks to their own efforts or those of the major parties.

While the party machinery was thus carrying out its task, the candidate also had tasks which were specifically his, and which can be summed up under the broad heading of making himself known to the electors. In this endeavour the sitting member naturally had an enormous lead since an M.P. has to be, as one member himself put it, 'a solicitor, a marriage counsellor, a welfare officer, a business advisor, a house-getter, a telephone applicant, a donor to charity and an attender at numerous functions'. His reward for all this is to be well known in the electorate. Some M.P.s take steps to improve even on this, as did the Labour M.P. who, since his first election, had canvassed an average of fifty houses a week, and the M.P. who made a point of sending letters and telegrams of congratulation to every potential voter who came of age and every elector who got married. Devoted members of this type are found usually, but not exclusively, in marginal seats. Even with the advantages of present tenure, some sitting members in these seats were still patently nervous as the election approached, particularly as the parliamentary session continued to confine them to Wellington while rivals made themselves known in the electorates.

To make themselves known most candidates took leave from their jobs for a month or more and were normally paid by the party for this period unless they were Social Crediters. The time was then spent by the candidates meeting groups of people where possible and visiting the electorate, or at least key areas of it, introducing themselves to the voters. Not all did this; a Labour candidate in a marginal Auckland seat strongly disliked door-to-door visiting and had almost to be forced into doing any of it, while sitting members in safe seats often afforded themselves the luxury of little or no visiting. On the other hand, there were candidates who were really enthusiastic in their visiting. By early September, the National candidate for Tamaki, contending for a likely gain, was estimating that he had worked his way around a quarter of the electorate. The Social Credit candidate in North Dunedin, with no such realistic hope, claimed to have visited 3000 houses during the course of the campaign. Such visiting was far more common in the compact urban electorates than in the larger rural ones. In the Wallace electorate, sprawling over 5600 square miles, it would have taken the candidate six nights a week for five weeks even to visit all the branches from the area headquarters. As a consequence, the sitting member in a rural electorate tended to have a slight advantage over his urban counterparts in that it was more difficult for a rival to make himself known. There were the inevitable exceptions: the Labour candidate in Hauraki made 2759 personal contacts through canvassing, but generally speaking, difficulties of size prevented any canvassing on a scale comparable with that in urban electorates.

In addition to visiting, candidates had to undergo the traditional election ordeal of public meetings, though in plenty of instances this was more of an ordeal for the audience. The year 1960 saw a continuation of the long-term trend towards a decline in the number of meetings held by candidates. The average number of indoor meetings held by National candidates in the Wellington division was only fourteen, while the average number held by Labour candidates in the Dunedin area was as low as twelve. There was also a continuation of the steady decline in the numbers attending the meetings. Since several newspapers gave attendances at those meetings which they reported it is possible to give some average attendance figures for various types of meeting. These figures are rough ones, and cover only the number of candidates listed in brackets beside the attendance figures.

	Attendance at National meetings	Attendance at Labour meetings	Attendance at Soc. Cred. meetings
Safe National seats	64 (14)	41 (14)	24 (5)
Safe Labour seats	52 (21)	41 (13)	23 (12)
Marginal seats (under 12% majority)	78 (17)	49 (12)	19 (9)

National candidates tended to draw audiences which were, on average, larger than those of Labour candidates, and it is hardly surprising to find that the audiences at meetings in marginal seats, where interest is naturally high, were larger than at those in safe seats, though attendances in safe National seats which are mostly rural were slightly larger than those in the urban safe Labour seats.

The most important thing shown by the figures is how small most meetings were and these figures may in fact exaggerate attendances slightly. On one or two occasions indeed, Social Credit and Independent candidates faced an audience of but three after including the inevitable policeman and reporter. Large or small, meetings all over the country had one thing in common: the audiences were mainly party loyalists, the already converted. The enthusiasm of these people might flag should meetings be drastically reduced in number or even, as some organizers suggested, abandoned. New Zealand might be a sadder, if hardly a duller place, but the net effect on the vote would probably be very slight indeed for those who attend are almost certain to vote anyway, while the conversion of an uncommitted voter by a meeting must be an extremely rare event.

Meetings were quieter in 1960 than they had been at the previous election. Odd incidents did disturb them, and a very few speakers met with warm receptions but the audiences were mostly quiet. Organized heckling was unusual. Devotees of the old-time election meeting will be saddened to learn that only one egg was thrown at a candidate during the 1960 campaign. It missed. Only one man was arrested and imprisoned for causing a disturbance at a political meeting. In part, these quieter meetings were due to the fact that the audiences were predominantly middle-aged and old people. The Labour and National candidates in New Plymouth both estimated their best attendance of new voters at four. Another gauge of the age level of Labour audiences at least was provided by loud applause at the ritual mention of the name of M. J. Savage, who died twenty years ago. At most meetings young people were conspicuous by their absence.

The shortest address in the election was given by the National candidate for Hutt, and consisted of fifty-eight words including a biblical text. It was not in giving shorter addresses, however, but by taking up other forms of electioneering that most candidates sought an answer to the problem posed by the decline of the traditional political meeting. One response was to take Mohammed to the mountain, for instance through lunch-time meetings at factories, a method which candidates particularly liked since they had a captive audience in yard or cafeteria. These were combined with visits to institutions, offices and anywhere where groups of people could be met. Another technique in increasing use was the holding of open-air meetings, with the candidate gathering a crowd by speaking through an amplifier. Friday, as the one late shopping night, was a favourite time for such meetings. Whatever the night, an open-air meeting could be relied on to gather a group of between fifteen and a hundred people to hear a short speech, and more than one a night could be held. Consequently these meetings were much used; the Labour candidate in Lyttelton held 121 meetings, most of them at street corners and in factories. A few candidates, mainly Labour candidates in the Auckland area, held even more, while some Communist candidates relied almost exclusively on these gatherings. Another type of event more frequently encountered in 1960 than in previous elections was the joint, inter-party meeting organized by junior chambers of commerce, church organizations, and a few other community groups. At these meetings candidates gave their views on questions which were usually set in advance. Less frequently the candidates were allowed to speak and then take questions from the audience. Audiences were usually large, ranging from a hundred to as many as six hundred, and were certainly more numerous than the average political gathering. Though party organizers tended to frown on such meetings, and sitting members to think that, like the Kennedy-Nixon television debates, they gave too much publicity to newcomers, they were much more frequent in 1960 than ever before. With the traditional type of meeting to inspire the party faithful in decline, face-to-face confrontations of candidates answering questions showed every sign of a popular future.

Other unusual means of electioneering were few. The voter could look in vain for departures, refreshing or otherwise, from the traditional routine of electioneering. In any case after the short, four-week period of the campaign, neither stunts nor traditional rituals could further influence the voters. After midnight on Friday, 25 November, the candidate, the show figure, moved into the background. On election day the voter and the party organizations shared the stage.

The election-day organization of both major parties is centred on a common objective; that of getting the maximum possible number of voters to the poll. For the National Party to aim at securing the highest possible turn-out may, nevertheless, be a mistake. Certainly in 1960, as in 1951, a falling vote favoured National even though the party was working to the reverse end. The basic policy may therefore need some adjustment to the circumstances of different elections but there is the compensation that with its superior organization, National can be more selective in choosing whom it gets out to vote than can Labour.

National Party organization varies from electorate to electorate, being at its most efficient in marginal seats and at its most rudimentary in very safe Labour seats. In the all-important marginal seats and other electorates where a card index existed this became the focal point of election-day organization, being kept either at a central electorate headquarters or being split and locally operated as in Wellington Central where only two of the four branches had compiled card indexes. The theory of the system is that scrutineers are appointed in every polling-booth to record the number and name of each elector as he casts his vote. Record sheets bearing these numbers are then taken back to headquarters at frequent intervals and cards are removed from the index as people are found to have voted. By late afternoon it is clear who has not voted and cars can be detailed to call on these non-voters who are known to be National supporters or whose allegiance is known to be doubtful.

This system is implemented in full only in a small number of electorates. It was so implemented in Palmerston North where 180 cars and 250 runners were used; canvassing began at 8.30 a.m. and by 10.30 a 'complete' door-to-door coverage of most areas had been carried out. Palmerston North's card index was centralized. The last sheets were brought in from the scrutineers at 4 p.m. and the last cards taken from the index by 4.15. The eight blocks into which the electorate had been divided were then notified of the non-voters and by 4.45 p.m. transport had been sent out to seek the 'National' and 'doubtful' electors.

Roskill operated a similar system, as did Manukau where the party had nearly two hundred cars and several hundred helpers. Most electorates, however, did not have the manpower available to work the system in full and in any case each division of the National Party tends to practise variations of its own. Often scrutineers were not used and in Otago the street books, instead of being arranged in a card index, were given to the drivers of cars who then called on all but Labour supporters. In Invercargill no attempt was made to 'beat up' the electorate, the organizer being convinced that a high turnout would favour Labour. Yet most electorate organizations did at least aim at an extensive, if not complete, coverage of the electorate by cars and canvassers and in the majority of cases National came rather nearer to achieving such an extensive coverage than did Labour.

Basically Labour Party organization was similar, with a central headquarters and a series of depots based on single branches at which cars were gathered or a series of 'blocks' each under a block captain. The chief weakness was that Labour usually had fewer helpers and cars. To follow up the Palmerston North example, there the party had 190 helpers and eighty-six cars. Elsewhere it was compelled to place more reliance on rental cars or, in the Auckland area, on radio taxis, two of which were made available to every electorate. In addition Labour was handicapped by the fact that, lacking canvassing returns as efficient as those of the Nationalists, it did not always know where its support came from. Election-day visiting had to be concentrated on those areas which, from a rough knowledge of previous booth returns, were thought to favour Labour. To venture into more marginal areas or into areas which favoured National was less rewarding because Labour supporters could not be singled out and lifts had to be offered indiscriminately. Even so, in Roskill the party claimed to have visited every house in the electorate, and some other marginal seats were well covered, though houses with cars outside were often not visited and on occasions entire streets were missed. At the other extreme many electorates were not canvassed at all and in one safe seat in Wellington, for example, the party cars on election day made no effort to work the electorate but waited around until telephone appeals for transport came in.

In the safer seats the organization of both parties is naturally weaker. Effort is normally proportional to the threat of defeat or the hope of victory, though the ambition to secure a full poll for reasons of local pride or considerations of the effect of nation-wide figures of polling is still found in many safe seats. This is particularly true of the National Party in the rural electorates where such canvassing as occurs is carried on mainly by telephone, cars being provided only for the aged or for sick votes, so ubiquitous is the farm car. In some cases, however, the extent of the envelope concessions in the 1956 Electoral Act made it possible to bring in the back-blocks and the sick votes in envelopes so as to have less trouble on election day.

Because of local pride and the autonomy of the electorates, neither party made much effort on election day to divert cars from the safe seats to the marginal ones where they could be of more use. In Dunedin, National, with 250 cars for the four city seats, held slightly more cars in Dunedin Central than in marginal St. Kilda. Labour, with 200 cars, only diverted extra ones to that electorate later in the day. In fact most marginal seats had enough cars and helpers, but the independence of the electorates and the slight co-ordination on a city-wide scale did mean that had cases of necessity arisen, little could have been done to meet them with transferred cars and helpers.

Nearly everywhere Labour and National worked under considerable pressure on the morning of polling day. So did Social Credit in the very few places where the League had any transport arrangements other than the candidate's car. As a fine day produced an early rush to the polls resources were strained to the maximum and officials began to forecast a high poll. By contrast, from three in the afternoon pressure was easing, cars were beginning to stand idle, and few calls were coming in. Several electorates still went ahead with a full-scale canvass at the end of the day.

More sat back in the easy confidence that a heavy poll had already taken place.

The result when it came was ascribed by some to National's superior organization, particularly in the marginal seats. It is true that over the Dominion as a whole, and less markedly in the marginal seats, Labour's local organization was inferior to that of their opponents. It suffered in fact from four main complaints. Labour had both a smaller body of volunteer workers and a smaller number of cars than National, but little could be done about this. It may be that Labour Party members are more devoted than National's since they have to make an effort to join, but an individual membership over four times the size of Labour's gives National a larger fund of members to draw on, and these members, being better-off, are better equipped with cars even in egalitarian New Zealand. A full-scale membership drive before the election might have helped Labour slightly, but even this was not attempted.

It was, however, the remaining three complaints which were the more serious and they could in some measure have been treated. One was an ingrained hostility on the part of older party workers to new developments such as card index systems. This was particularly serious because older people made up a higher proportion of Labour's forces than of National's, where the services of the Juniors were frequently used. Too little was done to combat this attitude. The third complaint afflicting Labour was a general state of low morale. Branch activity, membership and enthusiasm have not been high in the 1950s, though they picked up considerably before the 1957 election. This temporary vitality did not outlast 1958. The falling away of workers and branches was sporadic enough to mask its causes and, indeed, its probable result. In the months just before polling the customary surge of combative vigour was felt, but more than this is desirable in winning elections. Probably the real state of morale was at the bottom of many examples of branch inactivity, insufficiency of canvassing, inadequate pamphlet delivery, and half-hearted organization. Yet the fourth fault was a contradictory one, an undue feeling of optimism in many quarters and an almost complete failure to regard the dangers prophesied by the Gallup Poll. Officials at the top were too content with assurances that all was well and that organization was as efficient as in 1957. Local officials were too readily convinced of victory. The result was a relaxation of effort when additional attempts to tighten up organization and whip up enthusiasm were necessary. In Manukau for example, while Labour hoped, National organized.

Improved organization could not, of course, have won the election for Labour. What it could have done was improve the party's overall performance slightly, generate greater enthusiasm, and possibly save a couple of the seats won by National with very small majorities. It remains a central paradox of New Zealand politics that the party which probably stands to gain more from a heavy turn-out at the polls is the worse equipped, organizationally, to secure such a turnout.

X

THE VOTER AND THE ELECTION:
DUNEDIN CENTRAL

ANY study of a General election which did not include some
information about the voters who decided the issue, would
be like a study of Hamlet which left out the Prince of
Denmark. Yet the New Zealand voter is rather more difficult to
describe than his counterparts overseas because Gallup Polls
and voting surveys, the main descriptive tools, are comparatively
new arrivals in the dominion. As a compensatory factor both were
used in 1960, so that this study of the voter can be based on the
three Gallup Polls carried out at monthly intervals before the
election for the *Auckland Star* and the *Christchurch Star,* and on
a survey of voting in Dunedin Central, carried out by personal
interviews with electors in the two weeks after the general election.

Dunedin Central is an electorate which is very mixed in its social
composition, rising as it does from the low-cost housing and the
industrial areas of the city flat, through some very mixed housing,
to some of Dunedin's best residential areas at the top of the city
slopes, before descending on the other side to newer areas in which
State subdivision and group and private building are still going on.
Fundamentally a city centre seat, it also includes other areas
which, in larger cities, would make up seats more suburban in
character. It also differs from most other electorates because it
was contested by four candidates. Thus, although the rate of
Labour loss of votes at 4·89 per cent was practically the same as
the national average, this happy coincidence occurred for the
wrong reasons, being in part due to the success of the Independent
candidate, Mr. Warrington Taylor, in attracting a much larger
vote than any other Independent in New Zealand. For these
reasons, and leaving aside the vexed question of Dunedin's feeling
that it is distinct from the rest of the Dominion, it is clear that
though no electorate is typical, Dunedin Central is less typical
than many. Yet even though the information provided by one
survey cannot be exactly representative of national trends in the

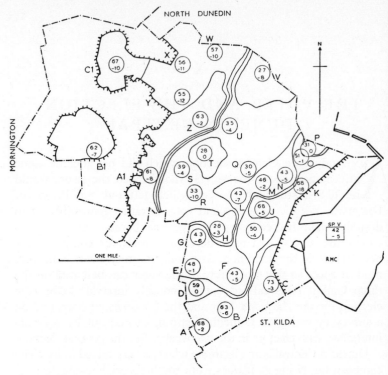

MAP A. DUNEDIN CENTRAL ELECTORATE

A	Caversham
B	Carisbrook
C	Kensington
D	Clyde Hill
E	Maryhill
F	Montecillo
G	Eglinton Rd.
H	Alva St.
I	Carroll St.
J	Clark St.
K	Stuart St.
L	Russell St.
M	St. Joseph's
N	Town-Hall
O	Hanover St.
P	King St. Hospl.
Q	Arthur St. Sch.
R	Belleknowes
S	South Highgate

T	Roslyn Institute
U	Roslyn, Sch. St.
V	Maori Hill
W	N.E. Wakari
X	North Wakari
Y	South Wakari
Z	Kaikorai North
AI	Kaikorai Vly.
BI	Brockville
CI	Halfway Bush

KEY

Circle = Polling Place.
1st Fig. = Lab. % of Valid Vote
2nd Fig. = Lab. Loss/Gain since 1957
Isopols = At Intervals of 10% in
Valid Vote for Labour
Barbed
Line = Excludes vacant areas

1960 election, these trends are clearly indicated and the coincidence of certain of the more general findings with those of the first university-sponsored interview survey, carried out by R. S. Milne in Wellington in 1957, also enables certain generalizations about voting habits in New Zealand urban electorates to be made.

The 1960 interview sample consisted of 594 people, or rather more than one in thirty of the electors, their names being taken out of the electoral roll at regular intervals. After substitutes had been provided for the 101 electors who had gone away, removed, died, or who were too sick to be interviewed, successful interviews were concluded with 551 electors, 44 per cent of whom voted Labour, 43 per cent voted National, 6 per cent Social Credit, while 2 per cent voted for the Independent candidate, and 5 per cent did not vote. As compared with the actual result therefore National voters were over-represented, while Independent voters were slightly under-represented, and non-voters were quite markedly so.[1]

I *Who Votes How*

Several voting surveys in other countries have indicated that young people are inclined to vote for the Left wing party and older people for the Right, a tendency illustrating, though certainly not caused by, the claim that 'If a man isn't a socialist when he's 20, he hasn't a heart. If he isn't a Tory when he's 40, he hasn't a head.' If measured by this adage the young people of Dunedin, unlike their counterparts in the 1957 Wellington survey, have no hearts, since the National Party took a higher proportion (50 per cent) of the votes of those aged 40 and under than did Labour (42 per cent), with 8 per cent going to Social Credit. By the same token some of those over 40 have no heads since Labour took 49 per cent in the age group 41–50 and 55 per cent in the one from 51–65, while National had only 45 per cent and 39 per cent in these two groups.

---

[1] For further methodological details see *Political Science*, Vol. 14, No. 1, March 1962. Here it is enough to point out that the sample conformed satisfactorily with the age and sex distribution of the total population of the census areas included in the electorate. When compared with the actual electorate vote, the results are:

Sample Lab. 44 per cent (244) Nat. 43 per cent (236)   S.C. 6 per cent (33)
              Ind. 2 per cent (12)   No votes 5 per cent (26)

Electorate Lab. 43 per cent (7175) Nat. 38 per cent (6333) S.C. 6 per cent (951)
              Ind. 3 per cent (471) No Votes 10 per cent (1707)

Professor Milne's survey is also found in *Political Science*, Vol. 10, No. 2.

The top age group, those over 65 years of age, divided fairly evenly between the two parties, 47 per cent voting Labour, 49 per cent National and 4 per cent Social Credit, a lower proportion than in any other group.

The contrast between this result and the indication from Wellington Central in 1957 that young people supported Labour and each succeeding age group was more National, probably arises in part from two factors. The first is the possibility of a slow change on the national scene. Labour may be losing support from young people, while at the same time it may be winning the support of older age groups, particularly those over 65, a trend indicated by the fact that the only age group where changers to Labour outnumbered changers to National was this last one. Such a trend was visible in the 1959 election in Britain, and, at the top end of the age scale, a more generous attitude to pensions may confer the same attractive power on Labour here that it did there. The second factor may be a local one. The Labour vote in Dunedin is heaviest in those generations which felt the influence of the depression, and this may have produced interactions between generations. The fact that the two youngest age groups support National by a slight majority may represent a local reaction against the previous generation and the long Labour domination of the city electorates.

American surveys and Milne's 1957 Wellington survey have pointed to religion as an influence conditioning voting. The same trends were found in Dunedin Central as Table I shows, though they were not quite as marked.

TABLE I

Religion and Vote (Two party vote only)

	Vote	
Religion	Labour	National
Presbyterian	49%	51%
Anglican	41%	59%
Roman Catholic	60%	40%
Others	60%	40%
No Religion	50%	50%

Labour attracted more of the Roman Catholic voters since they made up 17 per cent of the Labour vote as opposed to 12 per cent of the National vote. Anglicans on the other hand favoured

National, making up 26 per cent of its vote, as compared with 17 per cent of the Labour vote. Where, in Wellington Central, the remaining denominations supported National, in Dunedin they supported Labour partly because Presbyterianism, the local denomination, is considered as a separate group and a group very evenly divided between the parties.

It is now a commonplace of psephology in other countries that class is a potent influence on voting. Such findings are very difficult to check in New Zealand because weapons forged overseas are not always accurate in hunting out social groupings or classes in the New Zealand environment. There is even doubt in some quarters that the prey actually exists, and certainly social barriers are far less marked, far less tangible than in Britain or some other countries where classes differ in attitude, accent and way of life. The most that can be said is that classes, or social groups, do exist in New Zealand in the sense that society is to some extent socially stratified. When the electors of Dunedin Central are grouped on occupational lines it is found that these groups do have very different voting habits. In every case men and single women are included in the groups on the basis of their own occupation, and, though feminists may despair, married women are included on the basis of their husband's occupation.

Table II indicates a clear division in voting patterns between the professional and business groups, and the 'blue collar' workers, whether skilled or unskilled. Between these two groups comes the 'buffer zone' formed by the 'white collar' workers, who are, on the economic side, little if at all better off than the workers, but whose status aspirations are to the groups above them rather than to those below. In this middle position their votes show a mediating tendency, being fairly evenly divided, though with a slight majority going to National, and having a lower proportion than any other group voting for Social Credit. Each party draws the basis of its support from different sections of the community, but both of them must also, if they are to get a majority, draw support from this intermediate group. They therefore frame their policies so as to appeal to it.

The occupational and social group division of the vote is in many respects similar in Britain, just as is the tendency for different religious groups to lean towards certain parties. It would appear therefore from this survey, that the New Zealand voter

TABLE II
Vote and Occupational Group

Group[2]	Labour	National	Party Social Credit	No.
1. Upper professional and company directors	12%	86%	2%	59
2. Lower professional, self employed, and business people	25%	67%	8%	161
3. 'White collar', and 'uniform' workers	44%	55%	1%	91
4. Skilled and semi-skilled 'blue collar' workers	74%	15%	11%	142
5. Unskilled 'blue collar' workers	87%	8%	5%	60
Totals	244	236	33	513

does not differ fundamentally from his British cousin even though the politics on which he casts his vote differ in many respects, as does his social and economic environment. The rest of the survey will go far to confirm this preliminary impression.

II Sources of Information

The electors of Dunedin Central were asked where they got most of their information about the election and a list of alternatives was read out to them.[3] The answers showed that the newspapers were, for supporters of all parties, the most important single source of information, though Nationalists tended to rely on them rather more than Labour supporters. The rather general source

[2] The scale is based on a modified and contracted version of a social status scale worked out by A. A. Congalton (See R. J. Havighurst, *Studies of Children and Society in New Zealand*, Christchurch 1954, Appendix A.1.) This scale was based on social ranking. The main modification of Congalton's scale is to consider 'white collar' and 'uniform' workers together, instead of in order of rank. Group 1 includes doctors, dentists, veterinarians, accountants, lawyers and architects who have their own practices, together with directors or owners of large businesses. Group 2 includes all other professional people, owners of small businesses, and all employees of business firms from executive down to the level of traveller. Group 3 includes office, sales and clerical workers, policemen, customs officers, and storemen. These groups, though tentative, do appear to correspond to observable New Zealand stratification more clearly than would a grouping on English or American lines.

[3] In analysing this and the next few questions the views of all electors, voters and non-voters alike, are considered, the non-voters being allocated on the basis of the party they said they would have supported if they had voted. The totals are therefore slightly higher than those for voters only, being respectively—253 Labour, 249 National, and 34 Social Credit. Three non-voters did not know which party they would have supported and are not considered.

of 'talking to people' came next as a source of information, closely followed by the radio, while party pamphlets and meetings played very little part at all. Labour supporters were rather more prone than were Nationalists to get their information from the radio or conversations, the people talked to being mostly workmates in the case of men, and husbands in the case of married women.

TABLE III

Sources of Information

Source	Labour	Party National	Social Credit
From the newspapers	41%	56%	53%
From talking to people	25%	18%	12%
From listening to the radio	20%	16%	18%
From reading party pamphlets	4%	2%	3%
From going to meetings	2%	1%	3%
Combinations (mostly radio and newspaper)	3%	3%	9%
None of these/no information	5%	4%	2%
Totals	100% (253)	100% (249)	100% (34)

Before the election campaign began 52 per cent of the sample of 1000 voters interviewed by the Gallup Poll had stated that they intended to go to meetings addressed by the candidates in their electorate, and 41 per cent replied in answer to another question that they thought they would go and hear the party leaders if they spoke locally. Assuming that, as is quite likely, the electors of Dunedin Central would have expressed similar good intentions, they did not fulfil them, for only one-twelfth of the people in this sample, 14 per cent of the Labour supporters and 10 per cent of the National supporters, had actually been to any meetings at all. Not only did more Labour supporters go to meetings but those who did go went to more than did the National attenders. Two-thirds of the Labour supporters who had been to meetings attended more than one, compared with only just over a third among the National supporters who had been to any. The average was 2·4 meetings for Labour supporters and 1·7 for Nationalists.

Not all the people attending meetings had been to hear local candidates. In fact only just over half of the major party attenders had heard them, and only one man had heard all four. Almost as many had been to hear one or more of the national leaders of the parties as had heard the local candidates, while a third of those who had been to meetings had wandered into nearby electorates for their entertainment or information. Among Labour voters there was little difference between the sexes in respect of attendance at meetings but among Nationalists men were more likely to attend than women, while in both parties it was people in the age groups stretching from forty-one to sixty-five who were the most likely to have attended election meetings. Young people were a low proportion of the attenders. Young or old, male or female, the people who went to meetings were for the most part people who were strongly committed to their party. Changers and loosely committed voters were not strongly represented.

As the table on sources of information shows, radio has clearly displaced the old hustings. The intentions of people in respect of listening to broadcasting as revealed by the Gallup Poll were over-fulfilled, unlike intentions about meetings. Clearly it is easier to leave a radio on than to go out to a meeting. In the Gallup Poll 37 per cent had said they would 'practically never' listen to campaign broadcasts, but in Dunedin Central only 26 per cent of the Labour, National and Social Credit supporters taken together had heard no broadcasts. In each party the majority of these 'non-listeners' were women. Most of those who heard broadcasts had heard something from both major parties, though with a slight tendency to hear more of, and perhaps to listen more closely to, their own side. The average ratio was nearly two broadcasts of the elector's own side to just over one of the other. The interviewees were asked how many speakers, and whom they remembered having heard, and where necessary were prompted with the names of Messrs Holyoake, Marshall, Nash, Skinner, Matthews and O'Brien. They were not prompted beyond this, so that, for the other speakers, the information as to who was heard relates to who was remembered or who made an impression and is not an absolutely complete list. Of the supporters of the three parties who had heard broadcasts, 9 per cent had heard only Mr. Nash of the 'big three', 8 per cent had heard only Mr. Holyoake, and a mere 2 per cent only Mr. Matthews; 40 per cent had heard two of the big three, the great majority of these having heard Mr. Nash and Mr. Holyoake, and 33 per cent had heard the leaders of all three parties. The remaining 8 per cent either stated definitely that they had heard none of the three leaders or stated that they had heard broadcasts but could not remember whom. The other speakers with two-hour broadcasts did not attract anything like this wide audience, though Mr. Nordmeyer's two-hour broadcast from St. Kilda had been heard by 25 per cent of those who had listened to the radio broadcasts, a slight majority of these being Labour supporters, possibly because it was a local meeting in an electorate of some considerable local interest. The figures for the remaining two-hour broadcasts are very small. Mr. O'Brien had the next largest audience, but a total of only nineteen people mentioned having heard him speak. For the bulk of the fifteen-minute broadcasts the number of people who remembered specific speakers was very small, though the difficulty of remembering names is greatly increased here. It is, however, particularly striking that only nine Labour supporters remembered having heard Mr. Connolly, the sitting member for the electorate, make his broadcast.

The electors were also asked which of the local newspapers they read regularly. The results appear to confirm the conjecture in the chapter on the Press that the evening paper is read more by the workers than the morning paper. The local morning paper, the *Otago Daily Times*, was read by 78 per cent of the National voters, and 53 per cent of the Labour voters, while the *Evening Star* was read by 69 per cent of the National supporters and 83 per cent of the Labour supporters, the overlap being caused by the proportion of people who read both papers regularly. Incidentally, few electors supplemented their daily newspaper diet with extra calories from the political periodicals. *Freedom*, the National Party paper, which appeared weekly at the time of the election, was read by only 2·4 per cent of the total number

TABLE IV

Reading of Editorials and Correspondence Columns*

Editorials				Letters to the Editor		
Labour	Party Nat.	Soc. Cred.	Frequency	Labour	Party Nat.	Soc. Cred.
37%	35%	21%	Every day	52%	44%	67%
24%	29%	46%	Twice a week	25%	29%	15%
25%	31%	30%	Less	17%	20%	18%
14%	5%	3%	Never	6%	7%	—

* This table covers only those people who read a newspaper regularly.

interviewed, while the *New Zealand Guardian*, the Social Credit monthly, was read by only 1·3 per cent.

In view of the fact that the political bias of the newspapers normally comes out only in editorials, and in view also of the political discussion which goes on in the correspondence columns, it is interesting to discover what proportion of people do in fact read these two parts of the newspaper.

In fact both are read by a majority of the newspaper readership during the course of the week, though the correspondence columns are more popular than are the editorials and particularly among Labour and Social Credit supporters.

III *The Essential Differences between the Parties*

During the election campaign a considerable amount of attention centred on the question of the differences between Labour and National, with each party attempting to demonstrate to the electorate that it differed from the other. Mr. Holyoake challenged the audience at many of his meetings to say to his face that there was no difference between the two main parties. However, the Gallup Poll still indicated that, though no one took up Mr. Holyoake's challenge, many people were puzzled about the differences. Confronted with the statement: 'Some people say there isn't much difference between Labour and National', and asked whether they agreed with it, one-third of the 1000 people interviewed stated that they did agree.

The electors of Dunedin Central were also asked how much difference they thought existed between the parties and a list of possible degrees of difference was read out to them. Only one-fifth of those interviewed believed that there was a great deal of difference between the two parties, while exactly half believed that there was 'little', 'very little' or 'no' difference between them. When these figures are broken down into party groups, it is found that the National supporters were more inclined than the Labour supporters to believe that there is either a 'great deal' or a 'reasonable amount' of difference between their two parties: 61 per cent of them believed this compared with 41 per cent of the Labour electors. This would indicate that in stressing the differences between the parties National was not sowing its seeds upon stony ground while Labour could with profit have done rather more work in this field among its own supporters.

TABLE V

Differences between Labour and National

Party Supported

Amount	Labour	National	Social Credit
'A great deal of difference'	18%	26%	9%
'A reasonable amount'	23%	35%	21%
'Little difference'	23%	19%	26%
'Very little'	30%	18%	15%
'None'	4%	1%	26%
Don't know and no answer	2%	1%	3%
Totals	100%	100%	100%
	(253)	(249)	(34)

There is always the possibility of course, and to some it will appear a probability, that National supporters believe more strongly in the reality of party differentiation, not because of the party stress on it, but because they feel initially that their preference for National differentiates them personally from supporters of Labour, and desire that this differentiation shall have objective grounds. Social Credit was also carrying on a propaganda campaign on the same subject, its theme being: 'there is no difference between Labour and National'. In fact only about a quarter of the Social Crediters in the sample actually believed this, and some were even prepared to go to the other extreme and state that there was a great deal of difference, or at least a reasonable amount.

The next question on the questionnaire followed up by asking all electors, except those who thought there was no difference between the parties, what struck them as being the most important difference. Answering this question caused some puzzlement. Faced with it ninety-one electors, or nearly a fifth of the 502 supporters of the two major parties, were unable to think of any difference at all. Many of these people had replied 'very little', to the first question, so they simply repeated this or gave such replies as 'There is as much difference as there is between Woolworths and McKenzies'; or 'I'm damned if I know'. However, eight of them had earlier stated that there was a great deal of difference, and a further twenty-two had said that there was a reasonable amount. Two-thirds of both these groups were supporters of the National Party, which strengthens the hypothesis that it is their emotional involvement with their party and their opposition to the Labour Party which causes them to assert that the parties differ. Even though they were not asked the second question, some of the people who thought that there was no difference between the parties produced, in unsolicited comments, a more rational justification for their attitude. One reply is fairly typical if better expressed than most: 'In the twenties there was a big gap between the parties, but I see it closing more each election until this one, when it has completely closed. They could change speeches without anyone noticing it.' Disillusionment was the mood of most of these believers in party similarity.

TABLE VI

The Essential Differences between National and Labour

	Party Supported	
Difference	*Labour*	*National*
Labour stands for the workers or the less well-off. National for the farmers/bosses/well-off/or capitalists	41%	7%
Labour stands for socialism or State control. National stands for freedom or private enterprise	5%	39%
Differences centre on taxation	4%	10%
Differences centre on import controls	5%	4%
Differences centre on social security	5%	4%
Differences centre on relative honesty	1%	6%
Other	16%	12%
Don't know and can't think of any	19%	17%
Said initially 'no difference'	4%	1%
Totals	100%	100%
	(253)	(249)

The remaining interviewees, those supporters of the two major parties who were able to think of a difference, mostly produced party stereotypes, and two of these stand out head and shoulders above the others. Labour supporters tend to view the differences between the parties in human, group interest or occupational and monetary terms. National supporters, on the other hand, view the parties in terms of party dogma and see Labour as the party of socialism, and their own as the party encouraging freedom and private enterprise. This may, of course, be simply a more impersonal way of looking at the basic social division, or it may be a way of attempting to cover up that division, but whatever the explanation the antithesis between the two main stereotypes is quite marked. Differences between the parties in New Zealand, as in Britain and the U.S.A., are not necessarily related to specific contemporary policies, but are attitude formations long accreted. The three following differences on the table, all of them stressed by small proportions compared to the numbers using stereotypes, relate to specific policy differences. On taxation for example nearly all those citing this as the most important difference viewed Labour as a 'high tax' party, National as the party of reductions. On import controls Labour was viewed as the party of controls, National as the party of freer trade, while on the third, social security, Labour was viewed as the party initiating new developments or likely to spend more, a tendency which some National supporters thought would lead to the danger of 'spoiling the workers' and 'fostering idleness' or to 'hopeless extravagance'. On the taxation difference, and on the question of relative honesty, the views of supporters of the two main parties differ, since markedly more National than Labour supporters stress these. Both these two differences relate in some measure to the 1958 Budget, and it is presumably here that Press and National Party propaganda would be able to exercise an influence. The final category of replies, the 'other' group, includes a collection of diverse views. For example, four people thought that the National Party was composed of 'gentlemen' or men of 'better breeding, education and background', and a very few mentioned specific policy differences such as the Nelson railway or voluntary unionism.

IV *Party Policy*

In a country where a two-party system is firmly established, the voter has, for all practical purposes, only the alternative of supporting one or other of the main parties. An abstention, or a vote for a minor party, is reflected as the subtraction of a vote from one major party and so ultimately helps the other. In view of this limited range of choice it is quite probable that some voters will support a party on the grounds that it is the lesser of two evils, many on the grounds that it is good enough. In neither case does the voter believe that it is the height of perfection. This means that the average voter probably will not approve of every

item in the policy of the party he votes for, and is even less likely
to disapprove of every item in the policy of the other party. The
doctrine of the 'mandate' may be a necessary one if democracy is
not to deteriorate into an endless series of referenda, but it is not
a doctrine which accords with the facts of the electoral situation.

It was not possible to examine fully this situation in the 1960
election because policy differences between the parties were not
numerous and many of those which did exist were questions of
degree and qualification, not of clear opposition. However an
illustration is provided by five policy statements taken from party
manifestos and propaganda, on which the electors of Dunedin
Central were asked two questions. Electors were first of all asked
which party they thought would have made each statement in
order to assess not only how discerning each individual voter was,
but also how effectively the parties had been able to put their
views across to the electorate. In analysing the answers to the
questions the views of Labour and of National supporters were
considered separately.

TABLE VII

Attribution of Policy Statements: Labour Supporters[4]

Statement	Made by				
	Lab.	Nat.	S.C.	None	Don't Know
The Nelson railway is a necessary project	84%	2%	—	—	14%
Price Control should be used where necessary	69%	11%	2%	—	18%
Membership of trade unions should be made voluntary	8%	67%	4%	1%	20%
There should be stronger measures against juvenile delinquency	17%	67%	1%	1%	14%
There should be more scope for private enterprise	17%	61%	5%	1%	16%

If the statements are arranged in the tables in the order in
which they are most clearly recognized as having been made by
one party, the resulting pattern indicates that electors are most
likely to recognize statements which have been made by their own

[4] To avoid a multiplication of columns the small number of electors who
gave more than one party, but included in this number the correct one, are
included in the column for that party.

party. Thus the two statements most clearly attributed by Labour supporters are the one on the Nelson railway, which is hardly surprising since the issue had been well to the fore for some time before the election, and the statement on price control. The clarity of this second attribution is very surprising since the policy intention was little mentioned during the campaign. It was certainly a statement in the abridged manifesto sent to every householder, and had been in the news some time before at the time of the imposition of price control on meat, but it cannot be said to have been featured. The three National Party statements are all correctly attributed by about two-thirds of the Labour electors, though on each of them, just as there had been on the two Labour Party statements, there is a fairly constant proportion of don't knows and mistaken allocations, adding up in each case to a fifth or more of the total number of Labour electors.

TABLE VIII

Attribution of Policy Statements: National Supporters

	Made by				
Statement	Lab.	Nat.	S.C.	None	Don't Know
There should be more scope for private enterprise	1%	87%	1%	—	11%
The Nelson railway is a necessary project	86%	4%	—	—	10%
There should be stronger measures against juvenile delinquency	6%	80%	2%	—	12%
Membership of trade unions should be made voluntary	6%	72%	3%	—	19%
Price control should be used where necessary	50%	23%	2%	—	25%

The Nationalists are slightly more perspicacious than their Labour counterparts, but even here there is an irreducible minimum of 10 per cent or more who are unable to say which party made the statements, and on one National Party statement this proportion goes as high as a fifth, an indication that the voluntary unionism issue had not caught the public imagination. Once again the statement which is most clearly recognized is one from their own party, but it is followed by the ever newsworthy

Nelson railway. The statement on price control clearly caused a good deal of puzzlement.

The next question, on individual agreement or disagreement with the policy statement, also reveals interesting trends. In the tables the statements are arranged so that those with which most people in each party agreed are at the head of the list, those with which most people disagreed are at the bottom.

TABLE IX

Agreement with Policy Statements: Labour Supporters

| | | Reaction | |
Statement	Agree	Disagree	No Opinion
Price control should be used where necessary	95%	2%	3%
There should be stronger measures against juvenile delinquency	83%	13%	4%
There should be more scope for private enterprise	75%	16%	9%
The Nelson railway is a necessary project	58%	19%	23%
Membership of trade unions should be made voluntary	34%	54%	12%

The answers indicate that many people do not stand 'four square' on the party line, a tendency which is particularly clear with the Labour group, for although the most popular statement with them is one from their own party policy, it is followed by two statements, admittedly in rather general and undefined terms, from National party policy and propaganda. The Nelson railway, so vigorously forwarded by the Labour Party, has the support of only a bare majority of Labour supporters, with nearly a quarter having no opinion on it; and a proposal for voluntary unionism, which Labour strongly opposed during the campaign, is approved of by a third of the Labour supporters in this sample.

The tendency is similar, among the National supporters, though they do not stray quite so far from the party line. They approve wholeheartedly of private enterprise, but follow it with an item approved in Labour propaganda. Next come two other National Party statements, though a fifth either disagree with or have no opinion about both of them, and the second Labour statement is condemned, though by no means roundly

TABLE X

Agreement with Policy Statements: National Supporters

		Reaction	
Statement	Agree	Disagree	No Opinion
There should be more scope for private enterprise	92%	5%	3%
Price control should be used where necessary	86%	9%	5%
There should be stronger measures against juvenile delinquency	81%	16%	3%
Membership of trade unions should be made voluntary	77%	16%	7%
The Nelson railway is a necessary project	17%	64%	19%

since a third do not stand on the strict party positions. It would seem then that the *a priori* reasoning at the beginning of this section is justified. While the majority of electors approve on balance of policy items taken from their own party's policy, this approval can be unenthusiastic, and is not necessarily combined with condemnation of the policy of the opposing party. This they can approve of too.

V *Issues*

In an election which was quiet and unspectacular it is interesting to discover what the electors of Dunedin Central thought was the most important issue. Inevitably, because of this quietness, there were some who saw no issue at all. Of the supporters of the two major parties, 18 per cent replied that they did not know what the most important issue was, and a further 15 per cent answered that in their opinion there was no one issue which stood out among the others. Taken together, these two groups totalled one third of the two major party groups. The remaining two-thirds were, however, prepared to nominate one particular issue as having been more important than the others, as were most of the Social Crediters.

To those who recognized an issue, one seemed almost overwhelmingly important: taxation. This was mentioned as the most important issue by nearly three-tenths of all those interviewed. No other issue came anywhere near it, and, in fact, few others were mentioned by more than 5 per cent of the sample.

TABLE XI

The Most Important Issue

| | Party Supported | | |
Issue	Labour	National	Social Credit
Taxation	28%	27%	35%
Import controls	5%	4%	—
Nelson railway	4%	5%	3%
Defending private enterprise	—	10%	—
State of overseas funds in 1957	2%	2%	3%
Cost of living	2%	2%	3%
Voluntary unions	2%	2%	—
Broken promises	2%	2%	3%
Monetary reform	—	—	12%
Other issues	18%	18%	12%
There was no issue	17%	12%	12%
Don't know	20%	16%	17%

Cost of living, a perennial election issue, received surprisingly little mention or comment this time. The 'other' issues included several of no great significance, another indication that this was not a dramatic election. Some of the issues stressed by the National Party in the course of the campaign received very little mention in this or any other category. Defence policy, for example, was mentioned by only two people, one of whom was under the impression that the National Party would restore compulsory military training. The Bill of Rights was mentioned by only one person who thought that, once it was passed, New Zealand could never have another socialist government. The vexed question of the overseas posts was mentioned by only three people.

The results of this question are surprising when compared with a Gallup Poll taken in September for the *Auckland Star*. The voters were then presented with a list of issues specially drawn up by the *Star* and were asked: 'Which topics on this list seem most important to you, so important that they might affect the way you vote this year?' The three issues deemed most important by those interviewed were the cost of living, taxation, and changes in the liquor laws. The important place held by the liquor laws on this list is explained by the fact that they had just been discussed in Parliament. In the Dunedin survey only two people mentioned them. Similarly, the way in which the taxation issue had come further to the fore between Gallup in September and the survey in November is explained by the progress of the campaign itself, the way in which National hammered the theme, while Labour failed to produce a dramatic policy which would have ousted it from the centre of the stage. However, the much lower level of importance attached to the cost of living by November can only be explained by the difference between the two questions and the different interviewing methods used. In the Gallup Poll the electors were presented with a list and asked to pick the most important issue. This method would minimize any tendency to say that there was no issue and possibly encourage electors to pick one at random. If this happened cost of living was almost fated to be a popular choice.

At the end of the questionnaire the electors were asked another related question: why in their opinion the National Party had won the election. The aim of this question was not so much to reveal objective truth, as to assess general public impressions, since such impressions are not only a means of checking once again on what issues were thought to be important, but also shed some light on the politics of the next few years. After the last election the Opposition launched an onslaught on what it considered to be the means used by the Labour Party to secure power. This attack depended for its success partly on the skill of the Opposition campaign, partly on the facts of the two party cases, and partly on how people had felt about these facts in 1957 before either National campaign or Labour Budget interposed. The way people felt in Dunedin Central immediately after the election in 1960 is shown in the table which lists the views as numbers and not as percentages since some electors produced more than one reason for the victory.

A clear pattern emerges of the negative nature of the 1960 election. In spite of the fact that the question was loaded on the positive side, since it asked for reasons for a victory, explanations for a defeat in fact predominated among the answers. Electors of all parties agreed that the most important reason why National won the election was heavy taxation by the Labour Party, and to be more specific, the 1958 Budget, which was mentioned by forty-two electors. Nationalists commented more on the faults and failings of the party in power than on the virtues of their own party, and those who did mention National's ability or policy

TABLE XII

Why the National Party Won the Election

| | Party | | |
Reason	Mentions by Lab. voters	Mentions by Nat. voters	Mentions by S.C. voters
Taxation	77	63	17
The 1958 Budget	24	17	1
The virtues of N. Party leader, past administration, and organization	7	43	3
Betrayal by/indifference of/ Labour supporters	43	4	—
Broken promises	7	38	2
General dissatisfaction with Labour	12	29	7
Import controls	14	18	2
National Party promises	20	9	3
The £100 rebate	7	21	2
Vote splitting by Social Credit	24	5	2
Normal swing/time for a change	11	15	2
Age of Mr. Nash	7	9	—
Other reasons	36	34	8
Don't know/No answer	12	9	2
Number of Respondents	(249)	(243)	(34)

were outbalanced by the Labour supporters who thought that their party lost because many Labour voters, particularly the young ones, did not bother to vote. Promises and bribes on the part of the winning party, the traditional salve applied by the defeated to ease their discomfort, were mentioned by just over thirty. It may have been that a contrast between Labour's high taxation and National's promise to reduce it was implicit in the minds of some of those who gave taxation as the reason for Labour's defeat. This was not, however, specifically mentioned and the general concurrence is striking. When positive and negative formulations of the promises/Budget/tax issue are totalled, some version of essentially the same answer is found to have been offered by nearly half of Labour and well over half of the National and Social Credit supporters.

VI *The Party Leaders*

It is generally agreed that, compared with the policy and the 'image' of a party, a leader's role in winning votes is a minor one. Yet in a system where two parties are evenly balanced, minor factors all contribute something to election victories. Not only might a powerful leader attract a few votes to his party through his personal stature, but he could also modify slightly the image of that party in the public eye. It may be, for example, that the public view that Labour is a party of older men than National, a view which has earlier been shown to be mistaken, is in part produced by the age of the party leader.

In an attempt to discover what views the public had on the leaders of the two main parties, the electors of Dunedin Central were asked: 'Regardless of your own party preference whom do you prefer as a leader and Prime Minister, Mr. Holyoake or Mr. Nash?' The answers to this question suggest that to a large extent the preference for a leader is merely a reflection of the prior choice of party. The majority of the electors, 79 per cent of the National supporters and 82 per cent of the Labour supporters, preferred the leader of their own party to that of the other. Of those who preferred the leader of the other party, a slight majority preferred Mr. Nash, for 16 per cent of the National supporters preferred him to Mr. Holyoake, and 5 per cent had no preference either way or disliked both. The corresponding figures for Labour supporters were 13 per cent preferring Mr. Holyoake, and 5 per cent with no preference. If the supporters of the two parties are taken together, then Mr. Nash is preferred, but by a narrow margin. Only if we add in the Social Credit and Independent groups, who were compelled to choose between two leaders who were not theirs, does Mr. Nash have a real lead at all, since 74 per cent of these two groups preferred him.

The fact that the margin of the sample preferring Mr. Nash to Mr. Holyoake is as slight as 8 per cent, with 6 per cent having no preference, is surprising when one remembers that Mr. Nash had been before the public eye for three years as Prime Minister. It is also surprising when compared with the answers to a rather different question asked by the Gallup Poll before the campaign began: 'As between Mr. Nash and Mr. Holyoake whom do you consider to be the better campaigner?' Then, 55 per cent considered Mr. Nash to be the better campaigner, 30 per cent Mr. Holyoake, 10 per cent both equal, and 5 per cent had no opinion. Even though the questions are rather different it would still seem that two factors had been operating between the two surveys. Probably the campaign had helped to improve the standing of Mr. Holyoake, and it may even have slightly harmed Mr. Nash's standing. More important, as the election approached, party allegiances probably tightened, resulting in an increasing reluctance to admit that the other party had the better leader.

After the question on preference, the electors were asked why they preferred one leader to the other in order to secure a series of views on both leaders. Since many electors produced more than one view, the 'images' are listed numerically rather than as percentages.

The resulting pattern in Table XIII reveals that Mr. Nash's main political virtue, according to the electors of Dunedin Central, is his experience, which can be combined with the fact that he is, according to many of them, New Zealand's only statesman. The number of electors who emphasized experience was, however, outweighed by the number stressing the reverse side of this image, Mr. Nash's age. This was commented on by many, and only those specifically stating that Mr. Nash was too old have been listed. The remaining views on Mr. Nash need little comment except an expression of surprise that mention of his financial abilities came so low down the list of favourable views. The unfavourable replies in the 'other' category included those of six people who thought that Mr. Nash was either a Communist, or had Communistic inclinations, a clear demonstration of the impossibility of pleasing everyone. The group also included a woman who was convinced that Mr. Nash had been in business as a tailor, had robbed his partner, and was still wearing the suits he had then stolen. Evidently some exotic plants flourish in subconscious hot-houses.

In contrast with Mr. Nash, Mr. Holyoake was not as well known, nor had he made quite as clear an impression upon the elector. Cartoonists find it difficult to draw Mr. Holyoake: the electors of Dunedin Central found it difficult to describe him. In their view his chief political virtue is that he is young, or more frequently, 'younger', a virtue he acquired mainly by contrast with Mr. Nash. In this election, however, it would seem that of the two chief contestants, Mr. Holyoake managed to project the

TABLE XIII

Images of Party Leaders

Mr. Nash	*Mentions by* *Lab. voters*	*Mentions by* *Nat. voters*
A. Favourable:		
Experienced	52	13
Humanitarian	27	1
Able/good/leader	23	9
Statesman/respected internationally	17	6
Sincere/genuine	20	2
Good Christian	12	3
Skillful financier	11	2
'I just like him'	7	1
Other	11	4
B. Critical:		
Too old	38	71
Unreliable	1	13
Too fond of overseas trips	1	8
'I just don't like him'	1	8
Other	—	11
Mr. Holyoake		
A. Favourable:		
Young/'younger'	16	63
Able/good leader	1	23
Good speaker	2	19
Honest/keeps promises	1	17
Forceful/vigorous/energetic	5	15
'I just like him'	—	8
Other	3	21
B. Critical:		
Not tried/not proved himself	16	13
Opinionated/bumptious/sarcastic	21	6
Weak leader/not popular in own party	7	5
'I just don't like him'	9	1
Other	13	3
Other		
No preference	12	12
Prefer own leader for party reasons	9	18
Don't know	6	5

stronger image of energy and vigour, for more people made this sort of comment about him than about Mr. Nash. The remaining comments, favourable or unfavourable, need no explanation, except that several electors commented that Mr. Holyoake was untried or had not yet proved himself. For want of a better category this is included with the unfavourable views, but in fact most of these comments were not critical ones. There was the usual assortment of views in the 'other' category.

While the answers to these two questions indicate that Mr. Nash was better known than Mr. Holyoake and was preferred as leader and Prime Minister by a small majority, they do not indicate that he was the positive vote winner that many Labour officials had expected him to be. He can, however, be said to have influenced, if not actually won, two votes in this sample. When asked, 'What was your most important reason for voting the way you did?' two Labour voters, one voting for the first time and coming from a home background which was National, and the other a changer from National, mentioned Mr. Nash. The corresponding number in the whole electorate would be extremely small, certainly not more than a hundred votes, yet the personality of the leader clearly did have a slight effect. Mr. Holyoake was not mentioned in this question, though all but two of the changers to National stated in answer to the earlier question that they preferred Mr. Holyoake to Mr. Nash as leader and Prime Minister. There was in 1960, however, little to indicate that the leader was a factor of any but slight importance in vote-winning in the election.

VII *Mechanics of Voting*

Voting surveys in other countries have indicated that the actual election campaign has very little influence in winning or losing votes, since the majority of voters have made up their minds how to vote well before it begins and during the campaign stand 'unshook amidst a bursting world'. For real confirmation of this fact a survey with two interviews, one immediately before the campaign and one immediately after it, would be necessary. With a one-interview survey the best that can be done is to ask the elector after the election 'When did you decide which party or candidate you would vote for?' Such a question is faulty in some respects since it inevitably exaggerates the looseness of party allegiance, making it appear that people who eventually make up their minds to vote for their usual party have, at some time, been in danger of changing. What it exactly states is when people 'feel' they had made up their minds.

TABLE XIV

*Time of Decision**

	Vote		
Time	Labour	National	Social Credit
Before the 1957 election	62%	67%	36%
Since the 1957 election but before 1960	10%	15%	12%
In 1960 up to the month before the election	11%	8%	19%
In the last month, but before the last week	6%	2%	6%
In the last week but before the day	6%	4%	15%
On election day	5%	4%	12%
Totals	100%	100%	100%
	(244)	(236)	(33)

* This table, like the others in this section, includes only those who voted.

In this case, plainly, three-quarters of the major party voters felt that they had decided before the actual campaign, although it does seem that Labour voters were slower than National to redetermine on their customary allegiance. More National than Labour voters had made up their minds before 1957, and a higher proportion of them had also decided since that election but before 1960. This, even though it exaggerates the proportion of uncommitted voters, is exactly what one might expect given the effect of the 1958 Budget, for the period after this Budget was Labour's nadir so far as political popularity was concerned. This fact receives striking confirmation from a Gallup Poll carried out in Dunedin in March 1959 by the firm which carried out the 1960 Gallup Polls. A quota sample of voters in the Dunedin metropolitan area was asked how they would vote if an election were held tomorrow, and 44 per cent replied National, 39 per cent Labour and 4 per cent Social Credit, while 7 per cent, mostly former Labour voters, replied that they would not vote at all, and a further 6 per cent were undecided. The Labour vote had therefore undergone a heavy decline from the 54 per cent of voters in the same area who had supported the party in 1957.

However, as prosperity revived in 1960, as memories of the Budget faded and as old political loyalties reasserted themselves,

Labour began to reconsolidate its strength and, in Dunedin Central at any rate, was rallying support in the course of 1960, in the month, and in the week before the election, as well as on election day itself, faster than National. This again is not unexpected, though it is not confirmed by the Gallup Poll quoted in the chapter on the campaign, which indicates that Labour gained no support during the course of the campaign. Whether this difference is due to the difference between a local survey and a national poll, or to the different methods used, is not clear.

Survey and poll do concur in indicating that the Social Credit Political League was going through an exaggerated version of the same process as Labour. The March 1959 Gallup Poll indicated that by then the Social Credit vote had fallen to a very low level, probably a normal tendency between elections since a proportion of Social Credit voters are not firm Social Crediters, but drifters from the two major parties who may drift away again between elections. This is indicated by the fact that those among the Social Credit voters in the 1960 survey who gave the main reason for their vote as a desire for monetary reform had mostly decided how to vote before 1960, while the people giving reasons which indicated revulsion from the two main parties tended to decide later. Probably also the tendency to a decline in Social Credit support revealed by the 1959 Gallup Poll was accelerated by the splits in the party and the resignation of Mr. Owen. Eventually Social Credit began to rise again, and its support picked up in the course of 1960, and with gathering momentum, in the course of the month and the week before the election. This rise brought the Social Credit vote in Dunedin Central above the 1957 level.

The table on time of decision indicates that most people have always known which party they would vote for. This is confirmed by a detailed comparison of the 1957 vote of those in the sample with their vote of 1960.

This comparison makes it clear that nine-tenths of those who cast a vote in 1957 voted the same way in 1960. Even though the majority of the inhabitants of Dunedin Central vote Labour they are in fact very conservative in their voting habits.

Stability of voting is, however, a thing which not only endures between two successive elections. For most people in New Zealand it is as in other countries, a life-long feature. Three-quarters of the major party voters, or 78·9 per cent of Labour voters and

71·4 per cent of Nationalists, who were interviewed in Dunedin Central had never voted for any other party in the whole course of their lives. Only 8·8 per cent of Labour voters and 18·8 per cent of Nationalists had voted for the other major party, and 3·9 per cent and 2·8 per cent respectively had voted for Social Credit. The former Liberals (6·6 per cent and 6·0 per cent) had split neatly along occupational lines between the parties.

TABLE XV

1957 Vote and 1960 Vote Compared

1957 *Vote*	Labour	National	1960 *Vote* Soc. Cred.	Indep.	Non-Voter
Labour	89·0%	6·4%	27·3%	41·7%	26·9%
National	2·9%	84·3%	6·0%	41·7%	30·8%
Social Credit	1·2%	1·3%	57·6%		3·8%
No vote (not entitled)	6·1%	7·6%	9·1%	16·6%	26·9%
No vote (entitled)	0·8%	0·4%			3·8%
No answer					7·8%
Totals	100%	100%	100%	100%	100%
	(244)	(236)	(33)	(12)	(26)

Stability on this massive scale makes 'changers', those people who change their votes between elections, small in number (forty-nine or 9 per cent of the voters in this sample), but extremely interesting. If the changes are totalled then Social Credit made a net gain of four, and the Independent of ten, five from Labour, five from National. Labour's net loss was twenty-six and National lost four. These bald totals, though they conform satisfactorily to electorate trends, do, however, underestimate the complexity of movements. Thus Labour lost in all thirty-six votes, fifteen to National, nine to Social Credit, five to the Independent and seven to non-voting, but it also won three voters back from Social Credit and seven from National, one of these commenting wryly, 'I voted National in 1957 and they lost, I voted Labour in 1960 and they lost; perhaps next time I'd better vote Communist.' Quite clearly the impressive swell of the electoral tide can conceal a complexity of eddies beneath its surface.

An analysis of the time of decision of these changers revealed that two-thirds of the fifteen people changing from Labour to

National had decided on their change before 1960, during Labour's 'low' period, while exactly the same proportion of those who changed to Labour had made up their minds in the course of 1960, Labour's 'high'. The indications seem clear that by 1960 Labour had stanched the flow of losses to National and was even able to secure a small transfusion in return. What it did not do was to stanch the flow to the Independent or to Social Credit, for all the Independent voters made up their minds in 1960, as did all the nine former Labour voters who voted for Social Credit. This would indicate what the Gallup Poll does not, that most of the votes Social Credit was winning in the campaign were taken from Labour.

The time of decision of changers from Labour to National points the finger of suspicion at the 1958 Budget. Suspicion becomes certainty when the answers given by the changers to the question 'What was your most important reason for voting the way you did?' are analysed. Ten of the twenty-four people who changed from Labour to National or Social Credit gave either taxation or the 1958 Budget as their reason. The rest gave a collection of answers; two stressed import restrictions, two stated that they had lost confidence in Labour, one of these mentioning the *Truth* case with the comment that 'There's no smoke without fire', four covered the complexity of their motives with the simple comment that it was time for a change, and one gave the question of State aid for church schools as his main reason for changing to Social Credit which had made more effective promises on this issue. The remaining reasons were minor. Five of the ten voters that Labour won back gave as their main reason the fact that Labour had done well in its term and deserved another turn, while three gave the candidate as their main reason, remaining pro-National in their attitudes, but approving strongly of Mr. Connolly, the Labour candidate. One of the remainder gave Mr. Nash as his main reason, the other, a former Social Credit voter, thought that National was likely to borrow too much. The changers had a few clear characteristics. Two-thirds of them were men and just 35 per cent of them came from the age groups under 41 compared with 36 per cent of the rest of the voters, while rather more of them were drawn from the higher occupational groups than in the rest of the sample. They were not quite as likely to have been to meetings or listened to broadcasts but this did not mean that they were not as well informed on the policy statements.

Changers shared the key role in deciding the 1960 election with non-voters. Unfortunately the twenty-six non-voters in this sample are not a representative group, being a much lower proportion of the sample than were their counterparts in the electorate. Yet they are not without interest. The reasons they gave for not voting were in most cases trivial ones, such as forgetting or being too busy, too lazy, or too ill, and in only one case, that of a former Labour voter who refused to go to the poll even when a party car called, is deliberate abstention indicated, though three others were conscientious non-voters feeling that they did not know enough about politics. However, though there is little support here for the 'non-voting for revenge' theory and 'non-voting through apathy' would better fit the facts of the sample, it is to be remembered that some people would find a direct question of this nature embarrassing so that it might not always have elicited true reasons.

When they were asked which party they would have supported if they had voted, thirteen of the non-voters replied National, nine Labour, and one Social Credit, while three did not know which party they would have voted for. The sample does not therefore reveal uncalled reserves of Labour support, but once again its incomplete nature should be remembered, as should the possible existence of a band-wagon effect, a tendency to identify with the winning party. In some respects the non-voters were a clearly defined group, for two-thirds of them were women, almost two-thirds were under forty-one and exactly half were not married, most of these living alone. With such distinctive characteristics it is unfortunate that the sample is too small and possibly too distorted to allow of pleasantly sweeping generalizations.

VIII *Conclusions*

New Zealanders like to think of themselves as being in many ways distinct, yet voting habits in the Dominion are very much the same as in Britain, and other countries. Voting is conditioned by factors such as religion and social grouping, and this survey reveals two large and relatively unchanging blocks of voters facing each other across the electoral lines, just as a similar survey in Britain would do. These lines are not often crossed, and the two blocks swell and contract in response to demographic trends or fundamental changes on the national scene rather than to the appeals of party leaders, or the circumstances of particular elections. As a result stability is the basic feature of the political scene. Although changes occur, they are produced by marginal changes on the part of those groups who do not vote, or the loosely committed who change sides.

Coming down to the specific case of the 1960 election as distinct from the general long-term patterns of voting, the survey indicates clearly some of the reasons for Labour's defeat. In Dunedin Central at any rate Labour was winning a majority neither of the important younger age groups nor of the new voters. Some elements of National Party policy were almost as popular with Labour supporters as they were with Nationalists, and Labour supporters were certainly less convinced than Nationalists about the differences between the parties, and hence possibly less attached emotionally to their own party, while Labour's leader did not have quite the expected drawing power. Yet, so far as the actual result went, all these reasons are unimportant when compared with the effect of the 1958 Budget and heavy taxation. A large proportion of the electors viewed this, an issue on which Labour was fighting on the defensive, as being the most important issue of the campaign, and taxation was the largest single reason given by changers away from Labour. The improvement of circumstances in 1960 did bring a few votes back to Labour and did lead to a reassertion of old loyalties among habitual supporters, but was not enough to check the losses to Social Credit, to the Independent, or to abstention which weakened Labour in Dunedin Central, and, in the case of the first and last of these factors, over the country as a whole.

PART FOUR

THE RESULTS

XI

THE UNUSUAL ELECTORATES

EXAMINING the fall of the votes after an election to find out
what happened is a regular practice among members of the
general public, newspapermen and politicians. By scanning
the rises and sags in the majorities of candidates, which are the
most easily and quickly obtained of comparisons between one
election and its predecessor, the observer hopes to find a meaningful pattern which will show him such things as why his party went
out, how a specific candidate survived or whether the existing
electoral balance will be easily upset. In short, a century of
popular elections has persuaded the expert and inexpert that
voting is so consistent that major questions can in large part be
answered by watching minor variations in the voting trend from
place to place and from group to group. This chapter will ask
the same questions of the figures for the 1960 election as would a
candidate or newspaper editor; but it can afford to take more
detail into account and consider longer before answering. And if
the essence of the scientific method is to know exactly something
which could have been guessed at, then New Zealand is a very
suitable country in which to try refining common knowledge of
voter performance.

Our party system is well established, with but one considerable
alteration—the replacement of the Liberals by Labour—in seventy
years. Therefore, most electors know their preferred party and,
in voting regularly for it, clearly affirm the dominant harmonies
against which discords are detected.

Though New Zealand appears remarkably homogeneous to
visitors, it is in fact diversified both in landscape and townscape.
The high educational level of its inhabitants, their mobility and
the elaborateness of their organs for economic co-operation and
protection make for rapid discovery of divergent sectional interests
and for sharp awareness of even small differences of social status
and income. This lively awareness in turn affects party choice. So
the political map, especially of the urban districts, is divided
with the utmost nicety into areas of like socio-economic situation

and party opinion. Given a country of voters who can and do sort themselves neatly into explicable categories, the analyst finds it correspondingly rewarding to find out which categories did what.

We are helped here by the New Zealand Electoral Department which has long made its returns, not just in the form of figures for the voting in each electorate, or, as in Australia, by subdivisions, but on the basis of the molecule of electoral action, the voting at each polling booth.[1] Like the more elaborate molecules, the booth can contain hundreds of the elector atoms. A very few city polling places record over 2000 votes, but urban booths average about four hundred while polling places registering a hundred or less are usual in farming regions. Booths draw on small districts, then, and the character of those districts can be well defined accordingly.

A programme of research under my direction at the University of Auckland has used these returns to trace the voting history of every polling booth in the Auckland urban region since 1899. This area now contains 441 booths; it covers fourteen electorates and much of two more, and includes nearly a fifth of all voters in New Zealand. Knowing the history and the performance in the 1960 election of such a large sample in such detail, it is possible to check and to elaborate generalizations derived from trends among electorates as such. Further studies from the University of Auckland have covered Taranaki polling places since 1890 and booths in the Waikato region from the turn of the century, so that our detailed knowledge is not confined to the city.

In addition, polling place figures have been analysed for Miramar in Wellington, St. Albans in Christchurch, and for Dunedin Central, besides the examination of booth figures grouped by suburbs within Wellington Central, Lyttelton and St. Kilda. Thus something at this intensive level is known of each of the four main centres. As an additional check, Hamilton was examined, for it represented a large town electorate and also enjoyed the only by-election between 1957 and 1960,[2] so permitting the comparison

[1] This term 'booth' is no longer strictly accurate. 'Polling place' is the correct term and each set of boxes and officer at the 'polling place'—there may be one, two, or even more sets—is a 'booth'. In practice, however, only one combined return of votes comes from any one polling place. For variety, therefore, both terms, booth and polling place can and will be used interchangeably to mean one place of polling.

[2] One candidate for the Clutha electorate died on the eve of the General Election of 1957 so that the contest in Clutha had to be postponed for a month until 18 January 1958. In the legal sense only there were thus two by-elections.

of booth voting at three points across the period which is particularly germane. Lastly, the Rotorua booths were analysed for the example of a mixed urban and rural constituency which changed hands.

Altogether, the polling place results for almost a third of all the electorates were used to underpin this analysis. This reinsurance was in part made possible by New Zealand's size, for there are strict limits to the amount of raw data one man, or even a team, can process. But the opportunity of taking a second, closer look by examining the booths depended also on this country having an efficient and co-operative Electoral Department accustomed to putting into print all the worthwhile figures it collects.

One last advantage enjoyed here by the analyst should be noticed, the virtual absence of all those variables introduced by vigorous political organization on the basis of religious division, racial distinction, language rights, the repudiation of some former metropolitan authority or the entanglements of federalism. There are no such powerful cross-currents as are stirred by the presence of the French and their religion in Canada, the negro majority in South Africa, old history and young Ulstermen in Ireland, or the system of states and a written constitution in Australia. Issues connected with Roman Catholicism in New Zealand did appear for a time in the late 1910s and early twenties. They have tinged the 1960 election. But as with racial questions, which are nearly encapsulated in the four Maori electorates and do not dominate politics even there, religion may faintly colour but does not shape New Zealand politics. This narrowing of the field helps the investigation of the remaining types of political motive and response. What is left, when such complications as states' rights or a nationalities question are absent, may nevertheless be complex enough. Casual observers of New Zealand can too readily assume that ours are the politics of homogeneity or, with somewhat more justice, of equality. Actually it is the economic inequalities and diversities of status and occupation in our society which are reflected in the voting, elaborately graded and sectionalized as that is. They can show forth with force and precision, however, because they are unobstructed in their workings by countervailing values of extrinsic origin.

Given that New Zealand favours the analyst with a clear view, what does he make of such traditional questions as: Who threw out the Government? Are we faced with an accident of electoral mathematics or was there a real change of opinion? Was this the result of the National Party's organization and campaign or, since Labour lost, of Labour's lacks? What was the effect of the third party? of individual campaigners? of election issues? And what did the electorate mean to do?

Such enquiries are made, not because the voting figures always lend themselves to a ready reply, but because candidates and political organizers need to know how effective their operations were, voters want to understand just how typical or untypical their voting intentions were, and newspapermen hope, among other things, to comment and advise on party actions by referring to the contents of 'the mandate' supposedly given by voters at the general election. An analyst, however, is rather in the position of Gertrude Stein on her deathbed. Miss Stein's last words ran: 'Yes, that is the answer; but what, what is the question?' He is confronted by a massive answer; which must be broken down into its components, whereupon the inquirer can test various questions to find if they fit the parts of the answer he has. When he gets a matching pair he must then see whether the two correspond to a demand for information and a usable reply. We can speed this process by choosing to find out first who dismissed the Labour Government in 1960, for this query in itself will serve to break down our information into convenient sections.

The Electorates which Ejected Labour

In the narrowest sense the Labour tenure ended because electors in seven seats, Gisborne, Hastings, Palmerston North, Rotorua, St. Albans, Tamaki and Wellington Central, all changed their member. This might appear an unusually sharp change in a House of eighty seats until it is discovered that, over the last half century, the party in power has gained or lost an average of ten seats at general elections. The depression election of 1935 cost Coalition Government supporters thirty-five seats and, in the three-way division of 1928, Reform numbers dropped by twenty-seven. Even if we omit these instances as quite exceptional, the average change only declines to seven seats, while the post Second World War average is six. The 1960 movement of seven constituencies is thus neither more nor less than the norm.

Still concentrating on the seats which changed members, it is reasonable to ask whether the voting there altered to an unusual degree. If it did, the result of the 1960 election in general could have been the product of special factors such as local issues, strong opposition candidates or a weak Government defence operating in these particular seats. To test this it is first necessary to find what was the most consistent feature of the general election, whether Labour voting losses or National gains, or perhaps simply more people staying away from the polls. Then the constituencies can be ranked by their share in this characteristic and the changing seven seats can be located as abnormally high in the list or simply average or even poor exemplars of the common denominator.

The outstanding characteristic of the 1960 general election proved to be loss from the Labour vote. It greatly exceeded movement towards the National ranks or towards Social Credit. Indeed, it much exceeded the second most prominent feature, the increase in those not voting. Electorates were therefore put in order according to their proportion of Labour loss, beginning with the steepest Labour decline as No. 1 and ending with the least as No. 80. On this basis, the seven electorates where Labour members were turned out ranked thus: Rotorua, 9; Wellington Central, 15; Gisborne, 25; Tamaki, 27; Palmerston North, 35; Hastings, 40; and St. Albans, 69. The first six were thus above the national median and only one fell below. It is clear that there was a more than normal Labour sag in the changing seats and especially in Rotorua and Wellington Central. On the other hand, five out of seven are nowhere near far enough from the halfway point to lead the observer towards explaining the result of the entire election in terms of forces that displayed themselves in these seats alone. If we account, say, for Tamaki's drop of 6·81 per cent by local factors, what are we to make of Heretaunga where 12·08 per cent of all those qualified to vote moved out of the Labour column?

The hope of the defeated as a party is always that whatever felled them should be the result, not of general causes, but of particular limited factors. Thus if the seven lost seats had ranked near the top, then Labour as a whole could have ceased asking 'What have *we* done?' and justifiably begun enquiring what the seven ex-members or their opponents or their electors did. Our information has shown that particular enquiries about local factors could suitably be launched in the cases of Rotorua and Wellington Central, which leaves the party as a whole with plenty to concern it. This information, however, came from a test applied only to a limited class of electorates—those which replaced their M.P.s. Other and more surprising local deviations could lie concealed among the remaining seventy-three untested electorates.

Locating the Real Exceptions

To find out whether this was so, some method had to be found for putting to one side factors which moved all the electorates similarly so that individual variations would be left standing clear. Again a ranking test proved useful. The eighty electorates were arranged according to their 1957 position in the battle of the parties, with the largest majority for Labour at one extreme and the greatest majority for National at the other. A ladder of eighty constituency rungs was made which descended from Southern Maori, with a Labour majority over National of 53·20 per cent, down through ever smaller Labour leads like the 2·89 per cent in St. Albans, then passed to small National leads and placed at the bottom the largest National-over-Labour figure of 29·76 per cent in Wallace. A ladder was similarly constructed according to the order in 1960. If all general trends between the two elections had operated evenly up and down New Zealand and all electorates had responded to them alike, then there would be no alteration between the ladder for 1957 and the ladder for 1960. The only thing that would differentiate the two ladders would be the marking of the division between the two parties some seven rungs higher up. The constituency rungs themselves would each continue in the same place. Of course, if general trends were weak and the election was really the result of cancelling out a whole congeries of conflicting local forces, each going its own way, then the rungs of the two ladders would not parallel each other at all. They would be all over the place and we should know we needed eighty quite separate explanations of what happened in November 1960.

When the two ladders were constructed and compared they proved to be generally like enough to make sudden changes in the position of certain electorates significant. The total jumps up or down of just thirteen electorates were found to be almost equivalent to the sum of the small adjustments in position of the other sixty-seven. The exceptional thirteen, which show a minimum movement of $\pm$ seven, are set out below.

TABLE I

Exceptional Alterations of Rank between 1957 and 1960

Changes favourable to Labour		Changes favourable to Social Credit	Changes favourable to National	
Nelson	+16	Hobson +27	Rotorua	−11
Marlborough	+11		Mt. Albert	−10
Fendalton	+10		Wgtn. Cent.	−9
			Patea	−9
Waitakere	+8		Bay of Plenty	−8
St. Kilda	+8		Manawatu	−8
Nth. Dunedin	+7			

Hobson shows up as having changed between 1957 and 1960 more unusually than any other electorate. To put it the other way round, whatever factor altered the position in Hobson so markedly was not a major factor in shaping the general election yet was peculiarly forceful in this local situation. Hobson showed a majority for National over Labour of 20·55 per cent of the qualified vote in 1957[3] when it ranked seventy-first or near the extreme of National triumph. Three years later Mr. V. F. Cracknell of Social Credit had moved into second place and National were only 9·07 per cent ahead, which put Hobson in the forty-fourth place on the list. To reach this position there must certainly have been local factors at work, for Social Credit in this constituency climbed over eleven times as fast as it did in the nation as a whole, while not only did Labour drop a heavy 9·50 per cent but National also declined by 3·71 per cent, one of the eleven cases where its share of the vote was down.

[3] The qualified vote is the total of those on the roll, and those who demonstrated to their Returning Officer that their votes should be allowed despite the omission of their names from the roll. It thus includes everyone qualified to vote, regardless of whether they did or not. Percentages calculated on this basis reveal not only to what extent voters shifted across party lines but also to what degree they moved out of voting altogether.

Hobson: Tradition, Person, and Place

The Hobson seat, as drawn for both the elections we are considering,[4] includes rather more than all the territory of the old
Bay of Islands electorate, which returned Captain Rushworth in
1928, 1931 and 1935 as the only candidate of the Country Party
to enter Parliament.[5] Captain Rushworth preached Douglas
Social Credit across the electorate in season and out. As a pleasant
and popular member, he left many active groups of his persuasion
behind him. Mr. C. W. Elvidge contested the electorate both in
1954 and 1957 and described in an interview how farmers, storekeepers and townsmen had held to their faith from Rushworth's
time, and acted as the nuclei round which the Social Credit
Political League was able to build up rapidly from lingering
debating groups to active branches of the real opposition party in
that area.

Mr. Elvidge's enthusiasm and success promoted him out of the
electorate and into organizing Social Credit's 1960 national
campaign as their national secretary. But the advantages of
Hobson's unique local tradition and the booming condition of
the party there secured just the right kind of candidate in 1960
to continue the ascent. As a public accountant, Mr. V. F. Cracknell, Mr. Elvidge's successor, was well placed to convince his
mainly farmer constituents of his special competence with
financial transactions, a subject which looms large in any Social
Credit speech. Those that heard him represent his party on the
air are widely agreed that his was the most persuasive, cultivated
address heard from that quarter. He had not long joined the
League but emphasized in the party organ that he had previously
studied Social Credit doctrine for nine years. What mattered
more was his rapid rise to Dominion councillor of the League and
member of the policy committee, his vigour in opening new
sub-branches, and his large acquaintance in Kaikohe and Keri
Keri, both electorate centres where he had businesses. To this,

---

[4] Electoral boundaries are supposed to be redrawn every five years after each
census, and usually are. Fortunately for this survey, the census years 1956 and
1961 fell before and after the pair of elections in 1957 and 1960 which we need
to compare and are thus the same for both contests.

[5] An advertised Independent, with Country Party leanings, was elected for
one term at Franklin in 1935, but Labour stood no candidate.

Mr. Cracknell, an indubitably handsome man, added activity in fourteen local bodies and associations, usually as secretary or president.

Moreover, Mr. Cracknell was fortunate to be presented with a stirring local issue to take sides about. Rural electorates in New Zealand have always responded strongly to appeals based on developing the country and when country seats were proportionately more numerous, methods and projects for development were the staple of party controversy. When, in addition, some public work with wide effects was to be sited in one place, the parochial competition to capture the project could be fierce. The question of whether development should be concentrated on Northland's export port at Opua in Hobson, or whether money should be spent instead on expanding Whangarei in the Marsden electorate, gave rise to the kind of lively agitation political aspirants yearn after. The Whangarei Harbour Board Empowering Act had recently been passed to allow of £850,000 being borrowed for port works and a butter cool store, the latter being sought also by Opua. Mr. Cracknell was already a leading figure on one side of this dispute, for he had served as first chairman of the reconstituted Bay of Islands Harbour Board and was thus perhaps the leading proponent of Opua. Even if the local papers had not recognized that Mr. Cracknell's political views were widely supported, he could, as Opua's advocate, have counted on a fair and full local Press, for such journals must draw their readership with coverage of provincial concerns.

Naturally the National member for rival Marsden was identified with the cause of Whangarei. But, as it happened, the new National candidate for Hobson, Mr. L. F. Sloane, was not, by saving contrast, clearly an Opua man. The National Party in Hobson had just lost its sitting member by retirement. In the National selection contest for Mr. S. W. Smith's seat, a compromise candidate emerged after a struggle between Mr. I. J. Berghan, a Kaitaia contender and a member of the Bay of Islands Harbour Board, and the Hon. W. H. Fortune, an ex-Minister of Police and a former chairman of the Auckland division of the National Party who had recently bought property in the electorate. The victor over both Fortune, the major figure in the party, and Berghan, the representative of the far north and Opua, was Mr. Sloane, a farmer from Waihue near Dargaville in the south-western ex-

tremity of Hobson. The connexions of this portion of the electorate
go south to Auckland. As a director of the Northern Wairoa
Dairy Company, Mr. Sloane had approved of his company
shipping butter from that 'outside' port. Thus by a quirk of fate
the Social Credit representative was opposed, not by the respected
Mr. S. W. Smith, M.P., with his seventeen years of service and
settled attachments, but instead by a southern newcomer to the
National candidacy who, approve of Opua now as he might, had
chosen otherwise in practice.

The position of the Labour candidate in resisting the Social
Credit and Opua champion was little better. The Labour Government had, of course, presided over the passing of the Whangarei
Act which linked handily with the choice of nearby Marsden
Point for an oil refinery. Though the Marsden Labour representative pointed to jobs for the rising town population of Whangarei
as a local dividend from Labour's plainly fruitful policy of
industrial processing in New Zealand, his voting figures show no
grateful bound upward but rather a severe decline. How much
more might Mr. Webber, the Labour candidate in Hobson, expect
to suffer for favours showered by his party on the rival centre and
seat. Mr. Moyle, national organizer for the Labour Party
stationed in Auckland and a former candidate for Hobson, was
worried enough to see that two Auckland Labour members went
north to plead for Webber. City men in a rural constituency, they
addressed meetings at which Mr. Webber dwelt, perhaps in-
judiciously long, on his reserved-occupation status during the war.

At all events, the Opua issue had disarrayed the unexpectedly
weakened forces confronting Social Credit just when that party
had joined to an old local tradition of success an articulate,
widely reported and widely known campaigner in Mr. Cracknell.
Hobson's choice of Cracknell for second place is not so surprising
then. What surprises more is the fact that the National Party
share of the vote was just 3·71 per cent lower than in 1957 in the
face of a whole platoon of local factors gathered in the electorate
to distort the nationwide trends. Hobson has been investigated in
detail because its position in the ranks of the constituencies
changed more violently in response to local issues than did any
other. The particular factors at work prove on examination to
have been many and various and so conjoined that any exponent
of the importance of the man and the locality in politics would

expect a correspondingly large effect. Instead, the small size of the check administered to National in Hobson and the corresponding reflection that Labour's fall in that electorate and in Marsden were nearly identical, amount to a tribute to the strength of the general forces at work here as everywhere in New Zealand.

Nelson: The Maximum Public Work

The other peculiarly affected constituencies listed in Table I will have to be looked at. Nelson ranked after Hobson and is an even purer example of the power of the public work; though it should be noted that other elements of the Hobson scene were also present. The provincial Press, for example, treated kindly the man whose vote duly rose. A neighbouring National M.P., Mr. Shand, publicly and loudly advocated the opposite cause. Nelson even shares with Hobson a record of preferring political idiosyncracy. Nine times out of ten between 1911 and 1946 Nelson voted for Harry Atmore, who confounded cynics by moving to the Left politically as he got older. Having begun as an Independent Liberal, he thereafter passed through many shades of independence to finish as his own variety of consistently pro-Labour M.P. Like Mr. Cracknell in Hobson, Mr. Whitehead, the Labour man in Nelson, had a tradition to rest his case on. Meanwhile, in the present, the railway reclamation proceeding on the Nelson city foreshore gave substance to what was acquiring a legendary aura of extravagance wherever National candidates spoke. A *New Zealand Herald* staff correspondent reported a 'feeling, which is akin to one of victimisation' on the part of Nelsonians, being singled out for censure on the nation's hustings when what they wanted, a developmental railway, they felt had been granted decades before to a dozen other regions.

The Nelsonians' verdict was clear. Labour gained 2·76 per cent more of the qualified vote; Social Credit rose a paltry ·11 per cent; and National fell 4·17 per cent, their biggest loss in any seat. It was not so great an absolute gain in votes for Labour as that registered between 1954 and 1957 when the issue had first arisen, but it represented more of a cross-current working against the nationwide flow and it raised Nelson from fortieth to twenty-fifth place in Labour's battle order. Had the general result in 1960 realized the hopes of those Labour optimists who envisaged the election as a struggle to retain their Government by preventing the overturn of one seat, the Nelson seat, then Mr. Whitehead's survival with an enhanced majority would have justified all the wearisome night sittings, the protracted negotiations and concessions for the cotton mill and even the foundation-stone at the end of the unsettled route. As it stood, Nelson was in vain, but not alone.

Marlborough and the Failing Parish Pump

The next most oddly moved electorate after Nelson was its next-door neighbour, Marlborough, which was also disturbed by tremors passing down the proposed railway line to its intended terminus at Blenheim, the urban centre of the constituency and the home of more than a third of Marlborough voters. Much of Blenheim's growth had followed the completion by the first Labour Government of the South Island Main Trunk. The second Labour Government had decided in favour of a rail ferry across Cook Strait to Picton, Marlborough's second town. Traffic for Canterbury and the South Island generally would pass through Blenheim from Picton, as it would from Nelson, and only the labelling of the party fight as being concerned with 'the Nelson Railway' masked the fact that in terms of future profit it was more likely to prove a 'battle of Blenheim'.

The Hon. T. P. Shand, National member for the seat, cannot have worried unduly about the possible results of this local issue. In Parliament and in his constituency he joined Mr. Goosman who thought the Nelson connexion 'a fraud on the people', and Mr. Algie, who declared the people 'Hoodwinked', Mr. Shand adding for his part that the Nelsonians were being taken 'for a political ride'. The member, an ex-Minister of Civil Aviation, was so high in the policy-making circles of his party and the railway struck so near home for him that he must have participated in the decision to launch the hot attack on the Nelson connexion. Though he proved to have estimated the effects on Marlborough correctly, for his majority diminished by only $\frac{1}{2}$ per cent, nevertheless his decision involved political courage of a sort rarely manifested in New Zealand's past.

This example may lead members to assess more correctly the contemporary voting weight of local factors and give them heart to oppose in the future certain of the more gradiose projects for serving parochial interest. They should take care, however, to offer alternatives, for Mr. Shand did stress that there were, to his mind, other ways than Labour offered for advancing Blenheim and the electorate. The timorous politician will more probably note the 2·77 per cent decline in National's share of the qualified vote, a loss which did not much affect the National lead over Labour because Labour at the same time secured 2·27 per cent fewer of the electors.

In Marlborough, as in Marsden, Labour's attention to the constituency was thus ironically rewarded with a slipping vote, while Social Credit picked up 2·92 per cent and the proportion not voting was higher by 2·06 per cent. It will be argued later that the capture of votes by Social Credit over the whole of New Zealand in 1954 came mainly from ex-Nationalists, and that it was largely Labour supporters who retired into abstention in 1951 and 1960. Marlborough's results in 1960 appear to combine these processes, for the figures reveal dissatisfaction with both major parties and a consequent rise both for Social Credit and non-voting. The balance of figures also suggests that at least a fringe of ex-Labour voters crossed to the third party. What matters about Marlborough, however, is the small voting consequence of a large local factor. The nationwide trends appeared with sufficient power in the constituency to damp down an issue of great provincial consequence and a programme, in the Picton rail ferry, of direct financial benefit to this area. The analysis detected an unusual reaction in the electorate when it moved from sixtieth to forty-ninth in the ranking of constituencies. On investigation, Marlborough's display of voting contrary to the New Zealand pattern turns out to be quite minor, especially when the possible causes of parochial revolt are reviewed.

Rotorua: On the Loyalty and Leverage of Minorities

At the same level of local instability as Marlborough, but moving in the opposite direction, we encounter Rotorua, the first such constituency to have a part in actually ousting the Labour Government. In the National Party's opinion, their victory in this seat was the surprise of the election, the forecasters for the major dailies did not expect it and Rotorua has already been singled out earlier in this analysis as the seat with the highest Labour loss among those which ejected their member. There was a normal

crop of matters for local concern in Rotorua, such as whether the
Lands Department was hanging on to control of newly developed
country overlong, whether overseas tourists were being steered
past privately owned facilities to Government hotels, and whether
the rights of Maori owners on lake frontages were being wrongly
preserved against the demand for access. Yet these questions
scarcely rose to the status of local issues nor seemed capable of
causing an upset. The standing of the victim, Mr. Boord, both as
Labour Minister of Customs and Broadcasting and as member for
the seat since its creation, ought to have had a tonic effect on
Labour's fortunes, particularly since both his opponents, a
Rotorua grocer and a power-station operator, were standing for
the first time. The puzzlement was certainly deep and justified.

After the election Mr. Boord, who had campaigned hard and
been furiously shifted about not-very-adjacent country electorates
by his party, collapsed on to a sick-bed. Political Wellington, and
particularly the Labour Party, was frankly at a loss for a likely
explanation. Personal unpopularity in his home town, had it
existed, could hardly account for such a notable overturn. So a
supplementary theory appeared by which Mr. Boord, as the
much-cited Minister of Customs, had suffered from the odium of
inflicting the 1958 import cuts and had been cut down by the
revengeful shopkeepers and consumers of the sizeable town of
Rotorua. To test this theory it was necessary to break up the
constituency result into its components, the voting at the booths
in the town of Rotorua and at the various types of booth elsewhere. The result is set out below.

So far from the Rotorua townsmen's revenge falling upon the
Minister of Customs it will be seen from the bottom line of the
table that his losses in these particular booths were smaller in
proportion to his 1957 vote than in any other group. Indeed, if
the voting pattern of Rotorua town had held for the electorate as
a whole, Mr. Boord would have just contrived to keep his seat
with a majority of three-quarters of 1 per cent. The envelope or
special vote is so near in all its trends to the Rotorua town vote
that one can treat it as much the same vote and suspect that a
good deal of it comes from townsmen. The resorts near Rotorua
also performed like their large prototype. Thus it was not among
the town booths but in other sections of the electorate that the
execution was done.

TABLE II

Character of Booths	A Hydro-Electric Employees		B Forestry Workers		C Rotorua Town	
No. of Valid Votes in 1960	2300		724		7023	
% Labour in '57; '60 and change	77·26:66·26	−11·00	67·35:51·93	−15·42	52·62:45·74	−6·88
% National in '57; '60 and change	18·70:24·78	+6·08	25·29:32·18	+6·89	41·50:46·93	+5·43
% Social Credit in '57; '60 and change	4·04: 8·96	+4·92	7·36:15·89	+8·53	5·88: 7·33	+1·45
Loss or Gain in no. voting validly in '60 as % of no. in '57	−3·16		−6·58		+9·46	
Lab. loss in '60 as % Lab. '57 vote	−14·24		−22·90		−13·07	

Character of Booths	D Valid Envelope Vote		E Resorts near Rotorua		F Taupo Town	
No. of Valid Votes in 1960	1769		1312		1757	
% Labour in '57; '60 and change	51·07:43·98	−7·09	45·32:39·10	−6·22	42·07:34·49	−7·58
% National in '57; '60 and change	43·67:49·35	+5·68	47·32:51·22	+3·90	47·94:56·12	+8·18
% Social Credit in '57; '60 and change	5·26: 6·67	+1·41	7·36: 9·68	+2·32	9·99: 9·39	−0·60
Loss or Gain in no. voting validly in '60 as % of no. in '57	+14·80		+9·70		+29·00	
Lab. loss in '60 as % Lab. '57 vote	−13·88		−13·72		−18·02	

Character of Booths	G Mixed Farm and Forestry		H Farming		Whole Electorate	
No. of Valid Votes in 1960	414		1421		16,720	
% Labour in '57; '60 and change	37·68:26·81	−10·87	31·34:24·84	−6·50	53·28:44·69	−8·59
% National in '57; '60 and change	47·34:57·01	+9·67	61·00:67·91	+6·91	40·24:46·84	+6·60
% Social Credit in '57; '60 and change	14·98:16·18	+1·20	7·66:7·25	−0·41	6·48: 8·47	+1·99
Loss or Gain in no. voting validly in '60 as % of no. in '57	±0·00		+7·81		+8·59	
Lab. loss in '60 as % Lab. '57 vote	−28·85		−20·74		−16·12	

Among constituencies in the New Zealand countryside Rotorua is untypical. The Waikato River has been or is being dammed for power at several points within Rotorua's boundaries, while vast exotic forests and stands of native timber cover a third of the electorate. Employees at the hydro-electric stations, construction workers and loggers considerably outnumber the farming section of the voters. Throughout the twentieth century the centre of the North Island has always had at least one electorate—the old Taumaranui or Waimarino—where timber workers were important to the voting result. When the entirely rural North Island seats were Reform, Waimarino was Liberal and it first elected a Labour member in 1922, thirteen years before any other constituency of this class did so. Apart from Westland and Buller, where coal-miners play the role that hydro and timber workers fulfil in Rotorua, no electorate with less than 80 per cent of urban dwellers returned a Labour man in 1957 or 1960. The presence of a town as large as Rotorua, even when it is inclined so far towards Labour as Rotorua was in 1957, is not sufficient to tip the scale against the virtual unanimity of the farming community.

In the 1960 election the section of the Rotorua electorate which turned most fiercely against the Labour member worked in the forests. Polling places at or near mill sites show a heavy fall in the share of the total valid vote given to Labour, down 15 per cent; a drop in the number voting by 7 per cent, despite an increasing labour force; and a sharp diversion of votes past National to Social Credit, which more than doubled Social Credit's share. In the booths which mixed timber workers with farmers—generally settlers on recently opened and developed lands—the rate of Labour decline[6] was steepest of all. Here Labour lost 29 per cent of its 1957 vote compared to 23 per cent in pure forestry booths.

[6] This rate of decline is a separate measure from the share of the total vote lost. Suppose a booth of 1000 voters split in 1957 50 per cent:50 per cent, Labour:National. If Labour in 1960 loses 100 voters from its 1957 500 that is a Labour loss of 10 per cent of the valid vote and a 20 per cent rate of decline. Another booth of 1000 might be split 20 per cent:80 per cent, Labour:National. If Labour lost 40 voters the Labour vote would still have diminished 20 per cent and that would be the rate of decline but those 40 votes would only mean a loss of 4 per cent of the valid vote of 1000. Both measures are worth having, the percentage shares of the total vote lost or gained in a booth or constituency show how the whole population voting there altered its opinions, by how much, and in what direction. The rate of decline, offsetting one party's present loss against its former vote, makes clear how that party's adherents have reacted, regardless of whether they were a minority or a majority where they voted.

The hydro workers' booths, a more numerous section, show the second largest drop in Labour's share of the poll. At 77 per cent Labour in 1957 they had been nearly as vehemently for their party as any mid-city stronghold. When set against this, the 11 per cent loss in 1960 represents a rate of decline of but 14 per cent of the former Labour vote, only a shade worse than the town rate. That, however, makes the point. Labour's erstwhile hydro and timber champions fell away as fast or much faster than the sectionally mixed and socially middling townsmen. Only the farmer polling places could compete with the worker strongholds in rate of Labour decline but, since there were so few Labour votes cast there in the first place, the party's share of the total farmer vote went down only 6 per cent.

Was this unkind cut from Labour's fortress troops—a defection which cost Mr. Boord the seat—a local and unique phenomenon? Fortunately for our hope of understanding the cause of Rotorua's performance, it was not. At booths in the centre of Auckland, Wellington and Christchurch the Labour vote was declining at a rate quite comparable with that of the hydro workers, if not of the timber men. Moreover, the drop in the number voting, which especially characterizes the centre of the cities, appears in the timber centres and at the hydro sites. Instead of the fifth line of Table II showing a decline for columns A and B and zero for column G, there ought to have been an increase to represent a soaring voting population. It would seem on the figures that most of the abstention in the electorate took place at these booths, though Rotorua town might have supplied a fraction.

What the centres of the cities share with mill and work sites, besides a tradition of heavy Labour voting, is the presence of large numbers of young unmarried workers. Whether in boarding-house, hostel or tented camp, these men have a common pattern of expenditure on beer, cigarettes and the cars and motorbikes which make other diversions possible. In every sense the 1958 Budget hit these men 'where they lived'. The response can certainly be picked up in like places all over the country.

Rotorua's forestry men, initially less committed to Labour than the hydro workers, more highly paid, oftener doing contract work to accumulate capital, and even more isolated, were the ones who hit back hardest. Furthermore, during Labour's term there had been recurrent disputes at the timber centres which were tided over but which left the unionists no more satisfied with the management of the young industry and the company towns than newcomers to a raw, burgeoning establishment ever are. But the timber workers' pattern of reaction is there among the hydro men too: Labour's overall share is down 11 per cent, there is abstention, and nearly as many of the defecting votes go to Social Credit as to National, so that the third-party proportion more than doubles—the last two being trends which appear nowhere else in the electorate.

So far the analysis has deferred dealing with two sections of Rotorua's voters, the farmers and Taupo town. Farmers within the constituency, judging from their valid votes, acted just as did Hauraki, Waikato, Waitomo and Piako, neighbouring predominantly rural electorates. These seats and Rotorua's farming voters were already markedly conservative in 1957 and became more so in 1960, National taking Labour's loss and Social Credit declining or picking up by a little only. The Taupo town trends represent a cross between Rotorua town and farming patterns with a leaning towards the farmer. This is also the character of the voters gathered by Taupo's booths, which register the rapidly rising population catering to the wealthy holiday homes springing up round the lake and the farmers on the freshly profitable pumice lands quite close to the town.

Taken thus section by section, the Rotorua result, instead of being the puzzling effect of some unknown local factor or factors operating on all the voters alike, resolves itself into certain mild and several sharp sectional responses, each in the same direction as similar groups were taking elsewhere. The critical factor for Labour was the changed attitude of the two groups which handed the seat to the party in the first place. It is relevant to point out that, in the list of rates of Labour decline, Rotorua comes just before Avon and Auckland Central. What was peculiar about Rotorua was not its reaction but its composition—the presence in the countryside of groups fewer in numbers but equivalent in attitudes to the cities' industrial workers. That is what held Rotorua in twenty-ninth place in the ranks of Labour's 1957 majorities and when, in 1960, the groups reduced their powerful support, the constituency descended to fortieth place and received a Nationalist incumbent. The city centre electorates were doing the same thing but, since they were all near the top of the ladder of majorities, being more uniformly made up of workers, and because all the rungs declined more or less together, the order of rungs was not much disturbed and the test for the presence of local factors, therefore, did not pick them out on account of their behaviour under this New Zealand-wide trend as it picked out Rotorua.

In our examination of the list of peculiarly acting electorates we are already, at the fourth on the list, coming out of the domain of strong local factors—which proved, incidentally, not to be very potent—and are entering the realm either of the minor national trend which happens to be notably exposed in a particular electorate or of a major national or regional pattern which has been distorted in some one seat by the unusual way in which sections are balanced within that constituency. Undoubtedly further instances of the existence of local factors can be taken from the list, but less surely now and with increasing reservations about their power to accomplish much. The two electorates which altered their rank by ten rungs illustrate the alternatives. Fendalton looks to be an example of what happens when a major regional trend coincides in its thrust with a minor national trend; Mount Albert on the other hand, shows signs of the operation of local factors.

Fendalton; A Coincidence of Lesser Trends

The major regional trend carrying Fendalton along with it was the South Island's pronounced reluctance to join the rush from Labour. This will be examined later, but it is worth noting here that this reluctance was most manifest in Nelson, Lyttelton, Fendalton, St. Kilda, Waitaki, Marlborough and St. Albans, in that order. These seven seats, in fact, represent seven out of the eight lowest rates of Labour decline in the 1960 general election, and all four of the South Island's richer residential constituencies figure among the group. Fendalton, as the least socially mixed, most clearly wealthy seat in the South Island, shared in the trend to the full. If below Cook Strait for some reason the upper-income strata were not going to move farther from Labour, then this would be nowhere more apparent than in Sir Sidney Holland's old seat, the constituency twice selected for and selecting a Nationalist Minister of Finance. So it proved, and since other blue ribbon National electorates with farmer constituents were by contrast busily participating in the general shift against Labour, Fendalton, abandoned by its neighbours in a body, had its place on the ladder of majorities altered by ten rungs. At the same time St. Kilda, the nearest Dunedin equivalent to Fendalton, was shifted eight rungs in the same direction and thus also appears on our list of peculiarly acting electorates.

Paradoxically, the relatively favourable result for Labour in Fendalton, which was connected with Fendalton's nature as a constituency of the prosperous, was reinforced by extensive building in the north-west of the electorate which brought in more Labour voters and adversely modified the moneyed character of the electorate. Out beyond Fendalton North, in Burnside and below Harewood Road, State and group houses introduced a considerable voting population with young families who in their voting appeared as content with Labour's programme on behalf of the home-seekers as such people were in, say, Waitakere, Waitemata, Otahuhu or Manukau on Auckland's fast-growing fringes. Thus a minor national trend helpful to Labour among those younger married couples who had been driven by average or below-average income to settle in distant suburbs, co-operated in Fendalton with a South Island regional trend towards stable voting. In consequence all three parties' share of the qualified vote declined: Labour by 1·68 per cent, Social Credit by ·67 per cent, and National by ·54 per cent. Only informal and non-voting rose, the latter going from 6·45 per cent in 1957 to 9·29 per cent in 1960 with Labour contributing roughly three to one coming from National and one from Social Credit.

Mount Albert and the Personal Factor

The equally peculiar movement of Mount Albert from thirteenth to twenty-third among Labour majorities was a case of a very different colour. Here Mr. Freer, the sitting Labour member since 1947, saw his share of the whole vote decline steeply by 8·69 per cent and, more ominously, watched the Nationalist rise by an extra 6·95 per cent. This was really unusual, especially in Auckland where not National victory but a gain for non-voting was the counterpart to Labour loss. Those not voting in Mount Albert did increase by 3·22 per cent and a fifth of National's gain could have come out of Social Credit's loss of 1·58 per cent. But if all Social Credit's departed moved across to National and none ceased to vote, National was still managing to convert two-thirds of the ex-Freer voters, a considerable feat for 1960 and quite unequalled in any other of Labour's city strongholds throughout New Zealand. Moreover, if one maps the Auckland isthmus and shades it according to the rate of Labour decline, a band of light loss runs from Grey Lynn round to the south-west, along the shore of the Manukau through Waikowhai and Onehunga to Mount Wellington in the south-east—except where Mount Albert interrupts the band at Blockhouse Bay. Heavy loss occurs in the central city and to the north-east, but is unexpected in the long-established, middle to lower middle housing of Sandringham and Owairaka, the core of Mr. Freer's constituency. Extensive and more expensive housing is certainly filling up Blockhouse Bay and might account for the member's loss of 10 per cent of the entire valid vote in this statistical district, his home bailiwick. On the other hand, the Labour member for neighbouring Halsey-Waikowhai and Hillsborough districts, where similar homes are rising, lost only 3 and 1 per cent respectively.

Part of the contrast, of course, might be the product of the superior electoral organization in the latter districts, part of the Roskill electorate where Mr. A. J. Faulkner, a party organizer before he became an M.P., specialized in party branch work and bringing out the vote by post and by car. The rosters, staffing arrangements and checking of the turnout at his campaign head-quarters were indeed impressive, and the Roskill postal vote, a rough barometer, did climb by 253, or from 7·03 per cent of the qualified vote to 7·93 per cent, whereas Mount Albert's envelopes numbered just twenty-seven more than in 1957. Against this case for organization, however, we must bring the instance of Grey Lynn, Mount Albert's neighbour on the other side. There, special votes actually numbered 107 fewer than in 1957, there was no notable organizational thrust, yet overall Labour loss in Grey Lynn was also considerably smaller than in Mount Albert. Grey Lynn's record would have been about as favourable as Roskill's if it had not been for some punishing booth returns in the electorate's northerly projection into the central city area. As it was, National's tiny rise in Grey Lynn was even smaller than the rise in well-drilled Roskill and certainly only a fraction of National's gain in Mount Albert. After conceding, therefore, a very, very little to party organization and in the absence of any discoverable local issue on which Mr. Freer might have taken the 'wrong' side, we are left with the operations of the personal factor to account for Labour in Mount Albert dropping faster than in like constituencies and for the high rate of conversion to National.

Voting for Mrs. Anderson, the National candidate, was in Mount Albert no new experience, anyway indirectly. She had been Mayoress of the borough for twenty-three years and as she put it, 'After so many years of service on a non-political basis, I believe I have a lot to offer, particularly from the woman's point of view, in national affairs.' An M.B.E., mother of seven and a leading member of the Mount Albert Guild of Service, Mrs. Anderson was undoubtedly well liked and well known. Her energy and kindliness shone through the stock addresses of the apprentice politician. She epitomized an acceptable, bland combination of attitudes and concepts which she condensed thus: 'We have a welfare state, and to maintain it the people must be given freedom and opportunity to use their own initiative without harsh Government control.'

Against this challenger Mr. Warren Freer pitted his reputation as a fairly radical, articulate and vigorous Labour member who had met with considerable disapproval in his fifth term as member. Mr. Freer had been sufficiently consistent in advocating the recognition of China and a reappraisal of New Zealand's foreign policy to be known on the Right as a man of the Left. Then during the summer and autumn of 1958–9 he departed overseas for a six-month trip to Great Britain, Europe and on to the Soviet Union and mainland China. This proved to be unfortunate timing, for in the course of the Judd affair Mr. Freer was named in a published statement which alleged that a £2,200 commission was owing to Mr. Freer, inferentially for services in securing a licence to import glass from Czechoslovakia.

On 24 July 1959, in Parliament, Mr. Freer emphatically denied receiving 'from Judd and Company or any other firm or individual a commission for any services I have rendered to them in my duties as a Parliamentarian.' He offered to place 'the original and only statement of my financial affairs' on the table of the House and pointed out that £2,200 was not an asset but the amount he owed on a mortgage. The Prime Minister stated that no licence for £44,000 had been issued and cried, 'How can we charge the member for Mount Albert with having received a

commission on a licence that has never been issued?' Though
Mr. Sheat (Opposition—Egmont) accepted Mr. Nash's statement,
he believed that 'If any arrangement for commission were made . . .
it was in anticipation of that arrangement and that it was not
finalized', while Mr. Shand also continued to press for an enquiry:
'So long as the member for Mount Albert sits in this House
without having his name cleared, so long will the public doubt
continue to grow.' After hearing Mr. Freer, however, the Hon.
J. R. Marshall, Deputy Leader of the Opposition, concluded 'I
think the House will accept the statement of the member for
Mount Albert' and added that there was no need to produce the
statement.

In the meantime doubt and rumour had six months to enjoy a
field day. By 4 February the Press Association reported believing
the Labour caucus would discuss Mr. Freer's tour. On 5
February, Mr. McDonald, Labour's national secretary, affirmed
that 'Rumours have, of course, been circulating since the publication of certain allegations, but I repeat that the party has not had
any approach at all made to it. There are only rumours, so far as
the party is concerned, and it does not know that Mr. Freer has
any debts. There is not a grain of truth in the story that the party
has settled any such debts allegedly incurred by Mr. Freer.'

The context was, of course, that should anything untoward
happen to Mr. Freer's career, the Government would have to
rest on the casting vote of the Speaker and a National victory in a
by-election would leave the House divided 40:40. Tension
crackled around Labour circles. A sudden discharge was reported
in the *Auckland Star* on 7 February. The normally equable
Prime Minister 'was livid with anger'. The question had been put
' "Is there anything more, Sir, on Mr. Freer?"—and the storm
broke.' The Press conference rapidly adjourned leaving the
correspondent to wonder at the strain on a Prime Minister,
'personally antipathetic' to Mr. Freer as the result of past caucus
struggles, but determined to hear him before judging the matter
as 'influential men, particularly those on the industrial wing'
desired. Interest waned then waxed as the date appointed for the
1959 session drew near. There was quiet jubilation among
National supporters whilst newspapers published bulletins on the
trouble Mr. Freer had with booking his way south from China.
He arrived in the nick of time, there was a hush while the session

began, the Opposition raised the question of import licences on the Imprest Supply Bill and the Prime Minister and Mr. Freer dramatically confronted the doubt and issued their denials. Interest subsided but not, apparently, all memory of the tour and the suspense.

New Zealanders, in any case, habitually express a penny-pinching resentment of trips overseas by politicians, even those paid for privately or by external grant. 'Twice within about two years', complained 'Mt. Albert Elector' to the *Herald*, 'Mr. Freer . . . has spent several months abroad, even if "only on a shoestring." Who does the routine duties for which we pay our M.P.s a handsome salary—or do we pay them just to sit arguing and often being abusive in Wellington?' It is an odd attitude in a people so travelled and dependent on their understanding of the outside world; but it was as much there in 1959 as it was in the election of 1905 when Seddon was attacked. Mr. Freer was no magical King Dick to turn troubling to triumphant vindication. The suspicious continued to think he had been tripping round too long and in the wrong place.

His own party did not help by reversing custom and leaving until second to last among the Auckland seats the announcement that Mr. Freer, a sitting member, had been selected to stand again. The *New Zealand Herald* said softly that after his trip 'Mr. Freer fell into disfavour with some members of the Labour Party. As a result there was some doubt about his candidature being endorsed.' Mr. Freer himself underlined another result of his experience in his Press release for the campaign. 'I have seen communism operating. I know from my own studies that, despite the many advances it can give to backward people, it is the most formidable challenge in this age.'

Whether this added experience was to prove as positive as the trip and its circumstances were politically negative only his electors could decide. The figures on their response suggest that those who give thought to foreign affairs and tongue to unorthodox views should stay at home or, having anticipated all likely or un-likely charges, and with abundant private funds on view, confine themselves to short trips to Western Europe, Formosa or the United States.

Apart from this one instance there is little evidence in the New Zealand figures for believing the character of candidates to have been influential. According to the New Zealand Gallup Poll, 22 per cent of voters said 'they probably would vote for the better man' in reply to the question 'How would you be likely to vote if, while favouring one party in principle, you decided that its candidate for Parliament was not nearly as good a candidate as the man put up by an opposing party?' In almost all electorates in New Zealand voters acted as though this contingency had not arisen. And in Mount Albert, if—and it is still an 'if'—they thought after nationwide publicity that theirs was a case in point, something between 2 and 3 per cent more of the qualified voters, not 22 per cent, abandoned their party accordingly. Labour's loss of voters within the nine secure Auckland seats was 6·42 per cent. Mr. Freer's share of the vote declined 8·69 per cent, just 2·27 per cent more than the whole. The party's vote in eleven Labour-held constituencies in New Zealand, two of them Auckland seats, went down at a greater rate and eleven of them also lost a larger proportion of the qualified vote. However within reason one selects a group of constituencies in Auckland to compare with Mount Albert, the difference of the Mount Albert result from the average performance does not rise above 3 per cent.

It is only when we gaze at the destination of Mr. Freer's voters, into National and not abstention, that the case for the working of some special factor looks convincing. Among the fourteen wholly Auckland electorates, National registered a gain of 1 or less per cent in eleven. They picked up 3 per cent in Tamaki and North Shore, but 7 per cent in Mount Albert. If changing parties for one election be the test, then at the outside, 6, or at the inside, 4 per cent of the electors were so moved. Should this be a negative personal vote, the most likely example on the face of New Zealand's figures, it was not very large and certainly not so consequential as the general factors which removed 10 per cent from Auckland Central's Labour force.

Auckland Central well exemplified the national trend for customarily Labour voters in Labour constituencies to sit on their hands in 1960. This was most noticeable in the centres of the cities and undoubtedly the trend operated in Wellington Central, the other surprise National victory which has been indicated as worth closer examination. At this point one should recall Fendalton. There the South Island's regional tendencies and the minor national trend amongst outlying new suburbs worked together to cancel, or very nearly cancel, the major New Zealand movement from Labour. In Wellington Central the reverse happened. The notable regional feature was an intensification of the movement from Labour. Far from standing alone, Wellington Central shows less Labour loss than Heretaunga, Island Bay and Hutt, though more than Onslow, Miramar and Petone. At the same time the socio-economic balance in Wellington Central was slowly tipping against Labour as it was tipping towards them in Fendalton.

Wellington Central: Social Change or Special Issue

The Te Aro flatland, the heart of old Wellington and the New Zealand town planner's dream of a decadent area, has been losing houses and acquiring business and light industrial premises for years. Labour's strength was and is centred there as the Victoria University College survey of the constituency pointed out,[7] and fewer houses mean fewer voters. On one flank of the flatland, to the east of Kent Terrace, sits the lower middle class housing of Mount Victoria rising towards the town belt of parkland. Reminiscent of the northern end of Mount Eden in Auckland so far as social composition is concerned, it performs electorally likewise. It is clearly Labour in a good year for that party and marginally so in a poor year. The steady emptying of Te Aro made this margin, where depopulation was slight, ever more important.

Meanwhile, to the north-east and beyond the town belt, new flat-dwellers and even new houses perched on the hills were recruiting the well-to-do and traditionally anti-Labour areas of Oriental Bay, Roseneath and Haitaitai. Across the trough of Te Aro, on the other, western flank, is the strip just above and below The Terrace with its burden of big and little flats, last-ditch householders, hotels and boarding-houses. The voters here are often single, often young; a thorough social mixture with a liberal salting of junior executives in Government and business. Like its social and geographical parallel, the Symonds Street-Eden Crescent area in Auckland Central, The Terrace was either

[7] R. H. Brookes, 'Wellington Central, the Field and the Battle', and R. S. Milne, 'Voting in Wellington Central, 1957' in *The New Zealand General Election of 1957*, Wellington, 1958.

barely National as in 1957 or definitely so as in 1960. Certainly there was no help to be looked for from Haitaitai or The Terrace if matters went badly for Labour on the Te Aro bottomlands. And Thorndon, the fifth and remaining area of Wellington Central is so patchy an area—overall a slightly downgraded Terrace— that an evenly divided vote was as much as Labour might expect.

Basic changes of the sort that are thinning the population of Te Aro have caught political parties unaware before. When Lyttelton, in 1951, voted out Labour after a thirty-eight-year run casual observers of the political scene were startled. They had not realized that the port, cramped between the hills and the sea, had not been able to expand its population in proportion to the growing size of electorates. To make up the deficiency each boundary change had added fresh areas across the Port Hills in Cashmere, Opawa and Woolston until Christchurch suburbanites finally prevailed over the much outnumbered port workers. Likewise, social amendment and boundary revision had so balanced the markedly different elements in Wellington Central that it was necessary before the 1960 election to classify the seat in the marginal urban category—therefore vulnerable to National— despite its blue ribbon Labour history. This decision about the seat was confirmed by Labour's margin there in the fifties; 9 per cent in the bumper year of 1957, it had been 4 and 3 per cent in 1954 and 1951.

The political forces at large in 1960 were nicely calculated to overcome a party disposed as Labour was in this electorate. The single, the childless and the elderly, the occupants of flat and room and decayed house, were staying away from the poll. In Wellington Central the Labour share of the qualified vote went down 8·67 per cent and non-voting rose 6·39 per cent. National gathered in an additional 2·55 per cent while Social Credit went down ·78 per cent and a Communist candidate picked up ·72 per cent. The odd ·21 per cent is made up of a fall in informal voting from ·68 per cent to ·47 per cent. Since the minuscule Communist vote at the varying booths went higher where Labour was more numerous, it seems reasonable to think they had formerly voted Labour. This drew off about one-eleventh of Labour's loss. Unless ex-Social Crediters went into Labour as Labourites came out into National, one must suppose National's minor gain to have derived approximately one-third from Social Credit. Once these thin slices of the vote are accounted for, we are left with this picture of those qualified to vote: for every one ex-Labour elector who now voted Communist, two voted National and eight stayed in their rooms. The electorate had seen 1038 voters depart and come off the electoral roll, many of them from Te Aro. On top of that, instead of 1479 people who were qualified to vote not going to the polls as in 1957, 2531 refrained in 1960—a difference of 1052. The seat was lost by 381 votes.

In order to track down exactly where the movement was located I have added up the valid votes cast in 1957 and in 1960, both those cast as special votes and those cast at the booths in the five sections of the electorate. Between the two elections Labour dropped by 4·76 per cent of the formal votes cast in Haitaitai, Roseneath and Oriental Bay; by 5·43 per cent in The Terrace; by 5·75 per cent of the envelope vote; by 3·83 per cent in Thorndon; by 6·01 per cent in Mount Victoria and by 8·13 per cent in Te Aro. Apart from Thorndon, where there was some influx of Pacific Islanders who vote on the general roll, the cut taken from Labour's share in the regions grew larger in precise proportion as Labour voters were more numerous.

To identify where the stay-aways stayed away, the fall in the valid votes cast at the booths in each region was expressed as a percentage of the 1957 total valid vote. This method necessarily overstates the percentage of abstainers greatly, but it does show where they were located.[8] The Haitaitai vote went down 1·98 per cent; the special vote, 8·05 per cent; Mount Victoria, 8·18 per cent; and Te Aro, 15·42 per cent. The two predominantly flatting and rooming areas, Thorndon and The Terrace, went down 16·61 per cent and 18·90 per cent respectively. Booths in central Auckland, Wellington and Christchurch, and even Dunedin, tell the same story with figures of the same order.

[8] Because the thousand who left the electorate and the roll between 1957 and 1960 did vote in the first election but not in the second, they appear in booth figures as part of the decline in numbers at the second election along with the abstainers. Voters at neither election naturally appear nowhere in booth figures. So the decrease of 11·52 per cent from 1957 to 1960 at booths over the whole electorate is a combination of new non-voters and the legitimately departed. Knowing the roll change for the whole constituency, we also know that fresh non-voters alone constituted but 6·39 per cent, not 11·52 per cent. If sub-rolls were kept regionally we could assign the departed to their areas and deduct them, but we would learn little more than we can, with allowances, ascertain now.

It is therefore difficult to credit explanations which attribute the National victory in Wellington Central to causes not found elsewhere like the campaigning of Mr. Riddiford, his especial appeal for and to the Roman Catholic vote, the adverse consequences of Mr. Kitts's preoccupation with the Wellington mayoralty or the machinelike efficacy of National organization within the constituency.

Certainly National had a paid organizer working in the electorate who found in street visiting that he could mark down four out of ten as favourable, but he also encountered 'a high proportion of doubtfuls'. The steady conversion of old houses into flats and the large proportion of elderly people among those at home when canvassers called, or party volunteers were wanted, meant that a card index could be worked only for two branch areas out of four, and membership was still 'in the 1800s'. Indeed the party and the division were quite late in grasping that Wellington Central might conceivably turn over. The cars and helpers brought in on election day, though adequate, like the attention to pre-polling day organization, which was more than sufficient to match Labour's effort, nevertheless were not of an order to upset the situation that other forces had made. It is unlikely to have been superior National organization that beat Labour when the local envelope vote, the section of the vote most easily augmented by carefully planned visits and timely aid with paperwork, went down from 11·00 per cent of those qualified and on the roll in 1957 to 10·31 per cent of those still on the roll in 1960.

Some members of the Labour Party have been considerably disturbed since the election about the effects of a supposed change in voting by Roman Catholics which is said to have lost Wellington Central in particular. Both the Labour and the National candidates for the seat were of that religion. Mr. Riddiford, the Nationalist, however, was an active partisan for State aid to parochial schools and, as his organizer said, 'featured it in his speeches'. The organizer emphasized that State aid, for which Mr. Riddiford did not give the details of application, was not a party policy but something in which the candidate was a sincere believer and publicly offered as a cause he would personally press for if elected. This credo the organizer thought to have had 'a big influence'. At National's Dominion headquarters a senior official was sure that since they had 'never picked we would win Wellington

Central', and as the electorate was 'poorly organized',[9] it was 'the candidate who did it'. Mr. Riddiford was praised for good campaigning—he drew more newspaper photographs than anyone else in Minister-studded Wellington—and for utilizing the religious issue 'with great subtlety and painful honesty' so that the candidate 'got the automatic support of Catholics and the respect of Protestants'. Co-religionists and fellow professionals of Mr. Riddiford, who happened not to agree with his politics, have confirmed the transparent sincerity and outspokenness with which he raised the issue on his platform. So there we have both sides of the medal, each party containing those convinced that here was the unravelling of the mystery of the 'stronghold's' conversion.

As with many another colourful explanation attractive to men committed to politics because the explanation awards a big role to the candidate or his enthusiasms, this presumption of cause and effect in Wellington Central has left no confirmatory mark in the figures, which suggest instead a more mundane, impersonal conclusion. In the first place there was not much mystery to explain about the performance of a constituency which was fairly in the middle of a covey of seven Labour seats going the same way. Secondly, steady socio-economic alteration had already removed the constituency from the category of strongholds before it fell. The widespread astonishment which sought about for some very special trumpet to have levelled such walls was itself a reflection of how little is known of the cause of longterm political change in an area—its social transformation.

No booth, such as that at Dixon Street adjacent to St. Mary of the Angels and the huge State flats, stood out as being especially affected. The figures for the sixty Auckland statistical districts indicate that Roman Catholicism is like all other religions in being unevenly spread in New Zealand and that wealth and Anglicanism go together as do lower income and Catholicism. Therefore, perhaps, the increasing share lost from the Labour vote in proportionately poorer areas might support the thesis that Catholics went National. When, however, we extract the rate of Labour decline—in other words, express the Labour drop as a percentage of the Labour share, large or small, held in 1957—we find these

[9] This was a relative statement, of course, and gives as clear an indication as anything could of the high standard to which the National Party has been able to accustom itself, very high when compared with past conservative organization or present Labour machinery.

rates remarkably even: Haitaitai 13·02, Terrace 11·68, Special 11·45, Thorndon 7·52, Mount Victoria 10·87, Te Aro 12·25. This was no comfort to the Labour Party, which had to concern itself with the share it could retain of everybody's vote but worry most of all about keeping a larger portion in traditionally Labour regions.

What it demonstrates is this: if it was the Catholics, seduced by the siren call of State aid, who were thus leaving the Labour Party and crossing to National, they must have been quite un-typical in their even distribution across each region. Their conversion by this issue would have appeared likelier if the rates of Labour loss had been higher where there were more Catholics. This was not so and, in any case, there was not much conversion. Plenty of electors did not turn out for Labour but few, Catholic or otherwise, went over to support the Nationalist proponent of State aid. Lastly, the social composition and the polling returns for the electorate offer an alternative and altogether more con-vincing account of the matter.

No doubt active members of the Holy Name Society would have wished it otherwise and worked to see it so. Any candidate, particularly one who has triumphed unexpectedly, would resent the reminder that his platform oratory is heard by few and that only a small proportion of the electorate know of his pet projects. Any analysts with a proper respect for the importance of the individual, his ideas and his efforts, would delight in discovering proof of their effect. The case of Wellington Central gives them small opportunity.

A Conclusion on Individual Variation

Looking back over the cases picked out and examined earlier because they diverged most strongly from the general movement of New Zealand's electorates and would, therefore, best illustrate how parochial interest, local causes or attractive and unattractive political personalities changed the normal vote, one is struck instead by how little such factors managed to achieve. Approxi-mately one in twenty electors acted in Nelson and Mount Albert as they might not otherwise have done. Hobson, Marlborough, Rotorua, Fendalton and Wellington Central show decreasing divergence and diminishing individuality in their results. Gradually we have had to call in more information on national and regional trends, explain more particular situations by recourse to the balance of general forces they display. Looking forward over the details of constituencies which moved only eight, seven or six rungs on the ladder of majorities one sees that they deserve no more than passing mention as they illustrate features in the analysis of the results for the whole eighty seats. The review given of the seven cases has served its turn by disposing of the few exceptions, putting them in perspective and giving the small scale of their exceptionality, and by raising the issues and suggesting the trends which animated the other seventy-three constituencies. It has also operated as a pilot plant for the crushing mill of the general analysis itself, revealing how important it is to identify the social composition of an electorate, to group it correctly with its sectional peers and to watch lest regional cracks develop and generalizations about New Zealand split apart.

XII

THE GENERAL RESULT

I. *The Shape of the Analysis*

A BASIC social and sectional division in New Zealand separates city from country and this has revealed itself in our politics for as long as there have been parties. It is much more than a line separating two ways of making a living or two economic interest groups. The division passes between two approaches to social questions. It delineates different psychologies arising from two sorts of experience of life. It is so fundamental and arose so early—it is to be found in the 1840s—that it has long since found stable expression in the two-party structure itself, one party urban, one primarily rural, and within constituencies as a predictable and usually unequal balance of sections. Intercommunication between the two nations, rural and urban, is constant. Country families see their children go to the cities, parents retire to the towns and a high proportion of farmers, as recently as the 1930s, were city bred. Underneath the surface interchange, the geography of attitudes nevertheless remains fixed, while above it passes the political and economic weather, with an occasional cloudburst in one section or the other, but usually in fluctuations common to both because both sections are interdependent parts of the one economy.

The obvious first step towards understanding real movements of opinion was, therefore, to sort the thirty-three city seats in the four main centres into one group and place in another the twenty farmer seats with half or more of their population living outside any borough or town district. This left an uncomfortable balance of twenty-seven constituencies which were neither quite one thing nor the other. The four Maori seats, decided upon separate rolls and semi-autonomous issues, could be put to one side, though it should be noted that Maori voters are still mainly country folk.

A second level of urbanization in the provincial towns, large towns as New Zealanders think of them, provided another natural group of ten seats. The towns of Hastings, Napier, Nelson,

New Plymouth, Timaru and Wanganui just filled their constituencies. Hamilton, Palmerston North and Invercargill were so big as to overflow into the surrounding countryside. Only Gisborne included a sizeable sector of farmland and this was home to just over a tenth of the population.

The Nature of the Mixed Town and Country Seats

The remainder, after the Maori and the town seats were removed, were a group of thirteen constituencies with between 50 and 79 per cent of the population urban and, conversely, from 20 to 49 per cent of it rural. They made up the 'Mixed' category, yet the outstanding feature of their political behaviour was its likeness to the performance of the truly rural seats, despite the predominance of townsmen in the mixture. These townsmen were concentrated in one of the lesser provincial centres in five instances.[1] Waipa took up the overflow from Hamilton, Manawatu the surplus from Palmerston North, while Otaki received the northward outpour from Wellington. Another five spread their urban voters amongst several centres.[2] However they lived, together or apart, the townsmen's divisions left the decision to the relatively unanimous minority of farmers.

Explaining the mechanics of decision in the mixed seats does less than justice, perhaps, to the homogeneity of attitudes in electorates of this group, their quality as intermediate and mediating between town and country. A dozen years ago in analysing the elections between 1908 and 1935 I marked out a class of seats in which a distinct majority of farmers was admixed with a minority of townsmen. Changes of opinion in this class of seat won or lost the elections of the 1910s and twenties and they proved more, not less, responsive than purely rural seats to whatever was affecting the farming community. Merchants in these service towns felt the changes of the market in exaggerated form as their customers increased or cut their orders according to the pattern of receipts in London. It was always possible for the farm family to live lean on the farm's ancillary products, but a shopkeeper with full shelves and little trade in a stagnant district was driven to strike back at the situation by blaming the Govern-

---

[1] Marlborough, electorate (Blenheim, town); Marsden (Whangarei); Rotorua (Rotorua); Tauranga (Tauranga); Waitaki (Oamaru).

[2] Ashburton; Bay of Plenty; Rangitikei; Wairarapa; Westland.

ment or demanding of candidates that they secure developmental money and works or fresh settlers to get the district moving. These demands were not different from some, at least, of pure farmer demands; they were simply made more sharply and more speedily by sufferers from the economy who lived in little towns.

Since then the urban population has grown greatly in 'country' districts as it has in cities. The country quota, which gave nearly a third more representation to non-urban voters, has gone. So there are many fewer predominantly or wholly rural seats. A capture of larger and larger town centres by farmer or rural attitudes has, however, accompanied this urban growth within the countryside. In this way, and to a surprising extent, the representation of the country viewpoint has kept pace with and coped with the progressive dilution of the farm population. In 1960 the farmer seats gave 27·30 per cent of their votes to the Labour candidates; at the same election the 'mixed' seats with a majority of small townsmen rendered 33·59 per cent to the urban party.

TABLE III

Number of Electorates in all Categories of Seat having more than Half Non-Urban Population

	1908	1935	1960
'Rural'	24	20	—
'Country-Town'	18	16	—
Total of two old categories or present 'Farmer'	42	36	20

Since 1948 the detailed studies of the Waikato and of Taranaki by Graham, Malone and Bellringer have picked up and carried forward our knowledge of this likeness of view between the farmer and his towns. Now, as in the past, the correspondence in attitude has its limits. Booths in village nuclei are more heavily National and Social Credit—the farmer-approved parties—than little towns of around a thousand; the little towns are less for Labour than small towns like Stratford. And these examples are drawn from Egmont, which counts as a wholly farmer electorate. Add more dairy workers, garage hands or railwaymen and Labour rises as a proportion at the local booth. It is not the case that adding more merchants, professionals and agents has that result.

The crux of the political question posed by the growing towns seems to lie in whether multiplying the self-employed and service employees, the shop assistants and sales clerks and small shop and storekeepers, will result on balance in an addition to the Labour vote so heavy as to outweigh the farmer, or else give rise to a vote sufficiently split by sympathy with the customer and identification with his values that National wins because nowadays the customer is always to the Right. National may either win moderately by dividing the small towns and ruling with the farmer, or win handsomely by actually capturing a majority of townsmen while representing the farmer overwhelmingly. In the 1900s the ancestral party of welfare and the more urban of the parties, the Liberal and Labour Federation, utilized the townsmen in the country as a fifth column. It united them under the banners of development, public works and maximizing trade by financing new settlers on to cut-up estates. If the farmers divided in search of roading or a railway the Liberals won; and if there were enough townsmen, that meant Liberal victory regardless of the farmers. Now all is reversed. The figures for the fifties make clear that among the three possibilities issuing from the growth of urban population in the countryside—conversion to Labour, narrow National margins, or substantial National victories—it is the third which has occurred. The National Party does attract a majority of townsmen and represents between 70 and 80 per cent of farmers, and occasionally more. A whole new category of predominantly town seats has been engrossed, the mixed constituencies, and only Buller and Westland, with their unpersuaded and never-to-be-absorbed minority of miners, survive the country-minded, National flood which laps below the 80 per cent urban mark.

The Divided Past of the Large Town Constituencies

What, then, of the large towns, each a complete electorate of townsmen, but set in the country? Are they also mediators between the two nations? Have they chosen unitedly? Does the psychology of the country and its political judgement penetrate, or, indeed, grip these townsfolk as it holds the voters of the mixed constituencies? The short answer is that in 1960 41·28 per cent of the qualified 'large town' voters chose Labour and 43·13 per cent National. Three years before, the figures were reversed at 45·97 per cent Labour and 41·66 per cent National. These are not far from the figures of all New Zealand seats, city, town and country together. The perimeter of rural attitudes patently runs somewhere through these electorates.

This is a fact of long standing which appeared plainly while the Labour party was climbing slowly to power. The cities initiated Labour's solid progress by electing a core of Labour candidates in 1919 and adding more in 1922. Rural and country-town electorates remained quite unmoved by Labour appeals until 1935. But the large towns began shifting in 1928 and 1931. As Labour descended, the reciprocal phenomena appeared. Farming seats left Labour in 1938 or 1943. The hard core of the cities stays Labour to this day. Meanwhile the group of large towns divided and redivided. In the last seven elections, Wanganui and Timaru have consistently returned Labour members. Napier went National once in 1951 at that party's peak; Gisborne was National in 1951 and is now. Both Hastings and Palmerston North were National in 1949 and 1951 and replaced Labour by National in 1960. These six large-town seats out of the ten have more often been Labour in a period which has witnessed two Governments of each party. Just on the other side of the scale we find Nelson with Atmore still there in 1943 and a Labour member at the last two elections. Invercargill was Labour only in 1943 and New Plymouth and Hamilton have been National all through.

Is there a meaningful pattern or simply the confusion of chance division? For these voters are in fact, if not in attitude, all on one side of the urban/rural line and their shifting balance, when the large town environment is common to all of them, is puzzling— besides being vital to the making and unmaking of governments. Perhaps perfecting the pattern we already have will clarify the situation. After arranging the constituencies according to the number of times they were Labour, and then adding the percentage for the winning candidate, Table IV is arrived at.

The most striking feature of the table is its regularity and the the closeness of the contests throughout. Though candidates of opposed parties are chosen at the top and bottom of the scale, opinion change tends to affect all constituencies alike and moves them all in the same direction. The large town constituencies certainly act as a true group. National moves upward by equal, measured steps until 1951, then bounces down and up again in agreement, incidentally, with its percentage of the nationwide

TABLE IV

*Party Representation in the Large Town Seats and
Percentage of Valid Vote for Winning Candidates*

Election	1943	1946	1949	1951	1954	1957	1960
Timaru	L51	L52	L53	L52	L45	L54	L49
Wanganui	L50	L57	L54	L51	L38	L44	L40
Napier	L44	L57	L52	N50	L51	L55	L52
Gisborne	L56	L57	L52	N51	L49	L52	N48
Palmerston N.	L49	L53	N52	N51	L48	L51	N46
Hastings	L55*	L52	N53	N54	L47	L51	N47
Nelson	I51	N52	N54	N59	N46	L48	L52
Invercargill	L52	N51	N55	N57	N44	N50	N54
New Plymouth	N47	N51	N55	N58	N50	N50	N52
Hamilton	N48	N51	N56	N58	N50	N50	N55

* Then still labelled Hawkes Bay.

vote rather than in accord with the number of seats it obtained in New Zealand as a whole. The voting values are a trifle disordered in 1943 because in all large town seats, save Nelson, there were multiple contests. The almost perfect arrangements of 1946, 1949 and 1951 reflect undistracted two-party combat, while 1954 and Wanganui's gyrations mark the appearance of Social Credit. On the face of the figures, Nelson might or might not have gone Labour in 1957 without any railway issue ever having arisen. The table also emphasizes that Nelson performed inappropriately in 1960 by about 4 or 5 per cent, or one-twentieth of the electorate, an estimate arrived at earlier in another way. And at the top of the table the wavy curves of other people's electoral fortune are stilled and flattened by loyalty to the Rev. Clyde Carr, Labour M.P. for Timaru since 1928. In two out of three of the South Island large towns, in fact, the pattern is approximated rather than obeyed; the older-fashioned influences of local personalities, issues and loyalties moderating or skewing the result somewhat—a regional difference already encountered among the wealthier city seats.

Although opinion in these large towns surges together up and down the column of constituencies, they remain—railways apart —in an order preserved through population growth and political alternation, unaltered for seventeen years. At the Nationalist extremity stand Hamilton and New Plymouth, both of them notably service towns without the history of independent industrial development of say, Wanganui, almost at the other, Labour, extremity of the column. A long established and busy port, railway workshops, freezing works, woollen mills, processing plants and fertilizer works, light industrial factories arriving in search of employables, all set the constituency higher towards Labour. The absence of a few or several of these urban accompaniments, like the presence of large numbers of retired farmers, pulls the electorate towards National. Timaru seems rather too high in the column; Invercargill too low. Otherwise the order is not difficult to understand.

This understanding, however, incorporates two partially separate explanations. Looked at one way, the line above and including Nelson and below and excluding Hastings is the perimeter of that sense of identification which joins townsmen rendering service to countrymen contributing custom and new townsmen, the boundary where country finally passes over into city, the limit to general acceptance of farmer attitudes. Looked at another way, each large town is a city writ small, a microcosm of the quite different sectionalism to be found displayed across the constituencies of the four main centres. There a new dividing line appears between socio-economic grades, partly a matter of wealth, partly of occupation, partly of status. The line does not separate European-style classes, defined by fully differentiated ways of living, nor does it cut an inscrutable way through the homogeneous, unstratified, equalitarian lump so beloved of oratory idealizing or, oddly enough, condemning New Zealand. It parts some perfectly measurable but imperfectly recognized social grades from others, equally measurable and as well understood privately as they are de-emphasized publicly—much to the detriment of clear thinking.

The large towns balance within themselves grades which in a city might have a constituency largely to themselves. Add to the urban accompaniments in a large town and immediately the city-style sectional balance of grades is affected. The same addition of say, a fertilizer works and its labour force, will also alter the sectional balance between rural and urban orientations. Thus two kinds of analysis intersect, two sets of categories are found, two perimeters parallel one another in the large towns: rural/urban on the one hand and higher and lower socio-economic grades on the other.

Indeed there is an overlap, almost a fusing of viewpoints in the large towns between the attitude of those who think with the countryman, being themselves proprietors, agents, professionals and service employees, and those who, belonging to the same groups, base their political judgements on opposition to the party of the unionists, industrial workers and of the lesser grades generally. The converse is rather less true. Unionists and industrial workers give little evidence of thinking at all along the urban/rural dimension or in any way taking up a position governed by hostility to or identification with the rural community and its interests. Rather their attention and their politics seem rivetted to the vertical dimension of status and possessions visible in the cities. They treat their environment as though it were altogether urban, which in their factory and dormitory suburb environment it is, and recognize 'our party' accordingly. 'Our party' for the other side in the large towns may be 'ours' in the first place because it is the party of people like us or because it is thought to recognize enterprise in the small owner and keep an eye on the militant unions, or primarily because it is envisaged as understanding the farmer and we all depend on the farmer. Such attitudes, of course, sit easily in combination and together they make it possible for the National party to battle strongly in what at first glance ought to count as wholly urban and probably as enemy territory.

The result is an overriding likeness in this group of electorates which straddle the dividing lines of New Zealand sectionalism, predominantly service towns slightly to the Right, more industrial towns more to the Left, but all within reaching distance of the 50 per cent line. In consequence the class of large town electorates perform nearest to the New Zealand political norm for they contain both the major divisions of New Zealand life. Some are microcosms of all New Zealand, rurally oriented and urban minded in balance, some merely concentrate the sectional appositions of our cities; but together the swings of large town opinion contribute much to the fate of the parties and altogether they may be truer mediators between city and country, matching the inclinations of both, than the mixed electorates, committed as they are to one pole.

In plotting the boundaries of New Zealand sectionalism we have now discriminated out as many classes of electorate as we can by travelling along the rural/urban dimension. Farmer, mixed, large town and city seats have been classified and the first three classes display a satisfyingly homogeneous and comprehensible performance at the polls. The large town constituencies, however, introduced another sectionalism, that of socio-economic grade, while the city seats, simply by refusing to vote wholeheartedly for the more urban party, reveal that voters are measuring Labour and National upon some other scale than being more or else less for urban interests as against rural.

Drawing the Line in the Cities

Whilst working along the rural/urban axis a straightforward sequence of proportions could be used. Census figures directly supply nearly all one could want in fixing the ratio of rural people to town and city dwellers in any given constituency.[3] But on entering the cities we pass into *terra incognita*, the unmapped tribal territories of the sociologist's 'upper-upper', 'lower-middle', and so on. Here are the fabled regions of the land agent with his code words: 'desirable residence' and 'within sound of Merivale churches'; 'panoramic views' and 'near buslines'. The grocer knows the big houses begin 'up the top of X street' and the home-buyer eventually finds out that Y and Z are the districts where he can get something for a £3700 mortgage; but it is one of the features of our culture that we do not order this widespread knowledge precisely and that we draw from it as few and as temporary conclusions as possible. The credit manager and the valuer, the tax department clerk and the town planner can all rate areas exactly according to their profession's variant of a socio-economic scale, but no index figures for these facts of our common life are issued. The social grading of an area is related— just how closely, nobody knows—to the average of its inhabitants' incomes, and income, as has been observed, 'now is more private and secret than sex'.

Lacking a public index of social grade wherewith to measure all city constituencies and so parcel them into groups, it became necessary to invert the proper process and work backwards from voting performance to the underlying reasons for the classification. The first step was to measure the constituencies as now defined

[3] It would be most useful if Redistribution Commissions resumed the pre-1946 practice of stating the numbers living outside metropolitan boundaries in seats on the margin of the cities.

by sorting them into two groups: those with a 1957 Labour margin over National of at least 10 per cent of the qualified vote and those with less or, instead, a National preponderance. Provisionally, then, a first classification was obtained by putting into Group I the twenty-two Labour strongholds in 1957 and placing in Group II the eleven constituencies which were then either marginally Labour or National. Table V shows their disposition at that election.

Certain features of this second group stood out. Firstly, the listed constituencies contained all the four cities' wealthier and most of their middling upper grade regions which general knowledge could suggest, the exceptions being in Dunedin. As a classification, Group II thus passed its first test—common performance seemed likely to proceed from a common cause. Secondly, the group really contained two kinds of seat: the marginals of both parties and three constituencies, Fendalton, Karori and Remuera, as solid for National as their Labour equivalents in safety, Roskill, Riccarton and Hutt in Group I of Labour strongholds. If the analysis of the cities was to be checked and given more depth, this secondary line of fracture would have to be watched for and conservative city strongholds, though few, be put into their own class.

Working the wrong way around, from result to cause, it is doubly wise to check the present by the past. Groups I and II might have

TABLE V

1957 Performance of Group II of City Seats

	LABOUR HELD			NATIONAL HELD	
Seat	Lab. margin % over Nat.	Lab. % vote	Seat	Nat. margin % over Lab.	Nat. % vote
Wellington Central	9·07	48·33	Manukau	·96	44·96
			Eden	2·62	46·03
St. Kilda	4·68	47·64	North Shore	2·65	46·59
Tamaki	3·70	48·63	Fendalton	13·25	50·79
Lyttelton	3·24	46·03	Karori	17·19	53·24
St. Albans	2·90	46·01	Remuera	28·59	58·28

Percentages shown throughout the table are percentages of the entire qualified vote, i.e. all enrolled plus allowed voters.

been merely the chance products of the last electoral redistribution, their blue ribbons recent or their marginality temporary,
without a past, and with no assignable and sufficient cause in
social composition. The only convincing test was to apply time
to the matter. So a history, not of some, but of all the thirty-three
present city seats was compiled back to 1919, the year the New
Zealand Labour Party as such first fought a general election. Maps
of the seven redistributions over the period and the results at seats
and booths provide a direct lineal descent for our thirty-three city
seats, either for the whole forty years or from whenever the growth
of new suburbs created them. Maps show also that in the centre
of Auckland and Wellington four areas exist which were once
populous enough to support constituencies of their own but have
now lost that privilege, their voters being absorbed into surviving
electorates.

The whole thirty-seven, present and obsolete constituencies
alike, were put in order by finding the percentage of the valid vote
the Labour candidate obtained in the 307 individual elections and
then averaging the Labour vote for each seat over the last thirty
years, the figures for the 1920s being eliminated as rather too confused by three-party contests. Again two principal groups appeared,
solid Labour on one side, marginal or National on the other, and
again the second group divides clearly between the true marginals
and what prove to be National strongholds. The history of the true
city marginals is set out in Table VI.

Thirty Years of Decision in the Cities: The Marginals
What is so striking about Table VI is its revelation of the continuity of voting over three decades. Once a marginal always a
marginal. The limits for each area are fixed quite closely and only
within them can the flux of nationwide opinion float the candidate,
good, bad or indifferent, gently up or down. There is some change
of character in that Roskill and St. Albans alone have grown
slightly more Labour over the years. But the parties could at any
of the last ten elections have taken this table as a complete map[4]
of their ground of contention in the cities. Indeed the table maps
the far boundaries of the plain across which the actual battle-

---

[4] Just once in 207 times has a city electorate outside this marginal group let
in a candidate of the 'wrong' party. In 1938, Labour's peak year, Wellington
West, the predecessor of Karori, awarded 53 per cent of its vote to Labour.

TABLE VI

History of Marginal City Seats

Allegiance of Seat given by Letter. Figures give Labour per cent of Valid Votes

Election	'31	'35	'38	'43*	'43	'46	'49	'51	'54	'57	'60	Ave.
Lyttelton	L50	L59	L61	(58)	L52	L55	L53	N50	N41	L49	L48	51·8
St. Kilda	C49	L55	L63	(60)	L55	L54	L51	N49	N40	L50	L49	51·5
Wellington Cen.	L44	L44	L60	(58)	L51	L57	L53	L52	L49	L53	N47	51·0
Dunedin Cen.	C42	L53	L59	(55)	L55	L48	L54	L52	L43	L53	L48	50·7
Waitemata							L54		L47	L54	L50	50·3
Parnell	L42	L52	L59	(57)	L48	N49	N45	N43	N41	L55	L52	48·3
Roskill						L51	N41	N49	N41	N47	N47	48·2
Manukau			L60	(54)	L47	L51	N46	N44	N37	N47	N45	47·4
Tamaki						L51	N46	N46	N41	L51	N43	46·7
North Shore	C30	L52	L58	(52)	N46	L51	N45	N43	N43	N47	N42	45·8
Eden	C31	L46	L57	(51)	L46	N45	N41	N38	N48	N47	N42	44·1
St. Albans	C28	N39	N48	(41)	N38	N50	N46	N45	N40	L49	N47	43·0
Ave. Lab. V.V.	39·5	50·0	58·3	(54·0)	48·7	51·1	47·4	46·5	42·7	50·5	47·1	
Labour Held	3	7	8	(8)	7	8	4	2	3	8	5	
National Held	5	1	1	(1)	2	3	7	9	8	3	6	
Resulting Govt	C	L	L	(L)	L	L	N	N	N	L	N	

* Column estimates effect of eliminating splinter Labour group by adding Democratic Soldier Labour Candidates' Votes to Labour Candidates'.

N.B. Changes of constituency name occurred thus:

Before 1946:

St. Kilda = Dunedin Central   Parnell = Auckland East

Wellington Central = Wellington North   North Shore = Waitemata

Dunedin Central = Dunedin West   St. Albans = Christchurch North

Before 1954:   Manukau = Otahuhu

ground has migrated, first moving rapidly from Labour's country over to the edge of National's fastness for three elections, then back to middle ground for five contests during which lesser struggles broke out behind the lines. The distance from the lines of National's victories in St. Kilda and Lyttelton in 1951-4, or of Labour's 1957 victories in Tamaki and St. Albans, calls for explanation. Thus the table can be used to pinpoint anything unusual.

On examination the problem of 1951 dissolves. Roskill's Labour vote was artificially low in 1949 because the Hon. F. W. Langstone, formerly the Labour member and latterly the Social Credit candidate, stood independently and took 8 per cent of the total. Without Langstone to split the vote in 1951, Labour soared up 7 per cent instead of declining by 1. Remove this nominal gain from the calculation and the marginal seat trend between 1949 and 1915 becomes an average Labour loss of 2 per cent. St. Kilda declined 2 per cent that year and Lyttelton 3, so there was nothing out of the way about their conversion at this point; it had been advancing steadily since 1938. On the other hand, Labour in 1954 suffered severely from Social Credit's appearance in Lyttelton, St. Kilda and Dunedin Central, all South Island seats. It remained a matter of touch and go for the National men in St. Kilda and Lyttelton, however, both in 1951 and 1954; three margins of under 1 per cent and one of 2. The reversion of these seats to Labour in 1957 was a reversion to normal. Only in 1960 did they act somewhat irregularly by shedding too little of their Labour vote, as also did St. Albans and Fendalton. With an average performance Lyttelton would certainly have passed back to National in 1960 and St. Kilda might have.

Looking at the trend on the table from 1957 to 1960 one notices that the movement is medium to light and has about it an air of restoring normality. St. Albans and Tamaki cease their caprice of 1957. Only Wellington Central acts contrarily, though suffering no larger loss of the valid vote than Tamaki and only a shade more than Dunedin Central and Eden. Heavy movements of marginals characterized the previous election, 1957, not 1960. In 1957 the movement in St. Kilda, Dunedin Central, Roskill, Manukau and Tamaki was 10 or more per cent towards Labour while Lyttelton, Waitemata and St. Albans lurched 7 to 10 per cent. Roskill's 14 per cent jump Leftward was assisted by a narrowing of its boundaries which had the opposite effect on neighbouring Eden of helping it proceed untypically 1 per cent further to National.

Nevertheless, in these electorates of new building and young families the overwhelming trend was towards the party offering capitalization of the family benefit and 3 per cent housing loans. By the same token, the trend was away from the party that had presided over the credit squeeze which struck at the mortgage market, and away also from the party which had created the group house colonies of Roskill, Tamaki, Manukau, northern St. Albans and western Dunedin Central. Wellington Central and Eden, flatting and boarding electorates, did not join the rush to Labour; nor did North Shore, where the swelling population had incomes enabling them to build for themselves but debarring them from State aid for low-cost housing. The three wealthy or flatting exceptions thus prove the rule of the much moved eight new family constituencies, the latter managing, in their eagerness, to make the average movement of the whole group of seats the largest since 1943. The decline to 1960 was, by contrast, so soft as to suggest a substantial degree of content with what had been done on the young family front. But this is to anticipate.

For what Table VI also confirms is that as goes the marginal third of city seats, however softly, so goes the power to govern. By mounting on a graph the figures for the average vote of Labour candidates in marginal city seats and then adding equivalent figures for National we can follow the correspondence clearly.[5] Both parties began well below the halfway line because of the presence up to 1938 of numerous other party and independent candidates, almost all conservative. The decisive cross-over for the 1935 election duly transferred the Government to Labour despite these distracting competitors, and the fact that National as well as Labour rose to 1938 signifies the clearance of third, fourth and fifth candidates. From these eliminations National derived less benefit—4·4 per cent—than might have been expected when one remembers that almost all the eliminated would have been anti-Labour earlier. The reality of conversion is to be seen in Labour's vaulting line.

From the 1938 highpoint, an election fought on the issue of Labour's pledge to introduce its system of social security, that

---

[5] The official Coalition candidate in 1931 is taken as the Nationalist, that label not being employed until the 1935 election.

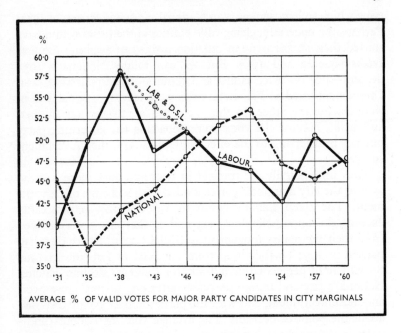

AVERAGE % OF VALID VOTES FOR MAJOR PARTY CANDIDATES IN CITY MARGINALS

party's way led only down for fourteen years. The wartime 1943 election saw a shambles of variant candidacies but the outline of affairs in the public mind was clear enough. National's steady gain continued, the party obtaining perhaps 1 per cent less than it would have had there been no independency at all. But official Labour tumbled very nearly as fast as it had ever climbed in the depression years. A third party drawing, as the graph shows, almost all its support from ex-Labour voters had interrupted the Labour–National dialogue. The ostensibly radical Democratic Soldier Labour Party had thus the power to attract from the ranks of Labour even in the better-off suburbs. When it disappeared, the Labour vote came back for 1946 almost to where it would have rested if J. A. Lee, the D.S.L. leader, had never held his dramatic quarrel with his party superiors.

The parties were now close in their shares of the marginal city suffrages. For three elections, 1946, 1949 and 1951, they competed undisturbed by others, and in 1949 the lines crossed and the government changed hands. We cannot now tell what would have happened in the 'normal' election year of 1952 without the strike issue which so handsomely won National the snap election of 1951. Perhaps the uncertain, changeable politics of the fifties would have started then on the issue of inflation instead of awaiting the first credit squeeze and 1954. But we can follow National's 1954 descent—just on twice as fast as Labour's—in response to Social Credit's appearance. Far more votes were leaving one party than were leaving the other. In this, 1954 was a pale version of 1943, and again, because the votes were departing the governing party but not transferring to the effective Opposition, the Government survived.

They undoubtedly did transfer in 1957 and once more a cross-over in the city marginals corresponded with a change of Government. The steep Labour climb to 1957, which so noticeably exceeds the minor National sag, reveals that city voters moved from their temporary lodgement in Social Credit, where they had paused in 1954 on their way from National to Labour. In 1960 Social Credit persuaded none back, for Labour's decline matches National's rise and the graph ceases after one further cross-over, another Government, and with the parties almost evenly disposed about the point of decision. The average vote for Labour candidates in the marginal city seats over thirty years has been 48·2 per cent. Whenever Labour's vote has fallen below this, for example, to 47·4 per cent in 1949, Labour has gone out. National now rests at 47·8 per cent and Labour at 47·1 per cent. It is apparent that the marginal city seats justify with continuity and sensitivity their grouping and their name.

Who Makes Governments and Who Concurs

To what are they sensitive and why? Do the shifts within this group of seats correspond with the fate of governments simply because it is here that governments are made? Only in part is this so. The unseating of two of the marginal city National members in 1957 was essential to making the second Labour Government, but so was Labour's capture of one large town seat in 1957 and of four such in 1954. Again, at the previous change of Government in 1949, shifts in both groups were necessary. The House would have been evenly split had not victories in four marginal and two large towns provided National with a sizeable majority of twelve. And in 1960, without National's three marginal city and three large town gains once more the House would have been divided equally.

A series of conclusions can be drawn. Firstly, that elections are decided by the ejection of members in these two classes of seat. Secondly, to have permitted this to be so, the other three-quarters of New Zealand's electorates must have been fairly evenly matched —farmer, mixed rural-urban, and the few wealthy city seats against the mass of city electorates and the few Maori constituencies.

A glance at the elections since the abolition of the country quota shows this to be strikingly true. The bulk of constituencies simply stayed stable through the surface gyrations of the fifties and took no action. At the end of the first Labour Government these underlying strata of our political landscape shook down to a more conservative position and, five elections later, made the minimum move of one, again to the Right. So, as was noted earlier, the more rural of the parties is not only coping with increasing urbanization but is slowly gaining ground.

TABLE VII

Party Seat Holdings apart from City Marginals and Large Towns

	1946	1949	1951	1954	1957	1960
National	31	33	33	33	33	34
Labour	28	26	26	26	26	25

Thirdly, since the underlying strata are tilted towards National and since that tilt has increased from a three-seat lead in 1946 to seven in the fifties and now nine in 1960, therefore Labour must win much more than an even share of city marginal and large town seats to get into power. In the first three elections of the first National Government that party secured not just equality but had a lead over Labour in the decisive classes of constituency, so National majorities were heavy. For Labour to reverse the position and secure the precarious hold on the Government they grasped in 1957 it was necessary for Labour to take fifteen of the debatable seats to six for National. Now that only a fraction of 1 per cent divides opinion on the two parties in the city marginals and National leads in the large towns by under 2 per cent, the even scores accompany a twelve seat National majority. The tilt of the underlying strata, which expresses the slow-changing balance be-

tween the two nations of country and city, makes it hard for
Labour to climb the slope to office.

Lastly, we can conclude that opinion among the hundreds of
thousands of electors in city marginals and large towns must be
very much in tune, for otherwise, if one class moved contrary to
the other, the shifts of opinion would cancel out instead of plotting
the zig-zag course of the fifties. Table VIII reveals just how
harmoniously political judgements have altered as between these
two separate eighths of the New Zealand electorate. Agreement
about the direction of movement, to or away from Labour, is total
and the difference in degree is tiny. For twenty-three years the
large towns were a trifle more favourable to Labour than the city
marginals; after 1954 Social Credit retained more support in the
large towns than it did in the cities, and so the large town figure
dipped slightly under its companion.

TABLE VIII

*The Correspondence between City Marginals and
Large Towns*

Average Percentage of Valid Vote received by Labour Candidates

	1931	1935	1938	1943	1946	1949	1951	1954	1957	1960
Large towns	42·2	49·4	59·4	49·9	52·3	48·6	46·5	44·3	49·0	45·1
Marginal city	39·5	50·0	58·3	48·7	51·1	47·4	46·5	42·7	50·5	47·1
Difference	2·7	0·6	1·1	1·2	1·2	1·2	0·0	1·6	1·5	2·0

Such long continued consonance in seats which are marginal
because they mix voters in differing economic circumstances and
of varying social standing raises the possibility that urban public
favour for the major parties is given or retrieved in fairly equal
measure regardless of the social grade of voters. In that event,
groups of electorates distinguished by being predominantly of one
or another social grade would each have a semi-permanent judgement of a party which would separate the results of that grade
from the others. But all grades could be taking much the same
view of what was common to all at a particular election, say a
credit squeeze or a welfare programme or a tax change, and all
would respond roughly alike, each at its own level. This is, in fact,
what happens as the following graph illustrates.

Over the whole thirty years the electors of the cities have judged
the changing political situation much the same way whatever their

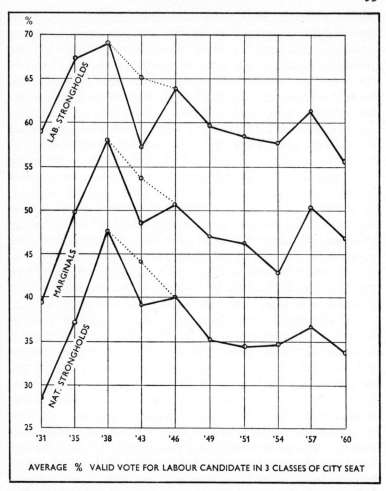

AVERAGE %   VALID VOTE FOR LABOUR CANDIDATE IN 3 CLASSES OF CITY SEAT

social background. That is, the judgements that high, middling
and lower income groups make begin with different initial weighting, as it were, but then proceed to rise and fall together. It
follows that the number of electors changing their minds and their
votes at an election are proportionately as numerous in seats of all
kinds.

Whether the ones to change their votes at election A are also
the ones who change again at election B—in other words, the much
sought after 'floating' voter—cannot be certainly told from these

figures, although, since voter movement has subsequently decreased when compared with that in the thirties, many must have stranded in one party. Yet we do have before us a far more telling reason for putting to one side that mythically decisive character, 'the floater' or 'swinger'. The graph makes superabundantly obvious that Democratic Soldier Labour votes in all classes of seat came straight out of and went back into normally Labour ranks. Ignoring the interposition of the D.S.L. then, we have a record of five successive Labour declines in Labour strongholds and in marginals and of a precipitous fall which finally levels out within the National bailiwicks. All the changing was one way; people 'floated' out of Labour but not back. In short, they did not 'float' or 'swing' or move back and forth at all. There is no evidence in the thirties and forties of a considerable number of voters regularly changing their minds. No doubt there was some fringe of unstable voting of the sort that appears in the Dunedin Central survey, but it must have been self-cancelling. All the evidence presented here says that at each election a fresh section of the electorate, well off as well as otherwise, altered its long-term opinion about Labour.

The facts negate the existence of an effectual mass of 'floating' voters in eight elections out of ten. The facts are quite positive about no one class of electorate holding a monopoly of the changeable, whether short or long term or at any time. Marginal city electorates in general change in the same direction as the strongholds of both parties. Their place between traditionally Labour constituencies and loyally National electorates has been held with great constancy. Like a naval squadron at sea, all groups keep station, tracking and wheeling together. Over thirty years the gap between Labour and marginal has averaged 12·9 per cent; that between marginal and National, 11·4 per cent. Conversion to Labour took place at different times—the strongholds of that party were fixed by 1935; the marginals and the National camp yielded most in 1938. But the movement from Labour took place at different rates. Measuring the second movement from 1938 to the present we find that the stations of the top two differ by an average of 11·4 per cent and of the bottom two by 11·2 per cent. We may safely take it that what makes an electorate marginal is not the residence there of greater numbers of 'floating' or even of 'long-term changers', but the balanced or middling political and social composition of the electorates themselves.

The Social Sectionalism of the Cities

The analysis is thus thrown back on to this question of the social composition of the three groups of city electorates, since we defined them by their continuing political preferences and have followed their remarkably constant variance in voting. What makes a National stronghold such? Why do the marginals cleave to a station 11·4 per cent less favourable to Labour than one group and 11·2 per cent more so than the other? The reply from a New Zealander who knows Eden, Ponsonby and Remuera, respectively, or St. Albans, Sydenham and Fendalton, will be that the initial weighting goes according to wealth. Here is something generally, indeed overwhelmingly, guessed at, which needs to be known more precisely. The obvious measure of average income in each electorate is, however, not available. Nor have we that measure for any area to which political figures might be adapted, so permitting direct comparison.

We can employ an indirect measure, however. Three years ago I was able to take a hand in designing some thesis research being done by Mr. Ian Pool with the object of classifying the regions of Auckland in various ways, among them by socially grading statistical districts on a Status and Possessions Index.[6] The proportion of managers, of professionals and of employers was found for each of the sixty-one districts into which the census divides the Auckland metropolitan area. Then the proportion in each of washing machines, refrigerators and hot water services was added into the index. These six factors were all found mathematically to be connected in fact, as common sense would suggest. None of them amounts to a pure test of wealth, but all together they measure adequately what enters into New Zealand social grading: type of job, ownership, amenities and possessions and, indirectly, occupational prestige.

Here, happily, was a measure of city areas, but unfortunately the areas, though built up, like electorates, from the tiny meshblocks used by the census, were not the same shape as the electorates. At this point it became necessary for me to retire on to the 882 individual booth figures for the 1957 and 1960 elections in the metropolitan area. Results for the booths in each statistical district

[6] For a brief report, see Pool, I., 'A Method for the Social Grading of Areas' in *Pacific Viewpoint*, Vol. 1, No. 2, September 1960, pp. 225-37.

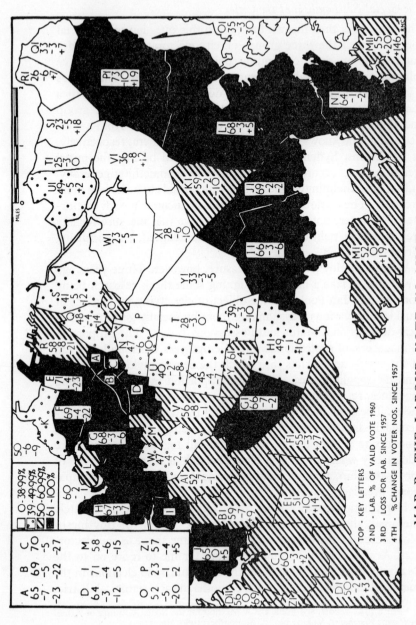

MAP B. THE LABOUR VOTE IN AUCKLAND IN 1960 BY
STATISTICAL DISTRICTS

were added up and the proportion voting Labour was worked out. The rank of each district was thus known on two scales: according to the index of status and possessions, and according to the percentage voting Labour. The two rankings were then matched mathematically first for 1957, then for 1960.[7] The result is expressed as a figure, a perfect relation showing as 1, and any figure above ·325 revealing a significant connexion between social grade and voting.

A coefficient of correlation of a very high order appeared for both elections: ·801 for 1957 and ·781 for 1960. Voters in an area do not merely choose National or Labour on a crude assessment of themselves and the parties. The voters discriminate with the utmost nicety and a district is National, for example, not just when it is well up on the status and possessions index but also to the degree in which it is so.

The fact that the coefficient of correlation is a shade lower in 1960 than in 1957 indicates the delicacy of the relation. The status and possessions ranking came from figures collected for the 1956 census. Growth in Auckland, with its attendant social amendments, has proceeded rapidly since then, the metropolitan area adding 18 per cent to its population in five years. The election of 1960 was three years farther than the previous one from social grading as it was in 1956 and the resultant fit was not quite so perfect. Yet, one reflects, even the torrent of new voters has scarcely disturbed the social and political character of the city's parts, as the thirty year record of the city's electorates bears witness.

The distribution of the city's sympathies and its social grades are visible on Map B opposite. These fifty-four districts on or near the isthmus fall into five large regions.[8] At the top of the social grading are the ten north-eastern districts—white on the map—running along the seaward, sunny slopes from the cliffs of Glendowie to the end of the Remuera ridge and thence south down Mountain Road or across northern One Tree Hill to the heights

[7] Spearman's Coefficient of Rank Order Correlation was used.

$$\rho = 1 - \left(\frac{6\varepsilon d^2}{n(n^2 - 1)} \right)$$

[8] To clarify voting, YI was separated from JI, though they are the two parts of one statistical district. DI, DII, MI, MII and OI are likewise but portions of awkwardly mixed census wholes. For ranking and correlating, these sub-districts were put back into their proper statistical units.

of St. Andrews Road in Epsom South. Towards the city's heart and towards the west and south-west, running down like a glacis from the walls of a fort, stretches the moderately National band of eight districts—the lightly dotted apron around the Nationalist heartland. Those nearest the commercial area, Parnell (S), Grafton (Q) and Mount Eden North (N), mix flats, boarding-houses and hostels with shops and residences and have been a political no-man's-land of fairly evenly divided sympathies for most of this century. The four running southward are solidly residential, ranging from 'lower-upper' in Hillsborough (HI) and Royal Oak (Z) to 'upper-middle' in Mount Eden South (X) and 'lower-middle' in Mount Eden Central (U).

The old heart of Liberal-voting Auckland and the modern core of Labour's strength lies in the third, black and barred block of eleven districts in the north-west. Stretching from the city proper (R) the black covers the seven lowest ranking districts on the status and possessions scale (A, B, C, D, E, F and G). Point Chevalier (H) is somewhat more prosperous so there is a per-ceptible element of tradition in its high Labour vote. Westmere (L) and Morningside (M) are flanking regions with patches of better housing intermixed. These long and heavily settled, lower-income areas are nearly as solidly Labour as the well-to-do ten are Nationalist on the north-east. Labour's core is supported by the predominantly barred block of thirteen in the south-west. In the 1910s and twenties, suburban building followed the tram-lines across the undulating plain, and in the forties, State house blocks were added (parts of H, BI and Y; most of I and GI). Then in the fifties a mixture of group building and moderately large bungalows rapidly filled in the remaining paddocks and surged over the crest to face the southern harbour. At present this thrust is carrying the same categories beyond the isthmus and to the north past the reaches of the upper Waitemata. This fourth, south-western block is almost entirely 'lower-middle' on Pool's index and is moderately Labour wherever State houses are not present to raise the count, or where no elevated view of the sea appears to depress it.

Lastly we have the south-eastern block, heavily Labour, and anchored on the bastion of Onehunga (II), which was heavily Liberal at the turn of the century and Labour by 1922. Small houses, State houses and group houses support Labour all the way up the six-mile crescent to the back of Glendowie. The lie of the land is away from the mid-day sun, offering glimpses of the shallow upper Manukau or tidal Tamaki, the houses descending the downward slopes and rocky outcrops, neglected until the inrush of population after the Second World War.

A few districts, isolated from their fellows, should be allowed to explain themselves. Tiny Newmarket (O) is a subordinate Auckland Central (R), a congeries of factories and shops with little old houses, and an occasional street of substantial residences. Ellerslie (KI) has an overflow of wealthier homes into its eastern corner and this lowers its Labour vote. Herne Bay (K) preserves the big houses from Auckland's second-best residential district of the 1890s. Looking out to sun and sea, the buildings are now mostly converted to flats, but flats sufficiently expensive to preserve Jervois Road to the south as the political watershed it has been for seventy years. Neighbouring Westmere (L) has also enough harbour view and elevation, particularly in the north-east, to have a long record of lessened enthusiasm for Labour. The influence of altitude all by itself is most patent, however, at Mount Albert (W) where larger homes rest on the sunny flanks of the hill and follow the rise along the main road. The island of conservatism so created has been perceptible on booth maps for forty years.

Across to the north-east in Orakei (UI), the hand of Government manages still to smooth the social consequences of topography. This district is made up of a western third of the wealthiest homes in modern Auckland and an eastern two-thirds of State houses built in the first wave of the late thirties and early forties and many of them now privately owned and extended to suit their unusually handsome siting. The compromise 49 per cent for Labour matches the social balance struck.

The fact is that these statistical districts are not always drawn to suit the sociologist or the political scientist. They serve to bare the strong relation between political preference on the one hand and status and possessions on the other. But they do less than justice to the delicacy with which voters measure out their support to parties according to their socio-economic grading. Map C, on the next page, is designed to illustrate more exactly the political regions which underlie the cruder statistical districts. The map is based on the use of hundreds of polling-booths as

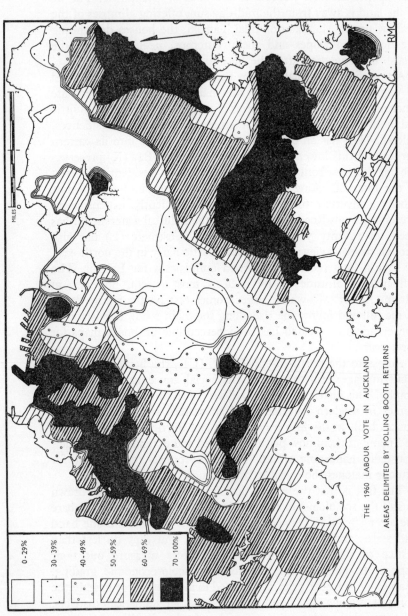

THE 1960 LABOUR VOTE IN AUCKLAND

AREAS DELIMITED BY POLLING BOOTH RETURNS

0 - 29%

30 - 39%

40 - 49%

50 - 59%

60 - 69%

70 - 100%

MILES

MAP C. THE POLITICAL FORM OF A CITY, SHOWING ISOPOLS
DERIVED FROM BOOTH RETURNS

reporting stations, just as meteorological stations supply observations which make up a weather map. Instead of isobars, lines joining points of equal barometric pressure, we have what might be termed 'isopols', lines joining points of equal political preference. To vary the comparison, the map shows the heights and depths of party preference in 1960, the lines being the political contours, which are likewise social contours and frequently, as has been suggested, physical contours as well.

This political topography of Auckland is very much fixed, subject to erosion by flats and leached out in spots by shop and factory development, but only to be sharply altered by fresh lava flows of housing. Elections leave this fundamental shape unaltered, but at all reporting points there is much the same rise or a fairly even fall in the pressure of opinion for Labour and conversely for National. Candidates change, and even parties come and go, but the outlines of the socio-political map reassert themselves election after election.[9]

It is on this basic form of the city and on the expectation of an even rise or fall of party preference that we can ground our reasoning as to particular elections. If Labour drops 7 per cent over its traditional core but only 2 and 3 per cent where new lower-income families are establishing themselves then, though the imbalance is not marked, it is sufficiently abnormal to alert the observer and isolate possible causes. Not only is the social composition of an area fundamental to its politics but the knowledge of that composition is basic to understanding why areas respond as they do to the legislative record and the proposals for the future of the parties.

To relate this information back to the performance of the three classes of city electorate is not difficult. If the map of the fifty-four districts on or near the Auckland isthmus was more crude than the map of polling-booth preferences, the electorates are simply more crude approximations again. This is unfair to Remuera alone, for it is built precisely and harmoniously of districts VI, WI, XI and YI, four of the wealthy, very Nationalist districts of the north-eastern block. This socially homogeneous electorate returned a resounding 68 per cent of its valid vote for National

[9] Cf. Aimer, E. P., *The Politics of a City*, 1958 (on Auckland, 1899–1935) and Orbell, J. M., *Politics of Prosperity*, 1960 (on Auckland, 1938–57); unpublished M.A.Hons. theses done under my supervision at the University of Auckland.

and permitted Labour just 27 per cent. At the other end of the scale stands the Onehunga seat, a Labour stronghold, straightforwardly made of districts II, JI and KI. The Labour share of 65 per cent requires no more comment than the opposite verdict of Remuera.

Tamaki, to Remuera's north-east and east, comprises PI, QI, RI, SI, TI, and UI. It was a marginal electorate not because it was made of middle-income voters, but because it balanced four 'upper' districts against the one populous 'lower' district of Tamaki (PI) and the internally balanced and outwardly compromising district of Orakei (UI). Eden constituency, at the National end of the spectrum of city marginals, is just as explicable but more evenly composed. All, save a shaving on the south, of 'upper' Epsom (P & T) and all of 'upper-middle' Mount Eden (X, U & N) once more minus three streets on the south, together constitute the basis for a very conservative to moderately conservative seat. To this is added a northern lower-income fringe made up of a third of Kingsland (D), all of Eden Terrace (C), the least well-off tenth of Grafton (Q) and half of moderately Labour Newmarket. This fringe counterbalances Epsom and the overall result—42 per cent Labour—corresponds to the sympathies of the three moderately National Mount Eden districts. This is the other kind of marginal city electorate, a type which, like St. Albans in Christchurch, contains and balances its extremes but also, like St. Albans, is decided by the preferences of a sizeable region of intermediate socio-economic grading (see Map D).

The other three cities have their characteristic social forms which impress their abiding shapes on the paper electorates fitted over them. As one consequence of these semi-permanent shapes, it is possible to discover classes of city seat and have them perform as consistently as they have been shown to do for thirty years. A second consequence is the establishment of a strong connexion between political result and social character which permits some confidence about reasoning back from the unequal electoral responses of the classes of seat towards the unequal way in which social groups were repelled or attracted by the parties.

Not, it should be emphasized, that a major party's responses from the various sectors of the New Zealand electorate is ever wildly unequal between sector and sector. Opinion in the three classes of city constituency has a history of moving broadly

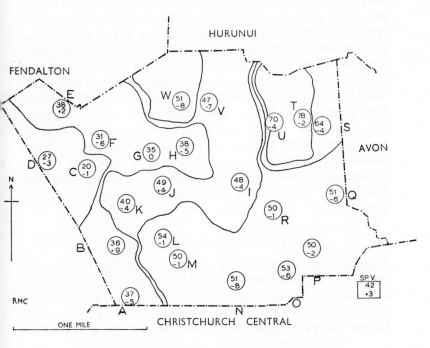

MAP D. ST. ALBANS ELECTORATE

A	East Merivale	M	South St. Albans
B	N.E. Merivale	N	S.E. St. Albans
C	Bretts Rd.	O	West Richmond
D	Papanui Rd.	P	N.E. Richmond
E	Paparoa St.	Q	S.E. Shirley
F	N.W. Malvern	R	S.W. Shirley
G	East Malvern	S	N.E. Shirley
H	North St. Albans	T	N.C. Shirley
I	East St. Albans	U	N.W. Shirley
J	St. Albans School	V	East Mairehau
K	West St. Albans	W	West Mairehau
L	St. Albans Centre		

together. The city marginals were as one with the large towns for three decades. Only the mixed rural and urban and the farming seats held to another course. A nation's opinion moves more steadily and by smaller amounts than one would gather from watching the dramatic ousting of a tenth of Parliament's membership. Therefore we must attend to the small differences and, to attend usefully, these variations on a common theme need to be tuned in clearly by a convincing and accurate sorting of the seats. This grouping has left us with seven classes of seat: farming, mixed rural and urban, and large towns on the country-city axis; upper-income National strongholds, balanced or middling-income marginals, and lower-income Labour fortresses on the socio-economic axis; and, in a class by themselves, the four Maori seats. What changes from 1957, then, did they register in 1960?

II. *The Analysis Applied: 1960*

Most notably, Labour lost the election in 1960, but National did not win it. The movement of opinion was away from Labour in every class of seat, the nationwide loss being 5·87 per cent. National gained 1·64 per cent, or between a third and a quarter of what Labour dropped. Table IX sets out how each group responded.

TABLE IX

Labour Loss and National Gain by Classes of Seat

Percentage Share of Total Qualified Vote in 1960 Subtracted from 1957 Percentage Share, or Vice Versa. (For nature of qualified vote, see footnote, p. 209)

	Maori	Poorer City	Farmer	Mixed	Large Town	Marginal City	Richer City
Lab. Loss	9·41	7·53	5·81	5·68	4·69	4·51	4·10
Nat. Gain	1·48	2·51	2·07	1·27	1·47	·91	·56
Nat. Gain as proportion of Lab. Loss	1/6	1/3	1/3	1/5	1/3	1/5	1/7

Labour's share of the vote dropped most heavily where it has been normally strongest—in the Maori and poorer city seats. The party's loss in the farmer and mixed rural and urban seats was close to the national average but, since Labour has not done well here for decades, this further cut meant a particularly heavy draining away of remaining supporters. Labour lost least among the mixed or higher-income urban seats. In the decisive large towns and marginals the sag was less than two-thirds of the decline in Labour strongholds, and least of all among the blue ribbon National city seats. But everywhere the great bulk of the vote did not transfer to National. At best National took a third of those social opposites, the farmer seats and the Labour city strongholds, at worst, only a seventh of Labour's departed in wealthy city constituencies.

Non-Voting; Effect and Cause

Where, then, did the voters go if not into National? To answer this it is essential to base one's calculations on all potential voters, whether they voted in 1957 and 1960, in one and not the other year, or in neither election. Non-voters must be tracked because the answer to where most ex-Labour voters went in 1960 is: out of voting entirely—for the time being. If one considers, as is usual, only shares of the valid vote, that is, of the people whose votes were properly cast and therefore counted in choosing the members, one neatly builds the non-voter and the informal voter out of the calculation. In this kind of detection, where the suspect has probably hidden in the cellar, it is useless to look only on the ground floor and upstairs, as the following model demonstrates.

	Numbers			Per cent of valid vote			Per cent of qualified vote		
	'57	'60	Change	'57	'60	Change	'57	'60	Change
Party A	1100	900	−200	57·89	52·94	−4·95	55·00	45·00	−10·00
Party B	800	800	0	42·11	47·06	+4·95	40·00	40·00	0
Valid voters	1900	1700	−200	100·00	100·00	±4·95			
Non-voters	100	300	+200				5·00	15·00	+10·00
Qualified	2000	2000	0				100·00	100·00	±10·00

The number qualified to vote in the model has been held constant for both elections and all the real movement of opinion is out of party A into non-voting. Working on qualified percentages the 200 shifting votes can be followed to their actual destination, whereas the valid vote calculation falsifies the trend into a simple exchange between party A and party B. It also seriously understates the amount of opinion movement there has been. Auckland Central is a case in point. Noting only valid voters, the apparent change is that Labour loses 5·86 per cent and National gains 5·02 per cent. Taking qualified voters, Labour is down 9·80 per cent, National up 1·15 per cent, and non-voting increases by 8·34 per cent.

Calculating on the basis of all qualified voters, therefore, we get the following relation between the diminishing Labour share and the expanding portion of the non-voters. Abstention is closely related on Table X to sagging enthusiasm for Labour

TABLE X

	Maori	Richer City	Poorer City	Marginal City	Mixed	Large Town	Farmer
Non-Voting Gains	+8·46	+4·13	+3·93	+3·22	+2·38	+2·36	+1·89
Lab. Loss	−9·41	−4·10	−7·53	−4·51	−5·68	−4·69	−5·81
Proportion	9/10	10/10	1/2	7/10	2/5	1/2	1/3

everywhere. The proportions coming out of Labour and just not voting are either greater or far greater than ex-Labourites going on to National in all save farming seats. In the wealthier and marginal city constituencies, and in the Maori seats too, this was the only important kind of voter movement there was. Since this transfer from Labour to non-voting is the crux of what happened in the 1960 general election it is as well to present a complete picture.

The Diagram opposite demonstrates just how opinion changed. Labour loss and non-voting glare starkly on each column and only the two rural pillars proclaim much true change of allegiance, with Social Credit taking an ominously large share there from the National Party's standpoint. So tall and black and white is the Maori column that, in Maori eyes, 1960 must have been an election

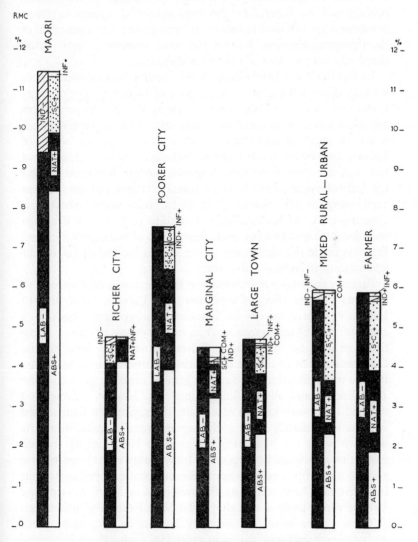

RMC

THE MOVEMENT OF VOTES

The Left of Columns shows Shares of Qualified Vote Lost,
the Right shows those Gained.

of a different order from the contest the farmer or suburbanite participated in. Therefore the explanation of events in those constituencies will have to follow on from a more thorough grasp of the European changes. But for the other seventy-six seats, what shape has the problem of 1960 now assumed?

In looking for a prime cause for Labour's decline everywhere we may dismiss the coupled attractions of National's programme, leader and past record because, in so far as National had a positive appeal, it was most unequally felt and, measured by positive gains, it was so much smaller than Labour's loss. There was plenty of Labour dust raised but the bag of National's vacuum cleaner was less than one-third full. If the National machine had been attracting Labour voters, most of these voters certainly did not confirm their liking for Mr. Holyoake's party by voting for it. And this is even more true of Social Credit. The third party's New Zealand-wide increase was 1·03 per cent, three-fifths of National's increase. But this made the alternative to the alternative the choice of but one-sixth of dislodged Labourites.

Patently the major movement was not the result of attraction to anything but the effect of repulsion from Labour. Something in Labour's record—or in its innocuous programme—became a cause of general annoyance so that, in every class of seat, a significant proportion of Labour adherents would not vote for the Government but could not quite bring themselves to vote against it. The most probable and suitable general cause is, of course, the 1958 Budget and all that hung therefrom. Here is a cause that reached into every kind of electorate, dismaying the fainthearted with its immediately adverse efficacy and remote justification. As we have seen, the Nationalist Opposition had shrewdly helped along this anticipated process, not by wielding trowel and mortar and building up a second home for disgruntled opponents, but by constantly hammering on the wedge of taxation, thus prying Labour voters loose so that they fell off on to a heap of abstention.

These voters were demonstrably Labour in 1957 and absent without leave, but with cause, in 1960. Has such a thing happened before? There is some evidence that Labour voters also reacted thus in 1951. Until a full study is made of the destination of movement by percentages of the qualified vote—or its near equivalent at the time, the enrolled vote—it is not possible to do more than suspect, as the election night figures for 1960 led me to suspect, that abstention would be the clue to the reasons for Labour's fall. The recent history of European non-voting, excluding 1943, a casualty of wartime rolls, is given in Table XI.

TABLE XI

	'35	'38	'46	'49	'51	'54	'57	'60
% not voting	9·25	7·15	6·54	6·47	11·17	8·75	6·86	9·71
Trend in non-voting		−2·10	−0·61	−0·07	+4·70	−2·42	−1·89	+2·85

Apart from the phenomenally high level of voluntary democratic participation which this table emphasizes, it also shows that when the voters have made up their minds, as the graphs earlier pointed to their doing in 1938, 1946, 1949 and 1957, then non-voting declines to around 7 per cent. When a three-party situation confuses them and they are caught in the process of remaking their allegiances and abandoning conservatism, as in 1935 and 1954, non-voting is about 9 per cent. But when Labour stalwarts are suddenly embarrassed about voting for the party, as they were in 1951 and 1960, then non-voting soars—comparatively. All the city and large town valid vote graphs show a moderate National increase in 1951 under the stimulus of the strike election. The lines rise steeply until 1949, then rather dispiritedly go up more slowly. They would do just that, on a calculation restricted to the votes actually cast, if Labour men had found they could not support the strikers, nor the equivocal position of Mr. Nash, nor the Holland Government's efforts, and had therefore stayed home. Undoubtedly an unusual number did not arrive at the polls. Labour losses in the cities were under 2 per cent everywhere. Transference to National in 1951 could well prove to be largely a mathematical figment when we consider that a more severe Labour decline in 1960 and a smaller increase in non-voting in 1960 proved to mean, on the undistorted measurement of all qualified voters, that two out of three who would leave Labour would not vote for anyone else.

The case for the Budget as prime cause should now be tested to the maximum where it is least applicable because Labour voters were fewest, that is, in the rurally oriented electorates. In 1960 Labour was 25·49 per cent of the thirteen North Island farmer seats and 30·57 per cent of the seven South Island farmer constituencies. This low point was plumbed following a setback more severe than it looks on the surface, as has been noted. When Labour's 1960 farm share is compared with their previously small portion, more than a sixth is found to be missing, a greater *rate* of loss than in any other class of seat, including the Maori. The first dozen constituencies, ranked by rate of Labour decline, include nine farmer and three mixed rural and urban electorates, and only five farmer seats fall below the national average—four of them, Franklin, Rodney, Hurunui and Selwyn, invaded by suburban growth, and Raglan, affected now and for the last thirty-five years by its miners.

The position of Labour among farmers, as studies of the Taranaki and the Rotorua booths confirm, is no position for a major party. Outside small towns and hamlets, polling places have been registering 70, 80 and more per cent for National, a phenomenon only to be matched by either major party in narrowly bounded, socially cohesive areas in the cities. This country singlemindedness dates back to the forties. The tilted strata, down which both Labour Governments tumbled along with their lost urban marginals, were inclined that way because the farming community do not recognize Labour as in any sense 'theirs'. Labour is held to be of the city, the unions, the civil servants; the party of the manufacturer sheltering behind import control while the farmer sells in a competitive market and buys New Zealand-made at a protected price.

And in 1960 Labour was the party of the Budget—a Budget raising death duties at a time when inflating land values had made it very expensive in mortgages for farm sons to continue on the land after the estate had yielded up its enlarged tribute. Such Labour farmers as remained no doubt matched these much trumpeted exactions against the negotiating success of the Hons. Nordmeyer and Skinner over butter dumping and the E.E.C., and some followed their neighbours out of the city party and into National or Social Credit. In Rotorua we can note settlers on the newly developed lands actually doing so.

Also in Rotorua a very different group was encountered, the hydro and forestry workers, and they were departing, it was suggested, because of other sections of the Budget affecting single spenders especially. Rotorua was the last non-mining rural or even partly rural electorate which Labour could have lost, and it went. There are milling, railway and construction camps in most rural constituencies, however, besides shearers, and if the farmer is fortunate, the single farm labourer in 'the room out the back'. No doubt they contributed their quota. Whether this group moved into a party, as well as out of one, we can rarely tell, since farm labour votes alongside the boss at the one booth. But the timber and hydro sites of Rotorua demonstrated that abstention and Social Credit were the refuges of these discontented ex-Labour Uitlanders in the countryside. Moreover, that third of all movement in farmer electorates which went into non-voting can only have come either from Labour deserters or from Labour failure to replace dead stalwarts with first voters.

There must have been some newly entitled voters in these seats who did not poll. Labour as a declining, discouraged party in the area, with a powerful disincentive for the free-spending new earner and a static, ageing organization, probably did suffer a deal of attrition thus, rather than simply get cut into by conversion. On the other hand, if the young were passing innocently from youth to non-voting, true non-voting without the colour of abstention which previous party commitment implies, then National must have failed to convince also. Yet that party has command of the community and a machine cared for and tended by all but a handful of the opinion leaders in each district.

Unfortunately our evidence on new citizens and non-voting comes from the cities. We must presume that the age of 'couldn't care less' and the repudiation of parents, the elderly, and of both their parties, has come to the country too. The perpetual revolt of youth against authority and the set minds of a united community normally recruits a certain minority into the opposite party. Labour in rural areas must have been resting on this in part. But the new turn nowadays given to revolt—opting out entirely from established patterns of social concern—would certainly be assisted if the Budget coloured Labour as black for the rebellious as community approval painted National. The young in the 'frontier' centres of the Rotorua electorate demonstrate that there is far from being anything incompatible about resenting taxed cigarettes, beer and petrol and not voting. The city results make the same point.

Whether the young and single had ever voted or never voted makes only a minor difference to the meaning of disapproval generated by resentment at taxation of leisure consumables.

Social Credit Regroups as the Alternative Country Party

The argument so far has covered the two largest slices, National and non-voting, to be cut from Labour in farming electorates, and dealt with the biggest and smallest shares, non-voting and National, removed in the mixed seats. It must now turn to Social Credit's gains of 2.24 per cent in the mixed rural-urban and 1·66 per cent in farmer areas. This contrasts with Social Credit losses in city National fortresses, a trifling one in 2000 more voters obtained in city marginals, and two-thirds of 1 per cent drawn in from large towns and poorer city seats. Social Credit, after an erratic electoral debut six years before as a third party for political protestants, in 1960 showed distinct signs of settling down as the new alternative conservative party of the countryman and his ally, the small townsman.

The ideological commitment of Social Credit, and the fact that its proffered cures are for the ills of the whole economy, seems to have obscured even from its leadership the party's probable function as a receiver for rural dissidence. This dissidence arises from a combination of resentment at the actions of either of the major parties when in power and rural discontent with their National member's incapacity to represent all his constituents in everything—a hard function to discharge and one falling only on the delegates of one-party regions. Social Credit campaigners still tend to misconstrue the push away from the old parties as being mainly a pull from Social Credit financial doctrine. So also did Social Credit's widespread initial reception lay false emphasis on its less enduring character as a nationwide party.

Between 1951 and 1954 National dropped over the whole country a dizzy 10 per cent of the valid vote. Meanwhile Labour parted with under 2 per cent; the newcomer, Social Credit, took over 11 per cent, while non-voting decreased, though remaining above the norm. Table XII demonstrates the movement. The abnormal non-voting in 1951 (mostly Labourites, I have argued) decreased markedly in 1954. Let us suppose for a moment the unlikeliest possibility: that every single one of the 2·4 per cent ceasing their 1951 abstention became a convert to Social Credit in 1954 and that every one of the 1·7 per cent moving out from Labour went to the new third party. Even under these improbable conditions Social Credit must have composed its membership in the ratio of 10 National: 1½ Labour: 2½ non-voter. In reality the proportion of one-time Nationalists was probably nearer 70 than 60 per cent.

TABLE XII

% *Valid Vote*	1951	1954	1957
Labour	45·8	44·1	48·3
National	54·0	44·3	44·2
Social Credit	0·0	11·1	7·2
Others	0·2	0·5	0·3
Non-voting as % of votes cast	11·2	8·8	6·9
Labour Seats	30	35	41
Nat. Seats	50	45	39

These voters were scattered over the electorates in the oddest, most inconsistent fashion, betraying the presence of people determined only to reject the works of the one major party without necessarily accepting the other's philosophy, an attitude which can be taken up least easily by true partisans. Labour strongholds were the only class of seat little affected. Some of the keepers of National forts appear to have gone over to the new camp, not acting like the indeterminants of the cities, but because they welcomed a second party in the countryside that they could join wholeheartedly. For it is there that Social Credit has since consolidated.

The year 1957 was the key year for Social Credit's fate, and changes effected in that election probably tell as much about the nature of what occurred in 1960 everywhere as changes between 1957 and 1960 themselves. Social Credit in 1957 survived a movement visible in city suburbs, namely, the departure of 1954's windfall gains from National, now proceeding on to Labour. Labour became the Government because it attracted in 1957 the voters who rested in the limbo of Social Credit and non-voting in 1954.

One can safely assume that those coming into the Labour fold in 1957 would include a disproportionate number of black sheep returning from a nibble at Social Credit in 1954, or a rest in the abstention paddock for 1951 and 1954. That would leave Social Credit even more a party of ex-Nationalists than it was at its first election.

Social Credit's geographical and sectional location in 1957 and 1960 tends strongly towards an additional conclusion. The classes of electorate were arranged to test just this kind of particularized appeal and Table XIII gives their unambiguous answer. Social Credit, after a largely adventitious capture of urban votes sent flying in the National collapse of 1954, is settling down in the country. There the party has picked up almost as much as National from among Labour leavers in a good year for National like 1960. In a bad year for National, like 1954, Social Credit takes largely from its rurally acceptable competitor and is able to hold voters in the country even when Labour is at its most seductive as in 1957. Labour certainly suffers but it now has no such seats to lose, and it lives inside the towns in the country anyway.

TABLE XIII

Seat Type	Richer City	Marginal City	Poorer City	Large Town	Mixed Rur. Urb.	Farmer
S.C. % Q.V. 1957	4·21	4·10	5·25	6·25	7·75	9·26
S.C. % Q.V. 1960	3·74	4·15	5·91	7·70	9·99	10·92

This process bodes no good for National if prices should prove hard, loan terms stiff, or marketing obstructed. The table above revives memories of the Liberal takings, hauled in when Liberal was an alternative country conservative party in 1922 and 1928; and it evokes again the spectre of the Country Party and its cry for credit in the twenties and thirties. The process has even redrawn the map of Douglas Social Credit enthusiasm in Northland and the Waikato; of the Country Party heresy in the north and whole middle of the North Island; and of that independency on financial questions shown by Taranaki. Social Credit in farming seats at the 1960 election scored 12·53 per cent in Northland and the Waikato and 13·80 per cent in Taranaki, but merely 8·53 per cent in the southern North Island and 8·37 per cent in the South Island. Mixed rural and urban seats were 10·89 per cent and 10·78 per cent for Social Credit in the north and south respectively of the North Island, but the party attained only 8·00 per cent in the South Island. There is certainly an ominous consistency about the whole rural evolution so far as the National Party, in particular, is concerned. For sectional and geographical concentration is the pathway by which third parties enter parliaments, as Maurice Duverger has amply demonstrated.

As for Social Credit's 1960 showing in the cities and large towns, it did reasonably well in the urban islands amidst the rural seas—revealing the far end of the phenomenon of country-mindedness—but obtained little from the annoyed Labour stalwarts of the poorer city constituencies. It received a derisory ·05 per cent in the marginals and lost in the wealthy seats. My own impression, derived from political meetings, discussion with party workers, and also from the somewhat higher booth results obtained by the party on the 1957 and 1960 Auckland maps in regions of 'lower middle' socio-economic grade—roughly, the lightly barred region on Map B—is that Social Credit makes its appeal in the cities to the smallest capitalist.

He is the skilled tradesman working for himself or the lone shopkeeper faced with large-scale competition, high labour costs, a maze of controls and sharp taxes. His party hits at taxation and 'the debt burden' which Labour's Budget raised, and National, says the Social Crediter, does not lower sufficiently. Yet his party, unlike National, does oppose banks and credit squeezes which must hit the small venturer first, as any bank manager will acknowledge. And Social Credit shows no special love of unions, following National in 1960 with an *ad hoc* modified form of the abolition of compulsory unionism plank. Penned amidst the party of bigger business and banks, the party of organized labour and controls, and the taxgatherers who are common to both parties, perhaps the smallest capitalist will continue to cleave to his own party, however ineffectual it proves at electing city members. What the 1960 result does say is that in the type of city seats where Social Credit had previously done best, whilst thousands of city Labourites were disoriented and when National was unable to gather in more than a third of them, Social Credit picked up just one-tenth. Its immediate future in the cities, therefore, is at best to hang on until help arrives from the country in the form of the exploits of a band of members in the House.

In the urban half of New Zealand, National made its biggest

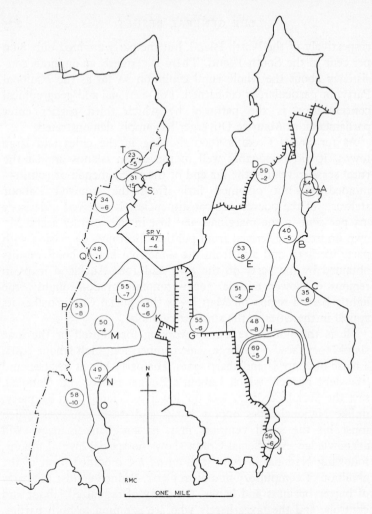

MAP E MIRAMAR ELECTORATE

A	Karaka Bay	K	Rongotai
B	Worser Bay Sch.	L	Kilbirnie South
C	Seatoun Sch.	M	Lyall Bay Sch.
D	Miramar North	N	Lyall Bay Pde.
E	Miramar Central	O	Houghton Valley
F	Argentine Av.	P	Melrose
G	Miramar South	Q	Kilbirnie Cres.
H	Glamis Av.	R	Kilbirnie Sch.
I	Strathmore Pk. Sch.	S	Evans Bay
J	Breaker Bay	T	Haitaitai South

gains where they were least useful, in Labour's safest city seats. On the other hand, with enough customary voters for Labour averting their eyes from the Budget-bedecked party image, Labour's forces were so depleted in the large towns and marginals that the small National gains of 1·47 per cent and 0·91 per cent, respectively, sufficed to tip over three members in each class of seat.

The Verdict in Labour Strongholds

The performance of the poorer city seats is worth a glance, not alone for itself, but because results there magnify trends present among minorities in the marginals. Maps B and C show how difficult it would be to draw any marginal constituency so as to include no areas of strong Labour sympathies and of matching socio-economic grade. The biggest continuous sheet of any persuasion is the wealthy Remuera-to-Glendowie area on the north-east, and this makes only one and a half electorates. Even then it is holed at three points by State houses: at Hapua Street, Purewa, and by the Orakei settlement. Map E of Miramar makes the same point in reverse. This is a 'safe Labour' seat which is rapidly approaching absolute marginality and has everything from elevated Haitaitai homes with a harbour view to a State house Labour keep. So what battalions of Labour men are doing *en masse* in their strongholds, companies of Labour men will be performing in the marginals, and with this the booth figures agree.

The manoeuvres being executed in the four centres can be traced in Table XIV. The one generally obeyed order of the day was, obviously: 'Go over the hill'. In Auckland and Dunedin not much else was done. Christchurch, historically the most pronouncedly Labour city in the Dominion, favoured National with nearly a third of its deserters from Labour, but another quarter went off to Social Credit as an escape from both. Only Wellington, the focus of the State, expressed slightly more confidence in the National Party than in the negative gesture of abstention. Even there National captured but four in every ten. The contrasts are not sufficiently marked, the movements towards National in Wellington and to National and Social Credit in Christchurch are not large enough, to do more than seek an indication of their origin.

TABLE XIV[10]

Change in % Q.V.	Auckland	Dunedin	Christchurch	Wellington
Labour	−6·42	−4·99	−8·41	−8·85
Non-voting	+4·50	+2·55	+3·51	+3·56
National	+1·85	+0·22	+2·55	+3·73
Social Credit	−0·60	+0·97	+2·24	+1·18
Independent	+0·02	+0·97	—	+0·11
Communist	+0·62	+0·22	+0·15	+0·15
Informal	+0·03	+0·06	−0·04	+0·12

But Wellington is the home of civil servants in rented State houses and the centre for young government and business head-quarters executives in flats. Perhaps they were slightly more politically sophisticated, more democratically responsible, appreciating that the right to vote must be operated to act twice, against one party and for another. Perhaps they were as irked by the Budget as the rest of the unmarried tenants but were precipitated into transferring more freely than elsewhere by the years-long battle over public service claims and conditions.

Heretaunga Labour lost the largest portion of voters of any electorate in the Dominion, 12·08 per cent. This disposes, rather, of the suspicion that Minister members were the target, since Mr. Bailey was a fresh candidate. Island Bay (Mr. Nordmeyer) at 10·00 per cent and Hutt (Mr. Nash) at 9·89 per cent did get into the top five for shares of the total vote lost; while Onslow (non-ministerial) and Miramar (Mr. Fox) showed almost as much movement in middling grade, residential regions as did the centres of the other cities. This leaves Petone, the industrial electorate *par excellence*, as the one Wellington Labour safe seat not above the average for loss. If the civil servants were having their revenge, they overlooked equal pay (lately Labour enacted, but approved by National) to take it; and still nearly as many stopped after leaving Labour as went on to help National.

As for Christchurch and the cross-trend to Social Credit, this was most unusual in being largely the work of one electorate,

[10] In this table a slightly different interpretation of 'safe Labour seat' has been adopted from the original 10 per cent Q.V. margin, so including the Roskill, Waitemata and Dunedin Central seats and raising the number covered from 19 to 22 and voters from 318,693 to 372,836.

Avon, with average assistance from Sydenham. Christchurch
Central was high in movement from Labour and in abstention,
while Riccarton, which includes areas like parts of Roskill in
Auckland and Mornington in Dunedin, was as moderately moved
as they. What the singular attractiveness of Social Credit was in
Avon neither the electorate's gross figures nor an outline knowledge of its social composition immediately suggests. A booth
study would be worth while, especially as in 1960 the smallness
of the Dunedin movement towards Social Credit and the definite
cross-trend towards it in Christchurch resulted in almost equaliz-
ing at 7·68 per cent and 7·77 per cent the markedly higher shares
that party holds in the safe Labour seats of the two South Island
cities. The third party now stands at 5·86 per cent in Wellington
and at 4·30 per cent in Auckland. Are we, one wonders, con-
templating a sign of the grinding force of heavy competition in
New Zealand's greatest city and watching the effects on society of
many civil servants and head offices? Has the age of the smallest
capitalist not retreated so far in the South Island?

We can be certain, however, that the southern cities share,
where they do not positively exaggerate, the grading out of
abstention and Labour loss from the epicentres in the hearts of
the cities. The bombs dropped on Labour's traditional core in
each metropolitan area. Thence the shock waves spread out with
generally diminishing force until they agitated only 2 or 3 per cent
in the domestic peace of their low-cost, mortgaged bungalows.
Ignoring Heretaunga, already touched on, the strict order by
Labour casualties in each centre is: Avon, Christchurch Central
and Sydenham; Auckland Central and Ponsonby; Island Bay,
Hutt and Wellington Central; and in the far south, Dunedin
Central. A recent article confirms several politically germane
features of the sketch of a city central region given in the previous
chapter when discussing the triumph of Mr. Riddiford.[11] Mr.
Neville contrasts the rest of Wellington City with the 'Central
Area'—almost identical with Labour's former safe seat. Since
1921 this region has been spilling out population, particularly
householders, at a steady thousand a year. Now the remaining
accommodation is one-third owner occupied and two-thirds rented,
precisely reversing the proportions in the rest of Wellington.

[11] Neville, R. J. W., 'The Changing Population of Wellington City, 1926–1956'
in *New Zealand Geographer*, vol. XVI, no. 2, October 1960, pp. 131–45.

Central inhabitants live half and half in flats and in detached dwellings, whereas the city proportion of flats is one-fifth. In consequence, 'by city standards the Central Area has a very large deficit of children under 15. This state of affairs is reversed in the 15–30 age group.' There is also an unusual concentration of the divorced hereabouts. Altogether, 'the most attracted to [the Central Area] are in the younger age groups, mostly unmarried, or married but childless; and older people, many of whom are widowed.'

Much the same could undoubtedly be said of the other city centres, and in saying it one would be describing those most sensitive to a sudden assault on free-floating purchasing power by means of levying 'indirect' taxes on leisure consumables. The Budget went off and the flat-dwellers, the tenants and the boarders were shocked into abstention.

It is useful to find the precise location of city booths where the numbers voting dropped sharply between 1957 and 1960. A survey of all booths in metropolitan Auckland reveals the pattern. Steep drops occurred in all the central area (on Map B, the districts of F, E, R, A, B, C, D, Q—apart from the wealthy residential eastern section—and O). Using contours, one sees that the reaction travels out along every main arterial street. It stops travelling south-west about four miles down the New North and the Great North highways, to resume at the Avondale shops and in New Lynn. The reaction reappears going south on Manukau Road at Royal Oak and travels through the heart of fortress Onehunga to the sea, and it runs south-east all the way down Great South Road from Newmarket, through Ellerslie to Penrose. The one type of booth where the reaction is found outside polling places in the city centre and along boarding and flatting axes, exists among State houses. The absence at the 1960 election of from ten to twenty-seven in every hundred who had voted in 1957 distinguishes Wesley-Owairaka, Western Springs, Oranga, Point England and even northern Orakei. State house areas continue to be towers in the outerworks of Labour's urban castle but one-tenth and more of the defenders were properly disgruntled. It seems likely that here is the reason for Heretaunga joining Hutt and Wellington Central.

The Unoffended

To leave the city core behind and turn off the main roads into the quiet streets of moderate and lower-income private houses is to discover those content with the second Labour Government's administration of the family welfare state. The square miles of new building to the south-east, north-west and north of the Auckland isthmus display little loss and less abstention. Mount Albert's peculiarities blur an otherwise perfect picture of a low-cost housing and subsidized building programme, the promise of which positively attracted the new family man to Labour and held him by being fulfilled through an adverse economic phase. Here the mass of Labour's city vote lives; which gives a measure of the infuriation of the minority who produced the effects generalized as a 7·53 per cent loss.

This picture is true for the normally least enthusiastic of Labour's safe city seats: Riccarton, Otahuhu, Mornington and Waitakere. It is true, likewise, for the middling income, domestic regions of the city marginals. Waitemata and Roskill lost very moderately and three-quarters of it went to non-voting; St. Kilda, Lyttelton and Manukau hardly moved at −2·34 per cent, −1·87 per cent and −0·08 per cent. The shaken marginals were the flatting and State house marginals.

Wellington Central at −8·67 per cent and Eden at −6·81 per cent need no further exegesis. Tamaki's very National half went along with Remuera across the border. Tamaki's Labour balance acted as the State and group house area it almost entirely is. In St. Albans the flats along the southern rim worked their will (Map D: Booths A, O, and N). However, one should note in the south-west (at B) that sufficiently rapid conversion of buildings could be offsetting the adverse effects to Labour in 1960 of a place being markedly childless and tenanted. Shirley, the St. Albans State settlement (T, U and partly S), held up remarkably well for Labour, but the new settlement of middling Mairehau (W and V) did not. Otherwise St. Albans turned in a quiet performance appropriate to its predominantly medium grading and it heads the South Island marginals for Labour loss at −3·35 per cent simply because of the immobility of the others.

And North Shore, the last, was betwixt and between. More like eastern Eden or eastern Wellington Central in its comparative

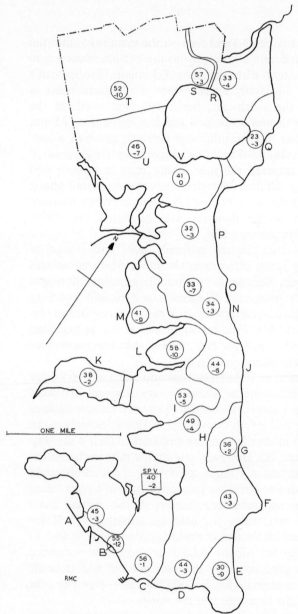

MAP F.
NORTH SHORE
ELECTORATE

A   Stanley Bay
B   Devonport Base
C   Devonport Centre
D   Devonport East
E   Cheltenham
F   Narrow Neck
G   Vauxhall
H   South Belmont
I   Belmont-Bayswater
J   N.E. Belmont
K   Bayswater
L   Eversleigh Rd.
M   Jutland Rd.
N   Clifton
O   Hauraki Cnr.
P   Central Takapuna
Q   Hurstmere Rd.
R   Milford Centre
S   West Milford
T   North Westlake
U   Taharoto Rd.
V   Takapuna Centre

wealth, it is nevertheless a family electorate into which the well-off are still moving, thus socially upgrading areas and lowering Labour (on Map F at J, O, M, U and probably, T, though there is a suggestion that this could be another Mairehau, a new Catholic centre). Established wealthy and comfortably-off areas (R, Q, P, N, G, F, D, A and K) declined 2 or 3 per cent or actually rose in two instances. The main shopping centres (C and V) hardly changed. E is an unexplained maverick. Long-established State houses (at H, I and L) gave Labour a fair drubbing and so did the naval barracks area at B. The North Shore's record underlines the importance to marginality of social transformations and emphasizes that, in an electorate which is marginal because well mixed, one encounters the trends in the parts that more single minded regions display *en grande*.

The North Shore, east Eden and north-west Tamaki are a guide to the action of the three National blue ribbon city seats. Non-voting there was high and matched Labour's lost share, while National's small profit nicely covered Social Credit's deficit. Fendalton, almost unmoved, was importing a new element into its social character. But it seems arguable that in Karori and Remuera the cause of non-voting was the same negative protest by the flatting singles as appeared everywhere, as witness the sag of 10 per cent in numbers voting in South Remuera along two axes of flats. Doubt must be stated as to whether only once-Labour or potential-Labour contributed to abstention. There is enough height in the columns on the diagram on p. 267, for a quarter or a third of Labour deserters to be going to National and for some 'first-voters', who would have favoured National if any party, to be supplying the deficiency in non-voting by just not bothering about politics. They, however, like the cross-changers who cancel out one another's movements beneath the visible, operative totals, cannot greatly affect an analysis resting on general trends so widely and exactly conformed to and executed.

The Maori Seats

The Maori seats remain for discussion and remain strongly Labour, but that loyalty has been much strained. Movement in the four seats is great; trends obvious and even. No Opposition candidate made much from Labour's staggering loss. In Western Maori, National took 2·44 per cent more while Social Credit received 3·19 per cent less, but non-voting rose 10·60 per cent. In Southern Maori, both opposition parties gained, 0·88 per cent and 0·19 per cent; while non-voting soared 11·01 per cent. The Eastern Maori figures have encouraged Social Credit, +3·86 per cent, and discouraged National, −0·95 per cent; but non-voting at 5·48 per cent really won. And in the Northern, most urban seat, the view is somewhat fogged by the wise disappearance between elections of unofficial Labour and Independent Social Credit candidates. Counting their old votes for their foster parties, Labour is found to have dropped a mighty 12·88 per cent, of which National retrieved 3·82 per cent and Social Credit 1·88 per cent. Meantime non-voting grasped a further 7·50 per cent.

The Maori voters struck Labour a stinging blow but withheld their votes from its rivals. We can check Maori inclination to vote only once before because they have been enrolled in the ordinary way only since 1956. At the election in 1957 non-voting was 14·45 per cent, double the proportion in non-Maori electorates. It now stands at 22·91 per cent, again double the non-Maori share. Past Labour totals and percentages of the valid vote, received since the Ratana Church members became Labour in that party's first term, have been rising, then standing steady and strong. My estimate would be that Maoris vote less than non-Maoris, but, such as do, vote very consistently and vote for their interest as a lower-income segment desiring welfare, much like the European-descended.

In that case, the Maori rebuke is far too heavy to have proceeded alone from the Budget. There are not enough young Maoris in the cities to be especially antagonized. Nor do I think it came much from the delay in producing a document, such as the recently issued Hunn Report, summing up many of the recommendations for action made at Young Maori Leaders' conferences during Labour's term. Maoris have proved singularly loyal to inactive administrators, once true benefits have won their gratitude—and they were so even in the 1910s and 1920s when small tokens sufficed. The conclusion is, I think, inevitable, that the Labour Government's handling of the Maori tour controversy earned it the deep disapproval of Maoris all over New Zealand and in this conflict of feelings—loyalty to Labour and disapproval at its attitude in this test case—they acted as others act when torn two ways politically, they ceased voting in large numbers.

The Weight of the Organizational Factor

Something quite different from the cluster of reasonable emotions and motives which has formed and been moulded round the Budget, something unlike a judgement on the Maori tour or a verdict on help with housing, has been suggested as a large factor in the 1960 election. This is organization—the mechanical factor. On the evidence in the rest of this book it is a factor which should have worked in National's favour. Unfortunately it must remain nearly imperceptible in its passage from cause, the gleaming machine, to effect, the turn-out of voters. For turn-out, as the analysis of past and present elections goes to illustrate, can be affected by other considerations.

Only one variable suggests itself for measurement, the number of special votes cast in each electorate for all parties together. Organizational efficiency ought to show up most in this field where party workers can provide advice, forms and visits for all those who want to vote earlier or otherwise than is normal. The faults of the measure are many. If booth non-voting goes up, so presumably does special non-voting. Both major parties are at work in an electorate and whose is to be the credit for a rising pile of envelopes? Organization may be thorough, but voters still prefer to express their feelings by driving to the polls and exchanging nods with overwhelmingly like-minded cronies. All the measure can achieve is humbly to suggest a few thoughts, while killing dead what cannot on the facts be held true. For the thousands of New Zealand's voluntary party workers and the dozens of paid organizers the data on special voting is set out in Table XV.

Whatever else this harmonious table sets forth, principally it shows that the improved and tuned National organization could not quite avert a loss in the share of special votes whilst simultaneously non-voting was eating its way into all voting. However, the rate of loss displayed by the New Zealand-cast envelope vote is only about half the rate of booth-cast votes. Possibly organization can be credited with braking the descent, although it could not prevent a descent. Ironically it was the least organized electorates, the Maori seats, which put up the only good clear gain in special voting in the face, also, of these seats having the maximum increase in abstention. The Maori voter had only lately been enrolled and there were necessarily fewer of his own polling booths per region. He is revealed learning to rely as heavily as the wealthy on special votes.

TABLE XV

The Percentage Share of Special Votes Obtained in the Total Qualified Vote at the 1957 and 1960 Elections

Cast In:	Richer city			Marginal city			Poorer city		
	1957	1960	Change	1957	1960	Change	1957	1960	Change
N.Z.	9·06	8·23	−0·83	8·47	8·16	−0·31	7·41	7·08	−0·33
Overseas	0·74	0·92	+0·18	0·43	0·63	+0·20	0·32	0·41	+0·09
Forces	0·02	0·02	—	0·16	0·08	−0·08	0·05	0·03	−0·02
Total	9·82	9·17	−0·65	9·06	8·87	−0·19	7·78	7·52	−0·26

Cast in:	Large town			Mixed rural-urban			Farmer		
	1957	1960	Change	1957	1960	Change	1957	1960	Change
N.Z.	7·97	8·08	+0·11	7·30	7·01	−0·29	6·60	6·36	−0·24
Overseas	0·27	0·39	+0·12	0·19	0·30	+0·11	0·13	0·27	+0·14
Forces	0·02	0·02	—	0·07	0·07	—	0·06	0·06	—
Total	8·26	8·49	+0·23	7·56	7·38	−0·18	6·79	6·69	−0·10

Cast in:	Maori			Total for all seats		
	1957	1960	Change	1957	1960	Change
N.Z.	8·20	9·17	+0·97	7·54	7·32	−0·22
Overseas	0·02	0·04	+0·02	0·27	0·40	+0·13
Forces	0·18	0·25	+0·07	0·07	0·06	−0·01
Total	8·40	9·46	+1·06	7·88	7·78	−0·10

In all types of seat—even the constituencies of the untravelled Maori—the general drop in special voting is considerably offset by an increase in the share of votes recorded overseas. In fact, the numbers touring or conferring in Australia, Britain and beyond had increased so surprisingly in the last few years and they were so costly in funds that the newly elected National Government made controls on expenses for foreign travel one of its first cuts. Correspondingly, there is probably no credit due to party organization for the fact that hundreds more people overseas meant hundreds more votes cast there. Therefore it is reasonable to read the top line of each column as a comment rather than the total shares below.

Lest it be taken that the high proportion of forces' votes coming back to city marginals as their 'home' electorates betoken unusual militancy in those of middling income, it should be explained that it just so happens that naval and air bases are in marginals. Whatever their origin, these men are now registered in or near their bases in New Zealand. The high Maori figures do mean just what they say, though. Maoris serve overseas in peacetime to a greatly disproportionate extent; and the number of their votes increased away from the tour dispute and in the presence in Malaya of New Zealand's first Maori ambassador.

Generally, special voting can be seen to increase in the cities in ratio to wealth and executive or travelling status. The Wellington sub-total outranks all others in special votes cast overseas. The rural–urban axis reappears so that the more countryfied an electorate is, the less special votes it will cast. Since National is strongest in such places and the party actively strives to bring in the backblocks vote early and by post, this low rural envelope vote is intriguing. The Egmont electorate, whose organization has been analysed and praised by a careful observer, scored 6·03 per cent of special votes.[12] It would appear that, masked by a social pattern like farmer preference for showing oneself at the booth, organization's best endeavours may flourish unmarked. They may even be unrewarded; for in Egmont as elsewhere non-voting inexorably rose, by 1·85 per cent.

A lone encouragement to organizers may possibly be descried in the rising special vote flaunted by large towns. These included several where National Party task forces had been sent in because they were rightly considered 'key' electorates. Here once more voters responded with their own ironies. In a group of five seats there are signs that worthwhile success crowned effort. Wanganui, Invercargill, Napier, Palmerston North and Hastings increased their special vote portions by between 0·55 per cent and 0·42 per cent, or by between one-twelfth and one-fifteenth of their envelope vote at the previous election. But the biggest gain rewarded no especial crisis planning, for Hamilton went up 0·96 per cent. Meanwhile in Nelson, that marginal of marginals for both parties, the envelope vote descended 0·01 per cent. Invercargill where National was secure, and Napier where Labour was safe, both show gains. Yet Gisborne, which turned over to National, suffered the very large fall of 1·02 per cent in special votes—task force and all.

---

[12] Mr B. Bellringer, who has brought his study of Taranaki politics up to date and has generously communicated his results.

When we look at the absolute share of envelope votes attained in 1960 in Labour-held and in National-held seats, however, there is again a little evidence of return on effort, for Labour large town constituencies gave in 7·89 per cent of their qualified vote as New Zealand-cast special votes and the Nationals, 8·21 per cent.

The facts in the cities do very little indeed to help the case for organization. Ten seats of the thirty-three show a rising envelope vote. Three of these gainers, as was proportionate to their numbers among city seats, were marginals: Manukau, St. Kilda and St. Albans. The median fell at −0·34 per cent and just above it came Lyttelton and well below were the rest. Considering the efforts poured into Tamaki, its figure of −1·32 per cent was positively disheartening, while Wellington Central's loss of −0·69 per cent does not argue that effective turn-out of special votes won the day there.

The only correlation is with abstention. Where non-voting was higher, on the whole special voting decreased more. This goes to confirm that organization cannot do much towards diverting or reversing a trend. To look at Roskill's gain of 0·78 per cent or St. Albans +0·30 per cent is to revive memories and accounts of vigorous campaigns, stoutly fought. But to look at Waitemata, down 0·45 per cent and Eden, less 0·68 per cent, is to know that hard work can be overborne. And in between the cited cases there are so many electorates where the effort was manifestly less, yet the response was just as good, that one tends to conclude, on this measure anyway, that the effect of good organization is itself marginal and organization should be justified in terms of morale and image building rather than by its specific, immediate rewards.

It could be argued that the nature of the measure is itself responsible for organization's poor showing. This is possible; but before the implications of the envelope vote are quite dismissed, one should perhaps gaze again at the orderly and reasonable progressions on Table XV and ponder the persuasive connexion between declining special voting and declining voting in general.

The Schools Question and Catholic Voting

It is traditional in New Zealand politics to point the moral to one's own party of the menacingly good organization of one's enemies. In the 1920s the *New Zealand Herald* was forever warning about the compact, disciplined ranks of Labour. What is uncommon is the suspicion of a religious voice at the ear of any significant body of voters. In the 1960 campaign, however, there were noteworthy efforts made by the Holy Name Society, by the Catholic Parent, Teacher, Friends' Associations, and by specific National candidates to have considered afresh and differently the questions of religion in schools or of concessions to the parents of parochial school-children, or both. The campaign speeches, special meetings with candidates, telegrams and questionnaires had their effect after the election in causing some politicians to ascribe Labour's defeat, at the very least in Wellington Central, St. Albans, Tamaki and Hastings, to bloc voting by Catholics.

The primary evidence of the results is that these electorates did not move in any peculiar way to answer the question automatically. The case of Wellington Central has been closely reviewed and no evidence was found for the hypothesis that the Catholics threw out Mr. Kitts. Against the hypothesis is the strongly defined pattern which agreed with other electorates and with a more likely general reason.

As for Hastings, it was one of a group of four large towns which altered their party shares of total vote very much together. Two did not change party; two did. Measured by rate of Labour loss, Hastings has more than six other large towns but less than another three, including Hamilton, with a most definitely Protestant National member, at the top of the list. The only shred of evidence that can be found to support this proposition about Hastings concerns voting for Social Credit. Gisborne and Hastings, which changed their members, increased their third party share by something over 2 per cent whereas in most large towns Social Credit either declined or gained under 1 per cent. Social Credit had made the only clear offer of financial aid. Unfortunately for the conclusiveness of these facts, New Plymouth, which had and kept a National member, also awarded 2 per cent more to Social Credit. New Plymouth is not cited nor suggested as an instance of parochial school promises being the cause of Catholic bloc voting. In any case, the trends for eight out of ten of the large towns are so close—the exceptions are Wanganui and Nelson, which Labour retained—that it is hard to believe in one electorate being separately moved towards the common fate.

In St. Albans and Tamaki there is a trifle more to go on. In both electorates National candidates took up attitudes likely to garner votes from such Catholics as would decide their ballot solely on religious issues. Tamaki's Mr. Muldoon, an Anglican, most definitely favoured more religious teaching in schools. The equally sincere and extensively reasoned negative of the Labour member, a secondary school teacher, would have done him no good with partisans of the cause of increased religious teaching in public schools. Tamaki was well up the list of marginals in voter movement while St. Albans was the most moved of the South Island marginals.

Again, however, they are too close to their confreres' performance for the case to be really convincing. Labour in Tamaki lost 6·81 per cent and in Eden, which is nowhere mentioned as bloc voting, Labour lost 6·61 per cent. Social Credit moved down, not up, in both. Social Credit lost also in St. Albans; which had just 1·01 per cent more movement from Labour than St. Kilda, an electorate not thought to have heard and acted upon these issues. If the hypothesis is to find any support, it can hardly be at the level of constituency totals.

A careful watch was kept throughout the booth analysis for any sign of results from the energetic raising of these questions encountered during the campaign. In the prosperous districts of Epsom, for instance, where there is some small and relative concentration of Catholics and where a large combined meeting of Catholic laymen and clergy was held on the issue, absolutely nothing unusual resulted at the polling places. In Tamaki, there was considerable movement against Labour in Mr. Tizard's best booths. Yet in the lower half of Tamaki's Labour State house section, losses were of exactly the same order as losses just over the electoral border in Otahuhu, which contains an extension of the settlement but where the candidates were not embattled on these questions.

Catholics sometimes congregate around their churches and schools, particularly those Catholics with families still growing, who will also, of course, be the most affected by the issue of State aid. The Catholic complex of buildings in the north of Tamaki district is near two booths which declined greatly in numbers voting Labour and another polling place where National rose suspiciously. Glenbrae booth had 938 Labour voters in 1957 and 649 in 1960; at Sacred Heart College Hall, Labour voters were 240, then 241, but National went from 57 to 150; and over at Point England School, which is rather stretching the description 'near', Labour went from 1057 to 733.

The Point England booth turned out to have emptied in part into a new booth one-third of a mile away. The old booth was 84 per cent Labour in 1957; the old and the new in 1960 were 80 per cent and 75 per cent Labour. Glenbrae lost a lot of voters, some going, no doubt, to another new polling place at Glen Taylor School. Glenbrae's degree of allegiance to Labour, however, dropped merely from 86 per cent to 82 per cent. The Sacred Heart booth itself dropped from 78 per cent to 60 per cent and so the case now rests on this, by elimination. A trip to the north of West Tamaki Road gives ample ground for believing in another cause for Labour's losses here. Dozens of brand new, privately owned houses, well above average in cost and size, have been erected between the elections in the area feeding the booth. They should suffice to account for the drop. The northern end of the Tamaki district is, in fact, grading out socially as Map C shows, and the booths have reacted most sensitively to an extraordinarily rapid transformation.

In St. Albans the Mairehau booths dropped 8 and 7 per cent and there is a new Catholic religious community nearby. It is conceivable that here is a case like the possible instance already noted of a booth near the Westlake Carmel College area in the North Shore electorate. If these are cases of Catholic-induced declines, and in all three instances new houses are going up, then the three are all that can be found among nearly a thousand polling places to support the generalization that Catholic bloc voting was a prime, or even sizeable secondary factor in 1960.

As a final, general check, all the statistical districts in Auckland were ranked by proportion of Catholic population. The long assumed connexion between Catholicism and a tendency to vote Labour was put to the test by taking the ranking of districts by 1960 Labour vote and matching the two rankings. The coefficient of correlation was a positive and definite ·590. Since Catholicism and Labour voting were connected thus, it followed that, if Catholics had moved more rapidly from Labour between 1957 and 1960, this too should show up. So districts were ranked by Labour loss and this matched against the ranking by proportion of Catholics. The answer was a negative correlation. If anything, Catholics were slower to leave Labour than people of other religions or none.

This result came as a considerable surprise. My personal expectation, based on attending meetings at which obviously primed questioners received patently pointed answers, was that the State aid and religion-in-schools questions would prove to be 'sleepers', issues quietly raised which explode into action in the polling booths. My conclusion on the evidence given leads me now to think instead that the lay leadership, not to mention the hierarchy, have not yet taken the kind of measures which will make the parochial schools question an important determinant of the voting of that 14 per cent of our citizenry who are Catholic. That the time will come, the course of recent American and Australian history leaves no doubt. Already candidates and members on all sides are alerted and some have promised what action they can take as individuals. But in general it seems doubtful whether more than a well scattered thousand or two votes were in any degree affected in 1960 and it would be careless of fact to think these matters at all decisive.

Conclusions

What was decisive was the hostility to the 1958 Budget among the young and old rather than the middle-aged, among the single and the childless rather than those with their families about them, among confirmed Labour supporters rather than those drawn into or kept Labour by the 1957 offers of 3 per cent loans and capitalization of the family benefit. The sections of the community most immediately affected by the cut at 'luxury' consumption took action in return by staying away from the polls in droves. Each man who decided thus, without consulting hundreds, lacking any organization, and in the absence of a public call for abstention, could hardly have anticipated how general his individual decision would prove.

Labour Ministers, members and candidates did what they could to recreate the atmosphere in which the Budget had been made and only helped to darken the clouds hanging over mid 1958. The much sunnier climate of 1960—perhaps the best year in history for New Zealand consumers—was unable to disperse the last of the feelings, so consciously cultivated and conserved by the Opposition and unconsciously fostered by Social Credit's ideological concentration on taxes, that the man with money to jingle had been had.

No tangible addition to the structure of welfare was offered to allay this resentment, which was simply not expected in the shape and size it assumed. Opinion polling might have given Labour researchers the warning that was an established expectation to the National organization. No concrete positive objective for Labour supporters was set up in the year of the campaign to which voters might press on, forgetting past hurts. Promises were puritanically eschewed on a strict assessment of New Zealand's prospects; the same assessment as prompted the Budget. And this gave added colour to the cry that promises had won in 1957, promises were incapable of fulfilment without penalty, promises were broken in 1958, and, now, a penitent Labour Government was acting as though it had learned the truth of all the Opposition said.

Instead of providing an objective for voting or repeating the tactics which had won before, Labour added to the black thunderheads over the 1957-8 crisis and its taxes a thick fog of statistics about industrializing New Zealand against some bleak future of too many adolescents and too few jobs. It was all very cold and confusing to the fully employed young. Nor did it mean much to the old Labour stalwart at the age when small pleasures in beer and tobacco mean most and some advance in welfare policy portends more ease and security soon.

All was made ready for a verdict by a minority of normally strong Labour supporters upon the one issue of the Black Budget, dressed up in a variety of guises. That verdict was rendered accordingly, say the results. It was an emotional verdict originally passed two years before. The anger prompting it had been slowly diminishing since. Given another three months while the contentments of 1960 sank into popular consciousness and the Government might have survived. Whether a four-year term would have helped, bringing with it the adverse prices of 1960's end and the looming, swelling threat of the Common Market, is another matter. Certainly it might have convinced the Labour man that the crisis of 1957–8 was real, since it had recurred, and suggested that a Labour Minister of Finance could have had his reasons for doing as he did. The darkening prospects of 1961 would undoubtedly have made all those speeches about rapid industrialization and planning for jobs into words of point and merit for Labourites, instead of boring diversions from the issue.

It would not, indeed, have taken much to preserve the second Labour Government. The turnover of seven seats looked large but the movement of voters was only middling strong against Labour, and in the cities and towns the movement was *for* nothing. National in 1954 dropped twice as fast in popular favour and survived; partly because Social Credit took the shifting votes out of harm's way, partly because Labour's strength was so concentrated within the cities that its surplus of votes there was wasted. If in the last two elections New Zealand had enjoyed the doubtful blessings of proportional representation, membership of the House would have looked like this, the actual membership being given in brackets for comparison. Proportional representation is, of course, myopic itself in being based solely on valid votes cast. A perfectly just representation of the movement of opinion in New Zealand in 1960 would have emptied some seats in the House since the principal movement among all those qualified to vote was the rejection of one party and the approval of none.

TABLE XVI

	1957						1960					
	Nth Is.		*Sth Is.*		*Both Is.*		*Nth Is.*		*Sth Is.*		*Both Is.*	
	P.R.	*Actual*	*P.R.*	*Actual*	*P.R.*	*Actual*	*P.R.*	*Actual*	*P.R.*	*Actual*	*P.R.*	*Actual*
Labour	26	(26)	13	(15)	39	(41)	23	(20)	12	(14)	35	(34)
National	24	(28)	11	(11)	35	(39)	26	(34)	12	(12)	38	(46)
Social Credit	4	(0)	2	(0)	6	(0)	5	(0)	2	(0)	7	(0)
Independents	—		—		—		—		—		—	
Communists	—		—		—		—		—		—	

But there is no quarrelling with the fact that National gets a very large advantage from the first-past-the-post system, principally at the expense of Social Credit and altogether in the

North Island. Labour gained its small but vital margin in 1957 by its over-representation in the South Island, but was under-represented on balance in New Zealand in 1960.[13] Thus a real opinion shift of $1\frac{1}{2}$ per cent towards National was exaggerated into seven more National members in a House of eighty. Five had margins over Labour of under 2 per cent of the qualified vote, so that a transfer of 1 per cent would have reversed them. Welling-ton Central's margin was 2·16 per cent and one, Tamaki, had a healthy 6·33 per cent between the parties.

This is a picture of an election in which deep and abiding sectional divisions expressed themselves consistently. An ex-plicable and strongly felt judgement was made by one definable portion of the citizens the net result of which was a close decision, mis-stated by the first-past-the-post system as a sound victory for one contender. The National Party, therefore, will find more in the result of the election to disturb it than a counting of party heads in Parliament would suggest. They can come off as easily as they went on, and the redrawing of boundaries will be of critical importance to this. More moderately safe Labour seats will be created to the north-west and south-east of the Auckland isthmus while credit constriction or a slow-down in aid to housing will strengthen the lessons of 1957 and 1960: that family suburbs vote for what aids the family man in his constant battle to better the standards of his little world. Meanwhile Social Credit has made gains in opinion three-fifths as large as National's, and is regrouping right where National has hitherto been safe, come price sag or stiff loan terms.

Labour can reflect that it was the chosen target of its own supporters in 1960 and it did nothing soundly calculated to disturb their aim. Labour is strongest now in the South Island, the home of dying parties. That is where the Liberals were dis-proportionately numerous after 1914, and ex-Reform and United members hung on in 1935. Social Credit may be cheered to realize that coming parties rise first in the island of fast population growth and swifter changing loyalties, because in the types of

---

[13] The mathematics of this kind of situation and a suggested cure for New Zealand are given in a useful article, 'Gerrymandering for Democracy' by K. J. Scott, in *Political Science*, Vol. 7, no. 2, September 1955. Paradoxically, though National is heavily over-represented and Labour under-represented in 1960, the average Labour-held seat is both smaller, 16,358 : 16,404, and held by a smaller average margin, 2,391 : 2,777, than National-held constituencies.

seats where Social Credit has a fighting chance, it is 3:2 a North Island party. Only the Communists, who drew two-fifths as many votes as were cast informally, have nothing much to worry over or hope for.

What the country at large will concern itself with in the 1960 result is its demonstration that voters act as though at elections they enter a contract with the party of their choice to produce not just some approved measures but continuously better times than ever before. In the fifties, long continued prosperity has inaugurated the politics of great expectations. No party could satisfy them and no party has. On my reading of our recent political history, the National Government was lucky to encounter the strike of 1951, and superbly fortunate to have Social Credit appear in 1954. In 1957 Labour clambered belatedly to power, in the sense that National had years since been disapproved. It carried out the terms of its contract with the family man, but could not avoid trying to write in afterwards an escape clause on indirect taxation. There was no escape. Disappointed expectation responded in 1960. The prospect before us suggests that all three parties face some odd gyrations of favour before New Zealanders reconcile themselves to reality.

INDEX

Aderman, E.P., 60
agricultural policy of National Party, 91, 94
Algie, R. M., 113, 214
Almore, H., 213
Amendment Act, 1950, 8
Anderson, Mrs. C. M., 224
Antarctic, policy on, 70
armed forces, 70–71
Arthur, Sir Basil, 146
Ashburton, 236
Auckland: absentee voters in, 230; campaign in, 97, 99, 163, 165, 167; Communist Party in, 26, 82; electorate in, 17; Labour vote in, 219, 222, 277, 278, 279, 281; newspapers in, 123, 132; party organization in, 81, 82; Social Credit in, 279; social sectionalization of, 256–61; strike threat in, 104
Auckland Star, election coverage by, 123, 125, 126, 127, 128, 131, 133; forecasting results, 108, 171, 188; Freer case report, 225; on foreign exchange crisis, 45; on racial discrimination, 72

Ballance, John 5
banks, policy on, 95, 102
Bay of Plenty, 209, 236
Bergham, I. J., 211
Bill of Rights, 93, 94, 188
Boord, R.: 20; illness of, 216; Minister of Customs, 32, 66; on broadcasting, 110
broadcasting: and the election, 109–122, 177; as election issue, 109; party allocations, 110–11; use by Labour, 111–12, 114–20; use by National, 111–12, 114–20; use by Social Credit, 113, 115, 118, 119; value of, 118; influence on election, 269, 270
Budget (1958), 48–50, 59, 60, 105, 292–3
Budget (1959), 62–64

Budget (1960), 64–66
Buller, 238
butter, exports of, 48

Canberra Times, The, 120
candidates: 139–51; ages of, 141–2, 154; differences between, 143–4, 147; educational background of, 145–6; experience of local government, 142–3; importance of personal factor, 224–7; numbers offering themselves, 139; occupations of, 144–5; organization by, 157; previous experience of, 140–1; selection of, 152–5; tasks of, 162–4; training of, 155–6; women, 146–7
canvassing, 161–2
Carr, Rev. Clyde, 240
Cheal, C. L., 85
child benefit, 31, 59, 60
Christchurch: 26; absentee voters in, 230; Labour vote in, 219, 277–9; Mr. Holyoake's speech at, 91; newspapers in, 132; voting in, 277, 278, 279
Christchurch Star, 124, 126, 127, 130, 131, 134, 171
church schools, state aid for, 103, 231, 289–92
city constituencies: 235, 243–5; Labour losses in, 277–80; marginal 245–50, 251, 252, 253; Social Credit in, 275; social sectionalization of, 255–64; special votes cast, 287, 288
Clutha, 204
Communist Party: age of candidates, 141–2; election policy, 97; experience of candidates, 143; finances, 80; gains, 229, 230; meetings, 165; occupation of candidates, 144–5; press coverage of, 127, 134; radio allocation, 111; seats contested, 140; staff, 82
Condliffe, Professor J. B., 56
Connolly, P. G. 112, 179, 198

Tamaki: Labour losses in, 206, 207,
289, 290; Labour Party in, 22, 30;
voting in, 244, 246, 247, 248, 281
Taranaki, 237
Taupo, 91
Tauranga, 236
taxation: 187, 189; in 1958 budget,
48, 49, 50, 58, 59; in 1959 budget,
63; in 1960 budget, 65; Labour
Party policy, 95, 105, 120; National
Party policy, 92, 105; press
opinions, 130; Social Credit policy,
97. *See also* income tax
Taylor, W., 171
television: 131; and election, 122;
National policy on, 92, 93
Timaru, 236, 239, 240, 241
Tirikatene, Sir Eruera, 112
Tizard, R. J., 290
town constituencies: 235; divided
past of, 238–43
trade unions: and Labour Party, 16–
17, 79; voluntary membership, 93,
100–1, 131, 134, 183–7, 188
treaty obligations, 69–70
Truth, 107, 123, 134, 198
two-party system, 10

United Kingdom, exports to, 51–53
United Nations, 68, 69, 83
United Party, 13

voters: 1957 and 1960 compared, 197;
abstaining, 207, 215, 218, 220, 222,
227, 230, 265–72, 283, 284; change
of party, 194–9; effect of age on
views, 174; 'floating', 253–4; importance of social caste, 175–6,
255–64; in Dunedin Central, 171–
200; in large towns, 238–43; in

voters: marginal seats, 252–3; in mixed
areas, 236–8; in Rotorua, 216–20;
motives of, 205; opinion of candidates, 226–7; qualifications, 7; role
of religion, 174–5; sources of
information, 176–80; special, 160–
1; views on issues involved, 187–90;
views on party differences, 180–3;
views on party leaders, 191–4;
views on party policy, 183–7

Waikato, 237
Wairarapa, 236
Waitakere, 9, 209
Waitaki, 221, 236
Waitomo, 160
Wallace, 22, 163
Walsh, F. P., 16, 100, 134
Wanganui: campaign, 100, 287;
Social Credit in, 113; voting in,
236, 239, 240
Watene, P. T., 72
Watene, S., 27
Watt, H., 32, 118
Watts, J. T., 35, 37, 64
Webber, E. G., 99,
Webber, R. J. M., 212
Wellington: 123; campaign in, 148,
150, 155, 156, 163; envelope votes
in, 288; party organization in, 26,
80, 81, 85, 88, 166; rail strike threat
in, 104; schools question in, 289;
voting in, 219, 244, 246, 248, 277,
278, 279, 281
Wellington Central, 204, 206, 207,
209; study of result, 228–33
Westland, 236, 238
Whakatane, 91
Whangarei, 211
Whitehead, S. A., 213
women's franchise, 5

Printed by Blackie & Sons Ltd.
at the Villafield Press, Bishopbriggs, Glasgow